Effective Sales Management

Effective Sales Management

JOHN STRAFFORD
and COLIN GRANT

NICHOLS PUBLISHING COMPANY : NEW YORK

First published in the United States of America in 1986 by
Nichols Publishing Company,
Post Office Box 96
New York, N.Y. 10024

Library of Congress Cataloging-in-Publication Data
Strafford, John.
 Effective sales management.
 1. Sales management. I. Grant, Colin. II. Title.
HF5438.4.S865 1986 658.8′1   85–28503
ISBN 0–89397–245–2

Author's note
Throughout this book,
the word 'salesman' has
been used to mean
salesman or saleswomen.
The use of this word does not imply that
saleswomen are not as
effective as salesmen.

Printed in Great Britain

Contents

Preface   xi
PART 1: THE TRANSITION FROM SELLING TO MANAGING   1

1 *Criteria for Promotion*   3
   Qualities essential for success as a manager   3
   Making the decision – commitment   3
   The super manager   4

2 *Maximising the Selector's Chances of Success*   5
   Will they make it?   5
   What can he do apart from sell?   5
   The filter factor   7
   Why all this trouble?   7

3 *The Sales Manager's Job*   8
   The sales manager's checklist   8
   Basic role of the sales manager   9
   Summary   11

4 *Seven Key Functions of Sales Management*   12
   Planning   12
   Organising the sales force   12
   Recruitment of sales people   13
   Staffing the sales organisation   13
   Training and developing job skills   13
   Motivating the sales force   14
   Controlling the sales operation   14
   Monitoring for success   15
   Summary   15

5 *Leadership*   16
   What is a leader?   16
   No one is perfect   16
   Qualities of leadership   16
   Leadership skills   18
   The boss and the leader   20
   Self-programming for leadership   20

6 *Motivating and Developing the Team*   22
   People developers   22
   Walking tall   23

7 *How to Obtain Maximum Job Satisfaction*   25

 8 *Managing and Working Relations*   27
   Relations with superiors   27
   Relations with equals   27
   Relations with subordinates   27
   Managing upwards   28
   Managing the junior management team   28
   Working with women   28

 9 *Managing Time*   30
   The time trap   30
   Delegation   33
   The Strafford/Grant approach to delegation   35
   The value of a good secretary   36

PART 2: CREATING AND BUILDING AN EFFECTIVE SALES
ORGANISATION   37

10 *Sales Organisation, Audit and Evaluation*   39
   Principles of organisation   39
   Need for stability with flexibility   40
   Evaluation of needs   40
   Writing the plan   41

11 *Marketing and the Role of the Field Sales Force*   42
   What is marketing?   42
   The marketing system   42
   Role of the sales force   44
   Conclusion   44

12 *Organising the Sales Force*   45
   Defining the market   45
   What type of sales force do you need?   46
   Segmentation   46
   Plan of action   47
   Conclusion   48

13 *More Concerning Structure*   49
   'By territory' organisation   49
   'By product' organisation   49
   'By market' organisation   50
   'By customer' organisation   50
   Multiple activity sales force   51
   Designing the individual territories   51
   Summary   52

14 *Importance of the Field Sales Manager*   54
   Stages of growth and the field sales manager   54
   Defining the FSM   54
   Field sales management and supervision   55
   Supervisor training   57
   Supervisor's remuneration   62
   Eight-point plan for the sales manager   62
   Importance of the supervisor as a field executive   63

PART 3: MANNING AND STAFFING YOUR ORGANISATION   65

15 *Job Analysis and Description*   67
    Specimen job description   68

16 *The Person Profile*   74
    Physical make-up   74
    Attainments   75
    General intelligence   75
    Special aptitudes   76
    Interests   76
    Disposition   76
    Circumstances   76

17 *Sources for Staff*   78
    The intensive search programme   78
    Internal applicants   78
    Advertising   79
    Selection consultants   81
    Headhunters   82
    Employment agencies   82
    Educational establishments   82
    Armed forces   82
    Professional bodies   83
    Government job centres   83

18 *Pre-interview Activity*   84
    Application form   84
    Dealing with 'phone ins'   84
    Writing to candidates   90
    Dealing with the paperwork   91
    The vital five minutes before the interview   91

19 *The Selection Interview*   94
    Aims   94
    Structure   95
    The seven deadly sins of interviewing   97
    Testing and checking   97
    Group selection techniques   102

20 *The Final Decision and Action*   103
    Contract of employment   104
    Conclusion   105
    Action checklist   106

PART 4: TRAINING AND DEVELOPING THE SALES FORCE   107

21 *The Need for Training*   109

22 *Formal Training*   111
    Defining programme objectives   111
    The pupils   111
    The syllabus   112

The teachers 112
The methods 113
Length of training 114
Locations 115
Motivation and measurement 116
Induction training 119

23 *The Use and Selection of Training Consultants* 121
Choosing the consultant 122

24 *Field Training* 124
Aims 124
Trainer's role 124
Content of field-training day 126
Field-training assessment forms 133

25 *Training the Trainer/Training the Manager* 139

PART 5: CONTROLLING YOUR SALES OPERATION 143

26 *Concept of Control* 144
Nature of control 144
Standards 144
Collecting the information 145
Analysis of variances 145
Corrective action 146
Designing and implementing an effective reporting system 146
Relation between planning and control 150

27 *Setting Goals* 151
Step by step 151
Goals are a must 152
Sales activity equals sales results 152
Management by objectives 152

28 *The Sales Process* 155
Merchandising 156
Average values 158
Professional selling 161
Appendices 1–22 162

PART 6: MOTIVATING YOUR SALES ORGANISATION 187

29 *Motivation* 189
By definition and responsibility 189
In practice 189

30 *Theories of Motivation* 193
Maslow – the father of modern motivation 193
Herzberg – action caused by desire 195
McGregor – the theory of X and Y 198

31 *The Hygiene Factors* 199
   Company policy and administration 199
   Working conditions 200
   Salary 200
   Technical supervision and interpersonal relations 203

32 *The Motivators* 204
   Achievement 204
   Recognition for achievement 214
   Meaningful and interesting work 216
   Increased responsibility 219
   Growth and advancement at work 221
   Summary 223

33 *Coping with Troughs and Levels* 225
   Troughs 225
   Levels 226

34 *Who Motivates the Motivator?* 230
   Checklist for self-motivation 230

PART 7: COMMUNICATIONS 233

35 *Communicating with your Sales Force* 235
   Your sales forces is out on a limb 235
   The plumber versus bureaucracy 240

36 *The Nature of Communication* 241
   Rules of good communication 248

37 *Sales Meetings* 250
   Suggested topics for presentations 255

38 *The Printed or Written Word* 258
   Sales bulletins and newsletters 258
   Correspondence 259

39 *The Infernal Telephone and Other Machines* 261

40 *The Sales Conference* 264
   Specialist speakers 266
   Working within a limited budget 269

41 *Dealer Meetings* 271

PART 8: WHAT OF THE FUTURE? 273

42 *Your Personal Role in the Community* 275

43 *Staying Abreast of Change* 277
   Impact of the micro chip 278

44 *Your Personal Development* 281
   The nature of management 281
   Decision-making 282
   Maintaining your own motivation 283

Further reading 284

Index 285

Preface

This book, written jointly by John Strafford and Colin Grant, is intended to help those who wish to become competent, professional sales managers. We have based our material on the assumption that, like so many prospective or even practising sales managers, the reader will fall into one of three categories.

1 A full-blooded practising sales manager who now realises that the balmy days of yore, when it was good enough to reign by being a super salesman, have now passed and that there is now a need to increase his/her practical ability.
2 An aspiring sales manager who, currently serving his/her time as a field manager, recognises the need for further knowledge.
3 A student who has to study the subject to qualify for his or her marketing diploma.

Whichever category you fall into, we do most earnestly recommend you to read on, as this book contains a wealth of practical 'How to' advice for the person who wishes to acquire the skills so necessary to function as a modern professional sales manager.

We have endeavoured to make references to people non-discrimatory. The title 'manager' is as appropriate to both male and female as is 'director' – whoever hears of 'directrix' or 'doctoress' in this day and age? However, if we appear to have erred on the side of 'him' at any stage, we hope the ladies will forgive us.

During the writing of this book the differences between the old-fashioned, swashbuckling, super salesman type of sales manager and the modern, well-informed, marketing-orientated sales manager became all too evident. We hope that our book bridges the gap and in so doing provides all those who read it with the key to prosperity and success.

We would like to thank our colleagues at InTech Training Ltd (especially John Donnelly, Ray Farmer and Bill Woods) and our families without whom etc.

Good luck to you, our readers, now and in the future.

F. Colin Grant   John R. Strafford

PART ONE

The Transition from Selling to Managing

The day you are promoted to sales manager will undoubtedly be one of the milestones of your career. It will be memorable, we hope, for all the right reasons.

For most people it will be accompanied by a rise in salary, a bigger, more splendid car, an office (possibly for the first time), a secretary and all the other goodies associated with the uplift in status. It will be taken for granted by those responsible for your promotion that because you are a good salesman you will automatically make a good manager.

That's one hell of an assumption!

In our experience the choice of a candidate for promotion to sales manager is all too often made on the basis of 'Let's promote Fred, he is the best salesman we have got'.

Perhaps the first question to ask the candidate should be 'Do you *want* to be a Manager?' If the answer is 'Yes', that's a good start. If the answer is 'No', then maybe it would be best for all concerned if the candidate was left to enjoy the status which goes with being the best salesman. Our assumption will be based on your answer being a firm 'Yes'.

Before proceeding any further we should remove any possible misunderstanding. We are not suggesting that a good salesman would not make a good manager. That would be ridiculous, as it would automatically exclude all star salesmen from being promoted.

What we are saying is simply this – it is wrong to promote the super salesman to sales manager on the assumption that because he is good at one job he will naturally be good at the other. Would you, for example, expect an accounts clerk to be made financial director just because he was good at double-entry bookkeeping? Would you expect an engineer to be made technical director just because he was a good toolmaker? No? Why then should there be a different set of conditions for the selection of a man or woman for the important job of sales manager?

So you want to be a manager?

1. *Criteria for Promotion*

Qualities essential for success as a manager

To have any chance of success in the highly competitive field of modern sales management the candidate must:

(a) Want to be a manager.
(b) Have the ability to lead and motivate others.
(c) Be a good organiser and planner.
(d) Be capable of control and administration.
(e) Fully understand the implications of finance.
(f) Have the skills required to recruit, train, motivate and develop those who will form part of the team.
(g) Accept the fact (and use it accordingly) that the computer is here to stay!

In addition it would be helpful if he or she has:

(a) The stamina required to work longer and harder than he or she did as a salesman.
(b) A reasonable degree of good health.
(c) A high degree of natural enthusiasm and integrity.
(d) The unqualified support of spouse and family, of whom he/she will see less than they did before their promotion!
(e) Commitment to being a successful manager.

How do you measure up against *this* checklist?

Making the decision – commitment

On the understanding that you have scored at least 100 per cent (!) on the checklist, the decision must now be taken. You must cross that invisible but very real dividing line which separates the salesman from the manager.

In most police forces a person will be transferred (from one district to another) on being promoted. That gives the person a chance to start the new job without any built-in prejudices and suspicions on the part of those about to be managed.

In selling, the options are:

(a) If promoted within the existing company,
   (i) to be transferred,
   (ii) to stay put.
(b) To take the new job in a new company.

3

With (a)(i) and (b) there is an opportunity to start afresh with new people. This can be an advantage. With (a)(ii) the new manager very often has the added difficulty of being the 'boss' of the team of which he was, until recently, a member. Either way the chances of success are governed by the competence, dedication and skill of the new sales manager. The team, be it all new boys or old lags, will be anxiously awaiting their first meeting with the person that is now their leader.

With the team that knows you the question will be 'I wonder how Fred is going to cope with the job of being our manager?' The team of strangers will be thinking 'I wonder what his track record is, where he came from, what he did before?'

So many newly promoted sales managers have failed at this stage. They have failed through lack of thought and preparation for what was the most important presentation of all; failed at the first hurdle because they couldn't make the transition from 'Good Old Fred, the Super Salesman', to 'Fred, the Sales Manager'; failed through lack of commitment to management.

The super manager

As we have said, being a super salesman does not give an automatic guarantee of success as a sales manager. To be a super manager means producing a team of highly motivated, dedicated professional salesmen. You have to *manage* the team, not try to outsell them!

There is a considerable difference between an architect and a bricklayer. Each is a skilled man in his own right. Which do you want to be, an architect or a bricklayer?

2. Maximising the Selector's Chances of Success

In this chapter, which applies especially to the selector, we suggest certain prudent measures that might be taken to minimise the risk of a costly and unsatisfactory failure.

Will they make it?

Promotion within the sales force of a company or organisation has all too often been a purely subjective judgement on the part of a manager who was himself chosen from the herd by a selector who believed in the infamous 'gut' feeling. The mistake is now in danger of being repeated.

How can we prevent this dubious method of selection? Simple.

The most likely candidate has emerged because he scored quite highly on the checklist in 'Qualities essential for success as a manager'. But what other precautions can the selector take to maximise success and minimise failure? It has been said that the best guide to what people will do in the future is what they have done in the past.

Looking at the candidate's history should tell us something about his loyalty, work rate, administrative skills, driving record, ambition, health and domestic circumstances. The last is critical to a manager's success. He needs the security of a stable home life to balance the commitment required for the hurly-burly of the modern business environment.

What can he do apart from sell?

To select a person for the critically important job of sales manager it is vital to formulate a checklist, loading the points by degrees of importance, as follows:

Quality/Ability	Marks	Actual
Sales record	5	
(Should be consistently good rather than spasmodically brilliant)		
Appearance	5	
(Businesslike, not flashy or 'with it'. Bangles, gold watch straps, gold medallions on gold chains, identity bracelets etc. are not a good sign)		

Quality/Ability	Marks	Actual
Loyalty	10	
(To company, colleagues, management, products, to things he believes in)		
Organisational ability	10	
(Look at his administration, reporting, documentation, record-keeping, planning)		
Humour	5	
(Not essential to be a comedian or an exponent of the 'have a nice day' brigade. Ability to inspire with cheerfulness in adversity is important)		
Intelligence	10	
(More important than outstanding sales ability. Essential if he is to succeed)		
Resilience	10	
(Has he the guts to keep going when the others give up)		
Integrity	10	
(Honest, reliable, knows the difference between telling lies and withholding the truth. Beware of him who continually tells you how honest he is!)		
Good health	10	
(Doesn't need to live on diet of yogurt and grated carrots but looks at the effects of too much smoking, overeating, too much drinking and under exercising. Healthy body, agile mind?)		
Leadership potential	10	
(Watch him in the presence of his contemporaries. Does he look and act like a leader, does he make it happen, or does he hang back and wait)		
Education	5	
(Academic qualities not so important as mental agility and native wit)		
Communication	10	
(Ever seen him 'up front' in a public speaking situation? Remember he will have to inspire by his word skills and presentation ability; not enough to have the gift of the gab!)		
Ambition	10	
(Essential that the person *wants* to be promoted and relishes the thought of the extra responsibility. Beware of the man who glibly says 'I want your job'!)		

Quality/Ability	Marks	Actual
Motivation	10	
(Must be a self-starter, able to keep going when the others have flagged or stopped. Should have the ability to 'make it happen')	(max. 120)	

Such qualities as experience ('in our industry') and background (technical or non-technical, commercial or not, industrial or consumer) have not been commented upon, as it has been assumed that the candidate is being promoted from within. Should the selection be made from 'outside', the selector should question the use and real need for such well-worn phrases as 'Must have experience related to our industry and must be a qualified mechanical engineer (or whatever)'. Our experience tells us that most industrial companies would benefit considerably by recruiting money-motivated, successful, well-trained salesmen with insurance or photo copying experience!

The filter factor

If our candidate is still scoring highly, there is a further action we can take to sift out the failure factors. Why not make the final selection process the responsibility of not one person but several, certainly two. The decision is too important to be based on even the most skilful techniques of one selector.

We suggest that he be put on an appropriate 'open course', where his activity and skills can be judged alongside those of similar people from other companies. Ask for a report from the course tutor regarding the delegate's interaction with other course members, his behaviour and performance and, most importantly, his potential for success as a *manager*.

Why all this trouble?

In 1984 it was reckoned that the cost of a salesman was in the order of £25,000 ($35,000) per annum. Applying the same formula it seems reasonable to calculate the cost of a sales manager to be no less than £45,000 ($63,000). That is a very considerable sum and like any other investment (for that surely is what it is), we must try to eliminate as many of the risk factors as possible.

The sales manager's influence on the sales force is more direct and certainly more personal than the influence of the chairman or managing director. It is, therefore, critical to ensure that the sales manager, who plays such a vital role in the success of the team, is the right person.

3. The Sales Manager's Job

It is essential at this stage to differentiate between the field sales executive and the sales manager. Generally the former is responsible for the training, motivation and development of the salesmen and achieves this by a programme of regular and frequent visits in the field. This vital function is covered in Part 4 of our book. We therefore now intend to concentrate on the role and function of the full sales manager, usually head office based and in control of the entire sales operation, including the sales office.

The sales manager's checklist

The role of the modern sales manager is both complex and demanding. Here is a list covering many of the different facets of the job for which he is either directly responsible or achieves through his subordinate managers:

1 Interviewing, selecting and recruiting salesmen.
2 Sales training and development.
3 Remuneration of salesmen.
4 Salesmen's expenses.
5 Control of salesmen.
6 Training staff in telephone selling.
7 Sales forecasting.
8 Budgetary control.
9 Profit improvement in selling.
10 Marketing policy and profits.
11 Sales manuals.
12 Successful sales bulletins.
13 Sales competitions.
14 Sales conferences and meetings.
15 Exhibition selling.
16 Merchandising.
17 Market research.
18 Direct mailing advertising.
19 Public relations.
20 Speaking in public.
21 Letter writing.
22 The use of consultancy organisations.
23 The computer as a marketing tool.
24 Human relations for management.
25 Audio-visual training.

26 Dealing with complaints.
27 Diplomacy.
28 Personal presentations.
29 Product launch.
30 Quotations.

Numbers 10, 16, 17, 22 and 23 come into play only if he is also concerned with the marketing function.

Basic role of the sales manager

What any individual sales manager does is conditioned by the size of his company, the products it makes and the way they are sold, the organisation of functions within it, and perhaps his own special ability. He may carry most or all of the responsibilities of a marketing manager if this position does not exist within the company.

Essentially, however, the task of the sales manager is to produce revenue for his company through the operations of the sales force for which he is responsible. The size of this revenue, and the profit (however defined) which it should show, are usually predetermined in order to achieve the aims of the company policy. The objectives he sets for the various activities necessary for carrying out this task should therefore be derived from, and be compatible with, company objectives, such as return on capital employed (ROCE), cash flow, market position, growth.

Characteristics of the sales manager's job

1 Many of the factors that affect his success are not within his control (such as competitors and government legislation) and may be imperfectly known.
2 He is nevertheless required to forecast future sales and to plan his operations accordingly, using his judgement and experience.
3 He must depend on other departments for the design, production, quality and delivery of the products for which he obtains orders, just as those departments must depend on him to get those orders.
4 The sales people on whom he relies to produce the results he has planned for are, for most of the time, working alone, not under his immediate control.
5 He is engaged in a constant struggle to obtain increased sales against competitors with the same aim.

Although the basic functions and skills of management, discussed later, apply to his job, it is clear that such qualities as creativeness, flexibility, pertinacity, and ability to deal effectively with people will be particularly important. At the same time the ability to analyse market situations and form sound judgements on them is equally necessary, but may not easily complement the kind of qualities mentioned.

The selling job

Like other managers, the sales manager depends on those who work for him to produce the results by which he is judged. Consideration of his job can usefully continue therefore by examining the nature and characteristics of selling and, hence, of the salesman's job.

Personal selling is only one of several possible ways of communicating with customers and potential customers but, particularly where industrial goods are concerned, is undoubtedly the most effective in terms of achieving the objective – influencing the decision to buy. It is also, even though selling costs may be a small percentage of revenue, expensive. Salesmen should therefore be treated as a scarce resource, to be used as effectively as possible.

Selling itself is a process of bringing persuasion to bear in the following ways:

(a) To awaken awareness of a need or a problem.
(b) To establish that the need can be satisfied by a particular type of product.
(c) To convince the prospective user that the salesperson's own product can offer superior satisfaction.

The actual selling job for a particular product or company may embrace all three of these stages, the last two, or the last only, depending on whether the situation concerns:

1 An innovatory product, hitherto unknown,
2 A product for which there are alternatives, eg, consumer items or forklift trucks and other forms of materials-handling equipment.
3 An established market in which the user can choose from a number of makes.

For economy of effort the salesperson's task (and perhaps the kind of person required) should be defined accordingly.

Other tasks of the salesperson

Although selling is the basic justification of the salesperson's existence and the sales manager's purpose in employing them, all sales people have to spend part of their time doing other things (eg, travelling and making reports). Many sales people are, moreover, often also required:

(a) To provide technical information other than that strictly needed to make a sale.
(b) To give some kind of after-sales service.
(c) To do market research (going beyond the normal, essential supply of market intelligence about customers, competitors, etc.).
(d) To check credit status of potential customers

The salesperson may or may not be best qualified to do such things as these. In addition, he/she is a scarce resource, expensive, and employed to get orders, so that the cost-effectiveness of using him/her for such purposes compared with other means should be examined – remembering also that there may be some loss of sales to take into account (the 'opportunity cost').

The sales manager's responsibility for sales people

Some modern characteristics common to most forms of selling are:

1 Smaller forces than in earlier years.
2 More responsibility and power to make decisions vested in the individual sales people.
3 The need often to deal with a number of people in the customer company in order to get buying decisions.

These characteristics must influence the nature of the sales manager's responsibility for his sales staff and the forms it takes.

One effect may well be that a good deal of market analysis and planning, which is part of the sales manager's responsibility, is often delegated to sales people who, to this extent, are the managers of their own territory. If this is so, the need for clear objectives and adequate general direction is stronger than if sales people were more closely controlled. This also emphasises the importance of good communications and information, flowing in both directions.

Summary

The successful modern sales manager must accept that on promotion the role has changed from doing to managing. Former No. 1 salespersons no longer have to prove how good at selling they are; they must now recruit, train and develop a team of sales people capable of becoming No. 1 salespersons themselves. If one is tempted to revert to the super salesperson oneself when selling is weak, remember the old saying: 'Give a man a fish and you feed him for a day. Show him how to fish and you feed him for a lifetime'.

4. *Seven Key Functions of Sales Management*

Success, like so many other worthwhile things in life, has to be worked for. There is no easy way to be good at anything. This is true for athletes who know all too well that to be above average requires considerable dedication and hard training.

It is also true of management where to be successful there has to be a structure for achieving the objective. Here is a format for successful sales management.

1	Planning	The setting of objectives for the team.
2	Organisation	The strategy for achieving the objectives.
3	Recruitment	Selecting the right people to staff the sales organisation.
4	Training	Developing the skills required to get the job done.
5	Motivation	Getting the best results from the team.
6	Control	Ensuring that results conform to the plan.
7	Monitor	Setting up a 'feed-back system'.

Planning

The sales manager is given resources, human and financial, and he has to plan to use them in the most effective combination to achieve predetermined results. He can only do this by knowing his staff and understanding the nature and the behaviour of costs.

The way in which he deploys his sales staff – whether on a general or a territorial basis, specialising in types of product, or by class of customer or end user – should derive from a study of the market, taking into account also the qualifications and experience of the individuals within that force.

Organising the sales force

The prime objective of all salesmen is to gain business directly. How they are to do this will dictate the kind and quality of skills they need and the way they are organised.

The sales effort must be organised to match customer requirements. The level and quality of customer service must be defined and personnel identified. This analysis will identify the workloads at each level and suggest ways of grouping people so they can be managed well.

Four basic factors need to be measured:

1 How many prospects and customers are to be called on by the salesperson.
2 How often does each category of call require to be visited.

3   The average call rate per salesperson.
4   How many selling/working days are there per year.

Thus total sales force size can be calculated from:

$$\frac{\text{Number of prospects and actual customers} \times \text{required call frequency}}{\text{Average daily call rate} \times \text{number of working days per year}}$$

Field sales management workload must also be assessed. The number of managers needed will depend on:

1   The degree of field training required by the company.
2   How much personal selling (if any) is carried out by the field manager.
3   Does the field manager do *all* the training or is he/she assisted by sales training specialists.
4   The need for different *types* of training required (induction on-going, advanced etc.).

Recruitment of sales people

Selecting men or women who will become successful sales people for any particular company is very difficult, whether they are appointed from within the company or are recruited from outside. It is often made more difficult than it need be by lack of an adequate specification of the kind of people who might be likely to succeed. Such specifications introduce some objectivity into the selection process and provide some measures of comparability between candidates.

The importance of the sales people to the company, and the considerable investment made in them, justify a systematic approach to the ways in which, as candidates, they are assessed and decisions are made about them. The validity of assumptions made about them at the time of appointment should be checked against subsequent performance and the reasons for mistakes investigated.

Staffing the sales organisation

A systematic staffing procedure will include the following steps:

1   Writing the job description.
2   Constructing the person profile.
3   Recruiting candidates.
4   Assessing application forms.
5   Checking references.
6   Interviewing.
7   Evaluating and placing successful candidates.

Training and developing job skills

In planning the development of members of the sales team the following must be considered:

1   What should be taught, including knowledge and skills relating to

   (a)   the company and its procedures,
   (b)   the products and their competitors' sales techniques,
   (c)   work organisation,
   (d)   reporting.

2   Where it should be taught, eg:

   (a)   the company factory and offices,
   (b)   the company training room (or hotel),
   (c)   in the field,
   (d)   on outside courses.

3   By whom it should be taught

   (a)   managers,
   (b)   company's training department,
   (c)   consultants,
   (d)   external courses.

4   How it should be taught.

Motivating the sales force

The sales manager must understand five major motivational forces and the importance of each to the individuals in his team:

1   Remuneration.
2   Direct incentives.
3   Job satisfaction.
4   Security.
5   Status.

Motivation implies two effects in the sales people: the right attitude to their job and willingness to play their part to the best of their ability in achieving aims agreed with the manager. It results partly from training, partly from incentives (financial and other) and perhaps most of all from the leadership given by the manager. Regular appraisal of performance and attitudes by discussion with each salesperson, and observation of their work, are important for this purpose.

Controlling the sales operation

Setting objectives, planning to achieve them, and controlling, ie, compelling events to conform to the plan, are a continuous process. To control the sales operation the sales manager needs accurate, timely information of the right kind so that he can compare actual performance with pre-set standards.

He needs to take action only if there is a significant variance between actual and planned performance. He must 'manage by exception'. This requires that:

1 Standards are set.
2 Actual information is collected.
3 Variances are produced and analysed.
4 Corrective action is taken.

To set standards for controlling salesmen, the manager must decide what constitutes success and what affects the achievement of success. The first point will be answered in terms of absolute and moving standards. Are sales targets being achieved? To answer the second point, the manager needs to consider the action a salesperson takes to reach the target.

He must ask:

1 How many people does the salesperson call on?
2 How often do they require a visit?
3 What kind of people are they?
4 What does the salesperson need to do during the visit?

Having identified the true nature of the variance, the sales manager has to decide how it has arisen and what action to take.

Monitoring for success

It is no good setting up a sophisticated system of activity and control without ensuring that those responsible for achieving the results are actually doing it. A method of feedback (of information and activity) must form part of the sales manager's total system. Remember, *Delegation without monitoring is abdication.*

Summary

Too many senior managements have in the past selected a sales manager for subjective reasons. Selection for this critically important job must be objective.

It is no longer sufficient for the prospective or even existing sales manager to be only a super salesman; he must be a complete businessman in his own right. He/she must be selected not for past skills in selling but for the possibility of being a future candidate for the job of sales or marketing director, or even managing director.

5. *Leadership*

Leadership and motivational abilities are very closely related, as strong leadership will motivate and strong motivation shows good leadership. Readers' abilities as potential leaders will vary, but if we can pinpoint just what leadership is, and define some of the attributes of good leadership, all can benefit.

What is a leader?

Leadership has been defined as 'the ability to inspire *willing* action'. Emphasis is placed on the *willing*. But to understand leadership we need to delve a little deeper than that.

One thing experience has proven over and over again down through the ages is that when any group of people are thrown together for any length of time or for any project, a leader will emerge from the group – one to whom they will listen and give their confidence and support.

His position on the organisation chart or his title alone can make no person a genuine leader. He must have certain *traits* and *skills*, or he will surely fail. In business it has been shown again and again that these skills can be learned and the traits can be developed in any individual who is willing to exert an effort based on strong desire and a true hunger for success.

Generally a leader or teacher does not actually 'develop' another person. He encourages and inspires that person to develop himself or herself from within. Thus, leadership is, in a large sense, self-initiated.

Once we understand and identify the methods and characteristics of an admired leader, we can take steps to develop these skills and traits ourselves. We can analyse ourselves – honestly, ruthlessly, objectively, – and which skills we need to acquire or improve (and those we need to play down).

No one is perfect!

The perfect leader has yet to be born. We all have room for self-improvement. If we can agree upon what it takes to be a good leader – on the traits and skills – we will at least have made a good start. We should analyse every genuine leader we know and try to learn which qualities influence us to consider him a good leader. We can probably agree upon at least five. You may have a leader in mind as we consider these.

Qualities of leadership

Enthusiasm

We will all agree that enthusiasm for what one is doing is one of the first traits. No man or woman can instil much enthusiasm in anyone else for something about which he himself is not enthusiastic. Genuine enthusiasm does not mean a glib, backslapping plastic smile type attitude. More often the genuine leader's enthusiasm is likely to be of a more quiet nature – but it is there! It is shown by the manner in which he goes about his work. His manner of handling his job seems to say to everyone 'This is important! It must be done right. It must be fairly and squarely done! and – *You can do it!*'

Unless a person feels right down in his bones that the work he is doing is worthwhile, he can never consistently (day in and day out) act as though he does. So, if he has any feelings or doubt about the importance of his work and cannot get enthusiastic about it, the trouble is in the person himself. And whether he realises it or not, those around him sense his feelings. His attitude is showing!

Courage

Leadership takes 'guts'. The true leader has the ability to 'take it' when the going gets rough. Often the leader has to 'take it' for the whole organisation to keep its morale high. The leader has to be able to deal with new problems all the time. Indeed, many successful leaders invite difficulties just for the sheer joy of coping with them. The genuine leader approaches each day with a sort of 'joy of battle'; the only people without problems are the ones with a tombstone over them.

Courage in leadership sometimes takes unexpected forms. It may mean standing up for a principle. (Has anyone ever known a real leader who was a 'yes man'?) It means having the character to stand up for what you believe in without compromising or cutting corners.

It may mean taking a bold approach to a new idea – sticking your neck out in support of something which you think is worth trying. It means loyalty to your convictions.

Self-confidence

An important requirement for the leader of today is self-confidence. However, in making decisions about people, their motivations and the way they act or react, the leader can never feel completely sure he is right. The best he can do is to make a sort of 'educated guess' from the facts he can assemble, and then depend upon his past experience and knowledge to interpret them.

However, a leader can be self-confident. A great help is to know and work within his personal assets and limitations. He knows what he can personally do and what he is unable to do. He is willing to listen to other opinions, assess them, and be big enough to adopt the meritorious ones even if they do not square with his original thinking. He can take small reverses in his stride.

A self-confident leader is never satisfied with his present accomplishments, but does not spend his time in useless longing for things he cannot have. Rather he sets about realising his immediate and realistic goals.

Integrity

A leader keeps his promises. He keeps his promises to his associates as meticulously as those made to his superiors. He keeps promises made to himself, which are the hardest to keep, and failure in this is the easiest to rationalise. He can keep all these promises because he never commits himself rashly, but always within the limits of reality and his present capabilities in terms of personal ability.

Part of this matter of integrity is certain, unquestioned loyalty to his organisation – to its reputation as well as his own. In addition, he must be loyal to his products and to his associates, and loyal to his industry. Loyalty to one's associates is extremely important in any leader. He should never allow himself or others in his group to ridicule or downgrade other leaders or people in the industry, as it is a sign of jealousy, and this is one trait that cannot exist in a true leader.

Part of this loyalty is a sense of stewardship – a feeling of responsibility for the welfare, progress and security of the industry as a whole, and that includes everybody who ethically runs a business, everyone in his organisation, his customers and his family.

Interest

A leader has a genuine and empathetic interest in, and a respect for, people as individuals. A very high percentage of any leader's day is spent working directly with individuals.

But be careful – do not go overboard. Here there *could* be a danger signal. Friendliness can, of course, be overdone. Although interested and empathetic, the true leader stays firm – never getting so involved in the personal lives of people that he forgets the implications of his role as a leader. He never plays favourites – and should never play one personality against another. He knows where to draw the line.

Even *Webster's Dictionary* seems to have a difficult time describing the word 'friendliness'. It says, 'it signifies befitting or worthy of a friend'.

Humour

Whilst not advocating that the leader be the 'life and soul of the party', it is essential that he has a keen sense of humour. There will be times when an appropriate joke or light-hearted remark will do more to relax and motivate than all the haranguing in the world.

These then are the six basic characteristics which help a person to be a successful leader. Think of others. Upon reflection, you will probably agree that your ideas are closely allied to or even a part of the six detailed here. They are not by any means a guaranteed panacea for success as a leader. Though all leaders possess them to a varying degree, all of us have known people who had them all but were still unsuccessful as leaders.

Leadership skills

Characteristics or traits by themselves do not make leaders. Certain skills are equally necessary – skills you must cultivate in yourself and in people you wish to develop as leaders.

No one has all the skills of management or leadership to the same degree, any more than they have the personality traits to the same degree. However, it is much easier to learn or acquire skills than it is to develop new personality traits. There are five basic skills, and the degree to which any individual cultivates those skills may well determine the degree of his success.

Co-operation

No one ever got very far completely by his own efforts. It has been said that none of us have ever accomplished anything without the help or the results of the work of someone else. No one walks alone through this life. Enlisting the help of the right people and at the right time is what we call the ability to enlist co-operation.

A genuine leader will understand that co-operation is a two-way thing, and that in order to enjoy the co-operation of others he must in turn be prepared to give co-operation in a like measure. He avoids unnecessary friction with associates in every possible way. He recognises that each person, whether superior or subordinate, has certain responsibilities and makes certain contributions to the group's success. He realises that they are all important – and he treats them as such.

The leader invites suggestions from others and gives each suggestion careful and courteous consideration. He sees that full credit is received by the originator. He knows that asking another's opinion is the sincerest form of praise. He understands that when associates have a part in the formulation of any plan or programme or in arriving at a decision which affects them, they will work all the harder to make that plan, programme, or decision turn out right.

Organising and planning

An effective leader must be an organiser. He must have the ability to see and grasp the whole big picture, separate it into its component parts, and determine what has to be done and in what sequence.

A true leader knows in advance that all is not going to be smooth sailing. He makes advance preparations and plans to meet needed changes and disappointments as they arise. He knows that there will always be some conditions arising which will necessitate an alteration or modification of plans, so he does not allow himself to become flustered by such things when they do come up.

Standards of conduct and performance

No measurement can be made without some basis from which to start and some sort of yardstick. One of the leader's greatest opportunities to lead others to high levels of performance is in the standards he sets himself and how well his personal performance squares with them. He must lead by example as well as by inspiration.

A man who sets high standards of performance and conduct for himself and sets an example of enthusiastic performance will be the more able to inspire others to outstanding performance. This means work and a strict adherence to the code of ethics and the rules of conduct required by your associates.

Decisions

A good leader does not avoid decisions. A procrastinating attitude towards decision-making has ruined more than one otherwise promising career. A good leader makes decisions whenever needed and at the time they are required. He weighs up the implications of his decisions after having carefully examined a number of alternative solutions.

Developing people

Most effective leaders try to make shrewd judgements of character. This does not mean that they are, or pretend to be, 'psychologists'. However, just because an individual seems to be a 'nice guy' or, on the other hand, seems personally obnoxious to the leader, he does not allow his personal likes and dislikes or his emotions to interfere with sound judgement.

Every able leader teaches his associates to learn and to grow. His proudest moment is when one of his people achieves success.

Do not be afraid of people who may appear to be more competent than you. You must replace yourself before you can move on, so develop your replacement to allow for your own progress.

The boss and the leader

The boss knows how things should be done –
    but the leader *shows* how.

The boss leans on his authority –
    but the leader counts on goodwill.

The boss drives his men –
    but the leader coaches them.

The boss always says 'I' –
    but the leader talks in terms of 'We'.

The boss tends to shout 'Go!' –
    but the leader tells his men 'Let's go!'

Avis had a slogan many years ago that said 'Instead of being the manager – be a leader – carry the water for your team'.

Self-programming for leadership

Veteran leaders can pass along valuable advice from their experience. In your leadership during the 'eighties' you can accelerate your effectiveness as a leader if you utilise basic tips such as the following:

Stick to subjects you know

Do not try to sound like an authority on subjects about which you are not sure.

Stay on the track! Stay with those topics you have prepared to talk about and have the background and knowledge with which to impress your listeners favourably.

Learn to think like a leader

This means being ever on the alert for ideas, quotations, figures, benefits – anything you hear, read, see or think about that might be valuable as ammunition for you. Examples always help to sell your points; keep on the lookout for them.

Prepare – prepare – prepare

Supposed leaders who have little worthwhile to say have been known to resort to tricks and camouflage to make themselves look good. Dropping names, blaming others, using meaningless technical terms, lamenting the shortage of time, quoting mysterious authorities – all these devices have been used!

Successful leaders agree, however, that the more you do your homework, the less the need for any tricks. Know your material. Prepare with care in advance – then you have confidence in your developed and natural leadership traits and skills.

6. *Motivating and Developing the Team*

Motivating is that leadership skill of developing other people to do a better job. Within every business you have recognised criteria for excellent development of your team leadership if you have developed your own personal leadership skills.

People developers

What are these criteria for developing others (let's call them people developers).

1   Achievement.
2   Recognition.
3   Participation.
4   Growth.

These four factors are interrelated. One factor may be more important to one individual than another. It is your job as a leader to ascertain what others require in their development.

Let us look at these motivators as related to the development of your team and your leadership.

Achievement

Achievement brings satisfaction, a sense of personal accomplishment that a challenge has been met and the job has been well done. For most people achievement is a reward in itself. It is the spur for people to go on and do a better job.

How do *you* as a leader use achievement as a developer? If someone knows that they have achieved something, they must first know what is expected of them. A goal must be set if they are to realise later they have achieved it or exceeded it. Thus, if you intend to use achievement as a developer, you must be sure you clearly outline goals for your people to strive for.

Recognition

Closely related to achievement, recognition is meaningless unless earned. It is an expression of approval or appreciation by others whose opinion and judgement is valued. Within the business world the many ways to show recognition include the following:

1   Pins.
2   Plaques.
3   Money.
4   Talks at seminars and meetings.
5   Mentions in company literature.
6   Titles.

Recognition or praise polishes the rough diamond of the personality, allowing latent talent to shine out.

Participation

People are more strongly motivated if they feel they have helped in the planning of their objectives rather than been given them. They should feel part not only of their own section but of the total group and company.

Remember inactivity is often caused by feelings of inadequacy. Participation can overcome this feeling.

Growth

The person who feels as if he is at a dead end is at a dead end. He must feel that there are the opportunities available for him to grow and that he is growing in experience, knowledge, skill and understanding. If we can help him to start growing, the person will, in fact, exert more effort. Even the rewarding of others can achieve motivation because it shows that the opportunity is available for growth.

Walking tall

I read a paragraph several years ago and it stuck in my mind. I'd like to share it with you:

THE PLEASURE OF WALKING TALL

Our security, believe it or not, affects the way you stand, the way you walk. In short, your physical well-being and self-confidence. A man without security is always running. He must take the first job offered, or nearly so. He sits nervously on life's chair because any small emergency throws him into the hands of others. Without security, a man must be too grateful. Gratitude is a fine thing in its place. But a constant state of gratitude is a horrible place in which to live. A man with security can walk tall. He may appraise opportunities in a relaxed way, have time for judicious estimates and not be rushed by economic necessity. A man with security can afford to resign from his job, if his principles so dictate. A man always concerned about necessities, such as food and rent, education for children, can't afford to think in long range career terms. He must dart to the most immediate opportunity for ready cash. Without security he will spend a lifetime of darting, dodging. A man with security can afford the wonderful privilege of being generous in family or neighbourhood emergencies. He can take a level stare into the eyes of any man – friend, stranger or enemy. It shapes his personality and character.

ANON

The best security you have in this world is *you*. Your efforts, your leadership and your ability to develop others as leaders will create for you, your company and your family a secure base on which to build a happy and successful career. Add to this your ability to achieve a sensible balance between work and play and you will have acquired the secret to being a leader.

7. How to Obtain Maximum Job Satisfaction

Let us assume that the selectors have done their job well and that you in turn have responded well to the training and the exciting environment of the job. What can you do to ensure that the challenge and the excitement continue? You can develop for yourself a Personal Action Plan.

Rather than allow yourself to drift or merely to respond to situations as they arise, it would be sensible to have a clear view of where you wish the future to take you. Treat your career as a marketable product and write a five-year marketing plan on that product.

Having projected your career into the next five years (or so), set up a number of check or monitoring points so that you can compare Actual with Target. You now have a PAP, which will provide the motive power to success in your career. In addition to the PAP it is essential to ensure your own growth and development. It is all too easy to settle into a cosy niche and forget about the need to continue the search for improvement. A checklist, then, for personal development as a professional sales manager, as follows:

1 Enrol in the appropriate, recognised professional body or institute that will enable you to exchange views and ideas with other like-minded professionals.
2 Set aside time to read magazines of your and associated professions, eg, magazines on sales management and/or marketing.
3 Take an intelligent and lively interest in the other job functions in the company, ie, Finance, Advertising, Distribution, Manufacturing, Computers, and if you cannot understand something, do not be afraid to *ask*!
4 Pick out for yourself the type of course likely to be of value to you and your company and positively plan to attend at least one per year. If you need a sounder foundation for your financial knowledge, choose a course such as 'Finance for the Non-Financial Manager'. If you require a deeper understanding of how the computer actually functions, there are plenty of courses giving 'Computer, Hands On' experience.

It is unlikely that you will have enough time to enjoy the luxury of acquiring knowledge for its own sake. But to gain knowledge for the benefit of greater efficiency is a different matter altogether. In being more efficient you gain the respect of your colleagues and your subordinates, which in turn gives you maximum job satisfaction.

Here is a thought about knowledge and wisdom.

He who knows not, and knows not he knows not,
He is a fool, shun him.

He who knows not, and knows he knows not,
He is simple, teach him.

He who knows, and knows not he knows,
He is asleep, wake him.

He who knows, and knows he knows,
He is wise, follow him.

ANON

8. Managing and Working Relations

A common mistake on being promoted into management is for the new manager to seek, too quickly, a new set of relations tailored to suit the new role. Here is some advice designed to help the newly promoted sales manager.

Relations with superiors

Despite the increasing tendency for informality in business relations, there are still certain rules which, having stood the test of time, have proven to be both workable and sensible. For example, it is usually wise (and prudent) to address one's superior as 'Mr' (or 'Mrs' or 'Miss') .... If superiors want to change that situation, they will invite the junior to use a more informal address (first or christian name). In the absence of an invitation, continue with the formal style. This degree of formality often includes the style known as 'One up, one down', where it is accepted that, although the superior addresses his subordinates by their first or christian names, the subordinate continues to use the formal style.

Remember, there is a very fine dividing line between informality and familiarity. If in doubt, use 'Mr'. Common courtesy should always be the best guide.

Relations with equals

To want to be friendly with equals is very natural, but there is a big difference between being friendly and being too close. It is therefore wise to encourage and maintain a good, friendly working relation with one's equals but at the same time not to encourage the one big happy family degree of closeness.

If you are ambitious and intend to rise in the organisation, it would be sensible and mutually beneficial to associate with others destined for promotion. Remember, a man is known by the company he keeps.

Relations with subordinates

If promoted from 'within', it is always difficult for you and your now subordinates (ex-equals) to establish a new working relation. It is easier if one goes from being a salesman with one company to being a sales manager with another company.

Generally speaking those whom you have now left behind will be pleased to see you promoted and will only want to help. For them it would be sensible to use the 'One up, one down' style.

Exactly how close the manager may wish to come to his subordinates depends very often on the size of the company and the calibre of those concerned. Where the organisation is small and the quality of the men is high, the relation is likely to be informal with no ill effects. As the company grows in size and the managing status increases, the more formal the relation should be.

Remember the golden rule, 'start as you intend to continue'. If you start 'formal', you can always ease up. If you start very informally, you may regret it but can do very little to change things.

Managing upwards

Subordinates should be encouraged to seek more responsibility for decisions they take and for the resultant action. With an intelligently written job description the salesperson should know exactly what can and cannot be done and also know precisely where and when certain decisions can be taken.

While the subordinate should be encouraged to take the decisions that are well within his/her scope of responsibility, the manager should ensure that the subordinate asks for guidance when the decisions are outside their personal terms of reference. Again there is the possibility that if subordinates seek help, advice and even permission from the manager when they are quite capable of taking the decision themselves, the manager is guilty of not developing the subordinates for future promotion.

Development is a vital part of the manager's role. He/she must constantly be aware of opportunities which present themselves to teach subordinates the elements of management, i.e., to manage upwards.

Managing the junior management team

This is different from managing subordinates. 'Junior management' would usually refer to the first line manager, who in most sales teams would be known as area sales manager or sales supervisor. Such persons would normally have in their charge three to six salespersons.

The job of the area sales manager (ASM) is a particularly difficult one and requires very skilful handling on the part of the sales manager. For example, whilst the full sales manager no longer has a territorial responsibility, the ASM may have the dual responsibility of managing people and a territory.

The sales manager should therefore use every opportunity to develop the ASM's man-management skills, concentrating on such subjects as training, motivation, leadership, counselling, and how to run meetings. The commonest mistake made by sales managers in this area is to continue to treat the ASM as merely a super salesperson rather than a junior manager. The ASM then has to learn his/her management skills the hard way, virtually by experimenting with members of the sales force.

Working with women

At the time of writing the question of women in sales and marketing is an accepted fact. This was not always so. But then the whole aspect of the so-called 'normal' job function has changed dramatically, not just in sales.

If one looks back in history, not too long ago lady doctors were classified as almost indecent. Now there are very few hospitals and medical practices which could survive without their quota of women doctors, surgeons and other specialists.

In selling, for the past ten years or so, it has been fairly normal to see a percentage of lady representatives in Fast Moving Consumer Goods (FMCG), pharmaceutical products, toiletries and other products which fitted the definition of 'normal' and therefore acceptable. But acceptable to whom? Why, men of course!

Increasingly the ladies have invaded such hallowed areas as industrial and even technical products, where, contrary to all expectations, they have generally been highly successful. Perhaps the most outstanding example of this is in the field of computers, both hardware and software.

Perhaps now is the time to issue a word of warning to the true male chauvinist sales manager. Do not make the fatal mistake of believing that the female of the species is less resilient than the male. Experience has proven that to be very far from the truth.

In the majority of cases the woman wishing to enter into what has previously been a traditionally male dominated profession has had to work harder than her male counterpart. She has had to be more skilful, more dedicated, more competent, harder working. In other words – generally better! It is therefore reasonable to assume that the reader has already, or will shortly have to, review his thoughts and perhaps his attitude towards the lady salesperson.

In the words of Professor Higgins of *My Fair Lady* fame, why can't women be reasonable, like us chaps? Perhaps they can if we treat them reasonably. Here are some guidelines calculated to ensure a good working relation with the ladies in your sales team.

1   They will ask you to treat them as equals – then do so. Only your pride stops you from letting her pay for the lunch or the drinks. Do as you would if it was a male salesperson.
2   Temper your criticisms with logic. You may be able to 'blast' your way through the problem with a man. You have to be logical with a woman.
3   Do not try too hard to be the 'gallant gentleman'. She does not need to be patronised, or even sympathised with. Offer constructive, objective advice and, above all, be natural. If you would, in a similar situation, tell a man not to be so 'bloody silly' then tell *her* not to be so 'bloody silly'!
4   Sorry chaps, but it has to be said. Please don't imagine that because this is a female, you have the right to exploit the fact. Just treat the situation as normal and keep the relation on a sound *professional* level, as you would with a man. She will respect you all the more for it.

Women in any sales team can be and usually are a great asset. As has already been said, the best guide for our behaviour is to apply common courtesy, (and commonsense). The same rules apply for working with men.

9. Managing Time

It took the authors twice as long to write this book as they thought it would. The publisher very kindly kept extending the manuscript deadline but kept saying it would be the last. One day he said, 'If you don't get that manuscript to me by such and such a date, no book!' They knew he meant it this time, so they finished the book. This they knew was *the* deadline. Time had run out.

Time is probably the largest single problem you are going to encounter in your management career. You will never have enough of it. How then are you going to get done all the things you must do? Simple, make better use of the time you have. Control it, do not let it control you.

The time trap

Here we can do no better than to recommend to you a most sensible, well written, eminently reasonable book – *The Time Trap* by R. Alec Mackenzie (published by McGraw-Hill Paperbacks; cased edition by the AMA). This book, subheaded 'How to Get More Done in Less Time', should be required reading for every manager. It is essential reading for every sales manager. Let us have a look at some of Mr MacKenzie's recommendations and comments.

Time is a unique resource. It cannot be accumulated like money or stockpiled like raw materials. We are forced to spend it at a fixed rate of 60 seconds every minute. While we cannot control its passing, we can determine how we spend it. The eminent Peter Drucker has said 'Time is the scarcest resource and unless it is managed, nothing else can be managed'.

Research has shown that if you were asked to list known time wasters you would produce something akin to List A, putting external influences first, then admitting your own fault. After a thorough discussion on the subject, it is likely that you would produce a list similar to List B, where most of the faults can be seen to be within oneself.

List A	List B
1 Incomplete information presented for solutions	1 Attempting too much at once
2 Employees with problems	2 Unrealistic time
3 Lack of delegation	3 Procrastinating
4 Telephone	4 Lack of organisation
5 Routine tasks	5 Failure to listen
6 Lunch	6 Doing it myself
7 Interruptions	7 Unable to say no
8 Meetings	8 Refusal to let others do the job
9 Lack of priorities	9 Delegating responsibility without authority

LIST A CONTINUED

10 Management by crisis
11 Personal attention to people
12 Outside activities
13 Poor communications
14 Mistakes

© R. Alec Mackenzie

LIST B CONTINUED

10 Involving everyone
11 Bypassing the chain of command
12 Snap decisions
13 Blaming others
14 Personal and outside activities

Here are four more lists from four different groups of managers. Take a sheet of paper and rank them in order of priority. Then ask yourself the question, which items are generated *internally* (by you) and which are generated externally by others. It is likely that in the majority of cases the cause lies within you; or if not the cause, the remedy certainly does.

LIST A

Unclear objectives
Poor information
Postponed decisions
Procrastination
Lack of information
Lack of feedback
Routine work
Too much reading
Interruptions
Telephone
No time planning
Meetings
Beautiful secretaries
Lack of competent personnel
Lack of delegation
Lack of self-discipline
Visitors
Training new staff
Lack of priorities
Management by crisis

LIST B

Scheduled meetings
Unscheduled meetings
Lack of priorities
Failure to delegate
Interruptions
Unavailability of people
Junk mail
Lack of planning
Outside (civic) demands
Poor filing system
Fatigue

LIST C

Junk mail
Socialising
Unnecessary meetings
Lack of concentration
Lack of managerial tools
Peer demands on time
Incompetent subordinates
Coffee breaks
Crisis management
Unintelligible communications
Procrastination
Lack of clerical staff
Poor physical fitness
Red tape
Pet projects
Lack of priorities

LIST D

Attempting too much at once
Lack of delegation
Talking too much
Inconsistent actions
No priorities
Span of control
Usurped authority
Can't say no
Lack of planning
Snap decisions
Procrastination
Low morale
Mistakes
Disorganised secretaries
Poor communication

LIST B CONTINUED
Procrastination
Telephone
Questionnaires
Lack of procedure for routine matters
© R. Alec Mackenzie

LIST D CONTINUED
Over-optimism
Responsibility without authority

And here is the rub. This must draw you to the conclusion that at the heart of time management is management of oneself!

It would be impossible in the space allowed to cover more than a fraction of the good advice given by Alec Mackenzie, but here are some of the key items which it is hoped will whet your appetite for reading the whole book.

Dangers of working long hours

Excuse: To cope with accumulation of work that has piled up during the day.
Cause: Too much non-work, ineffective activity while everyone else is getting on with their jobs.
Remedy: List of priorities; more personal discipline; try delegation; use secretary better; filter phone calls; stop managing by crisis.

Daily time management

Excuse: 'Can't plan my day like that.'
Cause: Too many interruptions; dealing with problems as they arise rather than in order of importance; not being able to differentiate between urgent and important.
Remedy: Draw up a daily time analysis chart and see where your time is going.

Matter of habit

Your present time problem has probably been brought about by a steady, slow growth of bad habits, eg, leaving reports until the last minute, doing things yourself and not delegating (you say it is quicker), procrastinating with decisions and many others. In other words, try to break old habits and set up a series of new good habits.

Planning time

Many managers resist planning because they claim that they do not have time. Sad! In truth, most of such people are merely busy being busy.

Planning will ensure that time is spent doing the important things, the things which only you can do and which have to be done to deadline. Planning time saves time. Set objectives and goals and measure progress by comparing what was *actually* achieved against original goal. Manage by exception – do not examine every situation that is working well, only look at it when it goes wrong. Learn to say no, let someone else do it. Organise your desk, your secretary and most of all yourself.

Do away with the pending tray, it is a trap for the procrastinator. Write short, fast answers to memos by writing answer on original memo and photocopy it. Return original to sender. Use dictation equipment rather than handwritten letters that have to be decoded and typed by secretary. Learn speed reading. Read selectively. Block interrupters, avoiding the infamous 'open door' policy.

Manage visits and visitors. Let secretary make appointments and wherever possible only see people by appointment. Socialising: don't, not in working hours, anyway. The telephone: let secretary filter all incoming calls and let her get your outgoing calls. Meetings: only hold meetings when they are the most effective way to communicate with the others.

Handling decisions

It has been said that procrastination is the thief of time. It is true. Indecision is a time waster and it is worrying to the person who is not making the decision. The procrastinators will say they have to have the facts. That is known as 'paralysis of analysis'.

In many instances the real reason behind the indecision lies in the fear of making a mistake. Even with all the facts at his fingertips the person lacks the confidence to take a decision.

All decisions are risky. The bigger the decision, the larger the risk. While it is impossible always to be right, there comes a time when all the facts have been weighed and a conclusion has emerged. The best that even a great manager can hope for is to make a higher percentage of good decisions than bad ones. It is to be hoped that most of the good ones concern important matters and the bad ones only the relatively unimportant matters.

Delegation

This is an essential tool for you to use if you are to manage your time properly. There are, however, a number of critical barriers to delegation and these are shown as follows:

Barriers in the delegator
1   Preference for operating rather than managing.
2   Demand that everyone 'knows all the details'.
3   'I can do it better myself' fallacy.
4   Lack of experience in the job or in delegating.
5   Insecurity.
6   Fear of being disliked.
7   Refusal to allow mistakes.
8   Lack of confidence in subordinates.
9   Perfectionism, leading to overcontrol.
10 Lack of organisational skill in balancing workloads.
11 Failure to delegate authority commensurate with responsibility.
12 Uncertainty over tasks and inability to explain.
13 Disinclination to develop subordinates.
14 Failure to establish effective controls and to follow up.

Barriers in the delegatee
1   Lack of experience.
2   Lack of competence.
3   Avoidance of responsibility.
4   Overdependence on the boss.
5   Disorganisation.
6   Overload of work.
7   Immersion in trivia.

Barriers in the situation
1   One-man-show policy.
2   No toleration of mistakes.
3   Criticality of decisions.
4   Urgency, leaving no time to explain (crisis management).
5   Confusion in responsibilities and authority.
6   Understaffing.

Managers and subordinates alike sometimes reject the advantage of delegation for the following reasons:

Managers	*Subordinates*
Unwillingness to let go some authority	Unwillingness to take additional responsibility
Failure to see delegation as a means of building team effort	Failure to see delegation as a means of growing and learning
Ignorance of what to delegate	Feeling that only distasteful chores are delegated
Ignorance of how to delegate	Confusion as to the manager's expectations
Restricting delegation to one or two subordinates	Group pressures not to volunteer
Failure to support subordinates executing delegated authority	An attitude of 'once bitten, twice shy'
Insistence that delegated duties be done as they would do them	Resentment at not being given credit for commonsense
Jealousy of their better people	Fear of incurring the boss's wrath
Preference for handling things personally	Eagerness to delegate upward in order to keep the boss busy
Lack of trust in their people	Lack of respect for the manager
Fear of taking prudent risks	Fear of being rebuked for even minor mistakes
Failure to develop their people	Lack of skill in handling delegated authority
Failure to reward achievement	Feeling of not being appreciated
Delegation by abdication	Feeling of being used and abused
Indian-giver delegation	Not knowing where one stands
Delegation of responsibility but little authority	Ignorance of the authority and its limits granted by delegation

Rate yourself as a delegator

How do you know how well you are delegating? Here is a checklist:

1   Do you take work home regularly?
2   Do you work longer hours than your subordinates?
3   Do you spend time doing for others what they could be doing themselves?
4   When you return from an absence from the office, do you find the in basket too full?
5   Are you still handling activities and problems you had before your last promotion?
6   Are you often interrupted with queries or requests on current projects or assignments?
7   Do you spend time on routine details that others could handle?
8   Do you like to keep a finger in every pie?
9   Do you rush to meet deadlines?
10 Are you unable to keep on top of priorities?

If you answer yes to none or one of the questions, your rating is excellent in delegating. If your yes answers total two to four, you should improve your delegating. If they total five or more, you appear to have a serious problem delegating and should place the highest priority on its solution.

Delegation is the transference to others of the authority and responsibility for carrying out certain tasks. Successful delegation implies that those to whom the tasks are delegated know what they have to achieve, actually want to achieve it, have the means to achieve it and have the ability to achieve it.

Every act of delegation is rooted in the relation that exists between the subordinate and his/her boss, the mutual respect they have for one another, the confidence they have in one another as people and the satisfaction that each perceives as coming from it.

The preceding material from *The Time Trap* by R. Alec Mackenzie, originally published by the AMACOM division of the American Management Association 1972.

The Strafford/Grant approach to delegation

1   Analyse the task(s):
    (a) Is it delegateable?
    (b) Is it worth delegating?
    (c) How does this task need to be performed to be successful?
    (d) What time factors are involved?
2   Analyse the people (person).
    Do they have the correct:
    (a) Ability: Now
                 With training
    (b) Attitude.
    (c) Work load (do they have the time?).
3   Decide on the monitoring system.

4   Communicate totally.
    – Sell the job.
5   Train (if necessary).
6   Start action.
7   Monitor and evaluate.
8   Be prepared to act.
9   Thank and praise the performer.

The value of a good secretary

Not mentioned to date but of tremendous importance, the value of a good secretary. Most managers are not good at organising their time. It is therefore critical that an ambitious manager has an ambitious, very competent secretary. This way most of the problems referred to can be overcome, certainly diminished. Perhaps the most explicit example of a secretary's value came from Coleman Hogan of the McCord Corporation: 'The best thing that ever happened to me was having a secretary who wanted to work for a president. I was not the president, so she set out to help me make it. She had a tremendous impact on my effectiveness, and yes, I made it'.

PART TWO

Creating and Building an Effective Sales Organisation

The function of the company should dictate the form of the sales organisation (consumer, industrial, etc.), and in the same way the business/marketing objectives of the organisation should dictate the structure and function of the sales force.

In the past many sales organisations have been put together in a haphazard fashion. Over the years almost panic reaction to the current needs has brought about a structure designed to cope with a particular situation: in many cases a classic case of management by crisis. To make matters worse, such structures have been changed by successive managements, which, without apparent rhyme or reason, have made changes almost for change's sake.

Modern sales managers, however, do adopt a more systematic approach to their decisions concerning the organisation of the sales force. Changes, when they are made are designed to increase profitability, decrease costs, improve efficiency, or effect a combination of all three. It is therefore reasonable to suggest that the well trained, well informed, intelligent sales manager will only reorganise or change some or all of the components (of the team) if he sees a way to make the team more efficient and thus more profitable to the company.

Here are some guidelines for those considering change:

1   Consider the activities and not the individual people currently employed.
2   Responsibility and authority should be assigned to each position/job, not to the individual.
3   Each function/position should be co-ordinated with each of the others, thus preventing overlap, encroaching or empire-building.
4   The span of control, supervision and responsibility of each position should be within the ability of one executive.
5   The organisation or structure should be stable but adaptable to change.

A good organisation is one that allows for expansion (or contraction) of personnel with the change in the value of business. It provides stability and the means to withstand the impact of such things as a change in government legislation, competition, or shifts in the economy. It provides for maximum efficiency (and thus profitability) during the span of the current business or marketing plan.

10. *Sales Organisation, Audit and Evaluation*

Principles of organisation

The first principle of organisation is that activities or functions, not people, should be organised. The major sales activities are sales planning and sales operations. These can be broadly classified as follows:

1   Market research (What does the customer want?).
2   Product (Which and how many?).
3   Distribution (Where and through whom?).
4   Promotion (advertising, selling, exhibitions, PR, etc.).
5   Sales force management.

Within each broad area lie many individual functions and duties which have to be arranged and co-ordinated.

The organisation should be built around each of these activities and not around the people already participating in them, for two reasons:

1   If the people are of limited potential, the activity will not grow.
2   A properly built structure is far more stable and permanent.

Naturally people perform the activities but ideally these people should be selected and placed *after* the basic duties have been defined.

The second principle of organisation is that there should be a proper relation between responsibility and authority. Responsibility for each individual activity should be clearly and specifically defined *in writing* and assigned to the appropriate executive. Without such attention to basic detail there is every likelihood that misunderstandings will occur, tempers flare, productivity drop and 'politicing' start – all because someone did not know what they were supposed to do in a particular job. Wasted efforts and personnel friction can often result.

The third principle of organisation is do not confuse responsibility and authority, and do not give one without the other. A person may be given responsibility for carrying out a particular task but no authority to make decisions concerning changing the direction of that task, ie, to change the rules. Perhaps that may work well for a car parking attendant but it does not achieve very much in a sales organisation.

A person given responsibility for carrying out the task of sales office correspondent should be given the authority to take limited decisions concerning his or her job, eg, minor price adjustments, questions concerning delivery, solutions to genuine complaints, even concerning methods of payment. Failure to delegate authority will most certainly weaken the organisation. If you are going to give a person a job to do or a task to perform, you must give him the tools to do the job.

The fourth principle of organisation is that no worker in a single job should have more than one boss. Selling is a good example of an activity where this principle can so easily be violated, eg, a salesman operating out of a branch where the branch manager is his immediate supervisor being visited by his area or field sales manager, or an executive from head office, any one of whom may go straight to the salesman and ask/order him to do something without first clearing that order through the branch manager.

Where there is a recognised and orderly chain of command, it should be used. No one in management should give orders to a subordinate without doing so through the immediate supervisor. This applies also to transfers, salary adjustments, and disciplinary matters. If this principle is not followed, the control and authority of the immediate supervisor will be undermined.

Need for stability with flexibility

A good organisation will be stable but flexible. Stability is the hallmark of a good organisation but there must be a high degree of flexibility to withstand the day to day blows inflicted on it, eg, people leaving the company, people retiring or dying, people being promoted. These blows should be catered for by there always being someone ready to fill the gap, an heir apparent ready and trained to take over the reins.

The concept of flexibility in an organisation refers more to the comparatively short-run situation. But a stable organisation will also be able to take in its stride such long-range changes as expansion or contraction of its business.

A company should be able to avoid frequent changes in its structure by anticipating demands on it. An organised change should not be necessary every time a new product, territory or activity is taken on by the sales department.

One final point regarding stability and flexibility. A good organisation will encourage change wherever and whenever necessary. It is all too easy in organisational situations to get into a convenient rut, following a policy of 'live and let live'. It is likely that such a policy will produce a situation where rather than make a change, however long overdue it may be, you will leave it rather than run the risk of stirring people up. Remember, 'the only difference between a rut and a grave is the depth'.

Evaluation of needs

As sales manager you may be concerned initially with the following:

1   What sales organisation is there now?
2   Is it appropriate for the task to be tackled?
3   What building is required?

The whys and wherefores of sales force type, size, structure, etc. will be dealt with in subsequent chapters. Now is the time to evaluate what has gone before and decide how you are going to cope with the organisational problems.

Writing the plan

To be a good organiser is a prerequisite for the ambitious manager. However, it is a fact that not all good sales managers are good organisers. If this is true of you, the problem has a simple solution – get yourself a secretary who is a good organiser. Having achieved this objective, give her both the responsibility and authority for carrying out the task of being your right hand.

Do not make the mistake of calling her your personal assistant. That can come later, if appropriate. Secondly, on taking up your appointment do not fall into the trap of 'making things happen' from day one. Much better to weigh up the situation first. Sit around in the sales office and hear what goes on. Go and visit other departments. Visit your existing distributors if you have them. Go out for at least a day with each member of the sales force. Call on some of your key customers, introduce yourself and ask some pointed questions. And lastly, visit your advertising agency, preferably at about 8.30 in the morning!

When, and only when, you have done all this, go back to your office, ask your secretary to keep you well supplied with black coffee, tell her to take all phone calls, etc. *and write your marketing plan.*

11. *Marketing and the Role of the Field Sales Force*

What is marketing?

Marketing is an extremely popular word in business organisations throughout the world now, but very few ever bother to define it for their staff. Many firms use it simply as a modern synonym for selling, others as a grander title for the advertising department.

The true concept of marketing is more than just a department, however. It is the whole question of which way the business is orientated and is one of the vital factors that can make the difference between success and failure.

The Institute of Marketing defines it as follows: 'Marketing is the management process responsible for identifying, anticipating and satisfying customer requirements profitably'. More simply we can say, 'looking at the business through the consumer's eyes', so that the interpretation stretches beyond just the marketing division into every facet of the company.

It is vital because it enables the enterprise to plan on the basis of the true objective and is the only single yardstick which will guarantee success, ie, supplying value satisfactions to the consumer at a profit.

The marketing system

If we examine the relation between a company and its markets, we can see why it is often so difficult for a company to practise this apparently simple concept, because not only is there inevitable conflict between the company and its customers, but also there is friction within the company that cannot be prevented.

The elements of the marketing system are:

1 The market and its segments.
2 The company and its functions.
3 The marketing mix.
4 The environment.

The market and its segments

Many companies presume there is a mass market for their product which can be exploited by mass marketing and advertising methods. Analysis reveals this is not strictly true. Within each market are a number of market segments, each segment representing a group of actual or potential consumers who satisfy the same need with the benefits of the same product. Each segment can also be differentiated by a degree of buyer loyalty ranging from total to nil.

Often these segments have to be tackled selectively to achieve minimum conflict to image and maximum profitability.

The company and its functions

Every company has three basic functions:

(a) production and/or purchasing,
(b) finance,
(c) marketing,

and the two major resources of capital and labour.

Each function has a different objective, operates to some extent on a different time-scale, attracts different types of people and regards money in a different way. Therefore, despite all of them contributing to the policy objectives of the company, there is inevitably internal conflict between, for example, marketing and production and finance and marketing.

The marketing mix

This term is used to describe the offering of the company to the market. It consists of three elements:

1 The product range.
2 The price and discount.
3 The means of communicating, ie, presentation.

It is the method by which the company balances its objectives with the objectives of the consumer (whose objectives in the ultimate are totally opposite), for prices are becoming increasingly similar between competing companies. They are becoming less important, not in absolute terms, but they are becoming less clearly differentiated.

In this situation therefore the element of presentation (ie, the way in which the product and price are communicated) becomes crucial. It is in many markets the only differentiating feature between companies. This element of presentation includes all the marketing tools from research, packaging, advertising, PR, promotion to selling, merchandising, display, etc.

The environment

This whole marketing system has to operate in a restrictive environment. These restrictions, which must be carefully considered as to their effect on the business, include:

1 Total demand.
2 Capital and labour market.

3 Competition.
4 Legal requirements.
5 Raw material supply.
6 Distributive channels.

Role of the sales force

It can now be seen that the function of marketing, ie, organising the firm to meet consumer needs, is the broad strategy. The sales force is one of the practical weapons that the chief marketing executive, who can be the managing director or general manager, can use to achieve his objectives. In most firms the bulk of the presentational effort is carried by the sales force, and thus it is often by far the most important tactical weapon.

In a situation where products and prices are becoming increasingly similar and the sales force is the chief tactical weapon, its efficiency is absolutely critical to the success of the whole enterprise. In fact, in many markets it can be said that the difference between competitors lies in the relative quality of their sales forces. The company with the best planned, selected, trained, motivated and controlled sales force will inevitably gain dominance in the market.

To a large extent, once the salesperson has been recruited and given basic training his/her success will depend on the quality of the field sales manager who controls that salesperson.

Conclusion

The marketing concept is vital to a company's survival in the future as it is the only way of ensuring that the business will continue. Despite this, it is difficult to practise because of its conflicts, both within the company and between the company and its consumers.

In a situation where products and prices are becoming similar, the means of communicating become increasingly important. The role of the sales force is a vital tactical one as part of the marketing strategy of the company.

In many situations it can be said that the quality of the sales force is the key factor in success or failure of the whole enterprise. The sales manager can therefore have a dramatic effect on the success of the organisation, since the quality of the sales force will largely depend on his/her efforts.

12. *Organising the Sales Force*

Defining the market

What market are you in? There is nothing more calculated to amaze, or even annoy, a salesperson than to ask him/her the question 'What do you sell?' But without knowing the proper answer to that question the sales manager has very little chance of producing an effective sales plan.

The sort of typical answers one might receive would be:

1 From a BP/Shell/Esso, etc. service station salesperson – 'Petrol and oil, of course'.
2 From a Dexion/Link 51 salesperson – 'Slotted angles, of course'.
3 From a financial services salesperson (bank, building society etc.) – 'Money, of course'.

But none of these would be the correct answer.

Surely it would be more accurate if the answers were as follows:

1 'Almost anything the motorist wants to buy.'
2 'The solution to materials-handling problems.'
3 'Investment, security, peace of mind, status.'

And so it can be seen that the sales manager must think beyond the product or service that his/her organisation supplies and should instead examine the *total* needs of the persons to whom they sell. If you sell bricks to people, why not sell other things that a housebuilder would want to buy, eg, tiles, timber, paint, etc.? If you sell radios and televisions, why not sell virtually anything that works off an electric plug?

Of course, everyone knows that in retailing they have been doing it for years. That is not, however, true of people in manufacturing or distribution of products and services. Look how long it took ice-cream manufacturers to realise that they could manufacture other products that would sell all year round. Look how long it took hotels to realise that they were ideally suited to provide for the conference business.

Look more thoroughly at the people you sell to. What other needs do they have that you might be able to produce for? When you have an idea of what else they buy, ask yourself the question 'Can we make it?' If not, can you buy it in from someone who does at a sufficiently keen price to be able to mark it up and merely distribute it.

Generally the other products and/or services which you market alongside your existing ones should be compatible with either your existing products/service or with your image. It would clearly be foolish for the manufacturer of fine bone china (say Royal Doulton) to market a range of cheap pottery mugs under the same name. There would obviously be a conflict of image. But that does leave open the further question, why not use your distribution skills and knowledge of the retail outlets to market such a product under another name?

What type of sales force do you need?

Let us first examine the factors which influence the choice of sales force.

Markets have already been discussed in the previous section, and you will now know into which market you are going to direct your efforts. With the use of the appropriate trade directory you will know how many prospects you will have. The industrial sales manager would do well to acquire a copy of *Kompass*, which will give him an excellent insight into the next point.

As for *size* of force, how many people are there (prospects) for you to sell to? This, and an idea of the number of calls you expect your salespersons to make, will give you the size of your sales force. You may not be able to afford immediately the number of salespersons you require. If not, concentrate initially in the areas of greatest potential for your product or service. The expansion can follow once the product/service is well established.

With regard to *structure*, if you are building a sales force from scratch, there will be no need for any structure other than deciding which salesperson operates which territory.

As the sales force grows in numbers, it would be prudent to develop an eye for the person most likely to be your first field sales manager. Before this appointment is made, all members of the sales force would report directly to you.

Much nonsense is talked about qualifications, background and experience – the necessity for the salesperson to have almost a degree, with a solid background in your industry and years of experience with products like yours. In reality none of these is absolutely necessary and very often a detailed knowledge of the product can be a disadvantage. Recruiting an experienced salesperson with intimate knowledge of your type of product will most certainly mean one or both of the following disadvantages:

1 He or she will have been trained (if at all) by someone else and will probably have ideas in conflict with your own.
2 Having previously worked with a competitor, he or she may lack loyalty to you.

If you can, build your own sales force, of inexperienced people with no previous sales or product knowledge. They will be more loyal and usually more productive. Such people will also give you a better return on your investment in them, in that they will probably stay longer with you before looking for greener grass.

Segmentation

As already mentioned in the previous chapter on marketing, there are a number of different ways in which you can set up your sales force. They are by territory, by product, or by market/customer.

By territory

This is the most common and perhaps the simplest way to organise the sales effort. It is only a matter of dividing your prospective market into a number of territories and then appointing a salesperson to each of those territories. That person will sell *all* the company's products/services to anyone who wishes to buy them irrespective of size of account. There will be no specialisation of any sort, just a number of salespersons, each with his/her territory in which he/she sells all the company's products irrespective of any other factor.

By product

This method is a slightly more sophisticated variation of the above. Here each product or group of products is divided up in such a way as to give special attention to that product or product group, thus ensuring very good market penetration for that particular product. The group of persons responsible for the marketing of that product or products would often be organised into a completely self-contained group and would then be headed by a product group manager. The PGM would be totally responsible for the profitable functioning of that group and to that end he/she would have in the team such people as R & D, promotion, distribution, finance and, most importantly, selling.

By market/customer

This is somewhat similar to the 'by product' method, except that instead of the specialist group marketing a group of products, it markets to a particular division of the buying public. For example, a company manufacturing pressure gauges may decide to divide its selling effort so that one group/person sells only to the marine industry, another to the aircraft industry, another to the automobile industry and a fourth group/person to general industry. In this way a high degree of specialisation takes place. It would be advisable when setting up such a degree of specialisation to make sure that the salesperson in each group is a genuine specialist in his/her own right.

Selling 'by market' differs from 'by product' in that here there is no likelihood of salespersons from the same complex calling on the same buyer as each 'specialist' would have a very clear definition of precisely which industry he/she should sell into.

Plan of action

If our previous advice has been noted and acted upon, you will now be ready to draw up a plan of action, a plan designed to ensure that you have given yourself the maximum chance of success. You will have taken your time to decide the best structure for your sales organisation (internal and external) and you will have carefully selected the persons most likely to help you to achieve your objective.

You will have decided whether to organise your outside sales force by territory, or by product or by market and you will have built the team accordingly.

Most importantly, you will have set up a series of systems which will control and monitor the activities of your team; and you will have made sure that with the aid of intelligent delegation you have given yourself time to think. Anything else you should have done? Yes, there is. You will need to make sure that if something goes wrong (which it inevitably will), you know about it. Even if the person to whom you delegated the responsibility and the authority solves the problem (or even crisis), you should know what happens, how and why it happened, what was the solution and how are you going to make certain it does not happen again.

Conclusion

Organising the sales force falls into the cateogory of prime tasks. You might not get it right first time but that does not matter as long as you know how to put it right.

It is essential to be flexible in your approach, but only so that you can make changes for the better, not so that you can continually change your mind. Do not be afraid to experiment, but only do so once you have thought through the implications of your action.

Finally, do not forget about the salesman/manager problem. Remember the question – which would you rather be, a bricklayer or an architect?

13. *More Concerning Structure*

In Chapter 12 reference was made to the importance of the question 'What type of sales force do you need?' There is unfortunately all too much evidence of sales managers not giving due consideration to this critical factor, often being content to only build on to the existing structure. This situation is usually the result of having inherited the structure from one's predecessor and either through lack of knowledge or just good old-fashioned fear, not being willing to examine the alternative. Never was there a better example of the saying 'Fortune favours the brave' than the possible benefit to be gained from possible reorganisation. Let us look more closely at the alternative material mentioned briefly in Chapter 12.

'By territory' organisation

This is the traditional and most often used method of organising a sales force. Each salesperson is allocated a clearly defined geographical territory into which that person sells all the company products. There would be no 'house accounts' or any other form of specialist activity.

Such a system is comparatively simple to construct and easy to administer from the salesperson's point of view and easy to control from the sales manager's angle.

There are limitations to this method, however. If the company have a large number of different products, it is difficult for the salesperson to be an expert in each. This, in turn, limits the penetration of the individual product and causes the salesperson to become a Jack-of-all-trades.

One word of warning to the sales manager. When deciding to organise the sales force activity by territory, it is essential to pay particular attention to the allocation of the territories. They should be as equal as possible as far as business is concerned, and should be of sufficient potential to ensure a good living for the salesperson.

It is not possible to be fair with the allocation of a territory in terms of work (and thus sales and income) without defining the *size* of the territory. For example, one person may have a territory in the middle of the city covering no more than 5 square miles. To give another salesperson the same amount of income potential, it may be necessary to allocate someone in the country as much as 100 square miles (or more).

'By product' organisation

As an alternative to organising the sales force by 'territory' the sales manager can examine the possibility of dividing the people into groups, each group being responsible for one specialised product.

An example of this might be where the company manufacture electronic equipment and allocate, say, computers to one group, office equipment to another group and high-tech medical analysis products to a third group. In such an organisation, each group could be in the charge of a product group manager and would have its own sales manager and sales force.

The job of product group manager in this type of company forms an excellent grounding for the ambitious marketing person as it calls for multi-discipline skills, and is a very good training ground for the prospective marketing manager and marketing director.

It can be seen that by dividing the products into a number of groups, each group having a specific particular responsibility, the members of the group sales force have specialist knowledge of their product, market and users and thus a high degree of individual product penetration can be achieved.

A disadvantage of this type of structure is that it is possible for different salespersons from different product groups of the same company to be calling on the same customer at the same time. It can also be seen that there would be the need for three levels of administration using these methods against the need for only one level of administration required for organising 'by territory'.

'By market' organisation

Here the sales force is organised so as to penetrate an individual market and is most often required for the sales manager to recruit people with specialist knowledge of that market segment for which that person be responsible.

For example, a company may decide to concentrate its sales activity into aeroplane, marine and defence as specific activities. It will therefore recruit persons with knowledge of these three areas and form these persons into three separate and specialised selling groups.

Again, this has the merit of increased market penetration as each particular market will be attacked by a person or persons who have a high degree of knowledge of the applications of and needs for the products in that particular industry.

As with organising 'by product' this has the disadvantage of requiring a duplicate of administration but the advantages will be carefully weighed against the benefits of the increased penetration.

'By customer' organisation

If the company's distribution includes marketing its products both direct (to the end or ultimate user) and through a network of distributors it may be felt beneficial to divide the activities of the sales force into two groups according to the company's distribution policy.

Thus one group will be responsible for selling to and supporting the distributors and the other group for selling the product(s) service(s) 'direct'.

If consulted prior to the plan being effected, it is unlikely that conflict will arise in the sales force as a result of this split in their activities. Distributors have, for many years, felt that manufacturers pursue a 'best of both worlds' policy and would feel more secure in the knowledge that their principals are in full support to the extent of having a separate sales group for distributor sales.

Multiple activity sales force

It would not be unusual in this day and age for the sales manager to decide to combine some, if not all, of the previously mentioned methods of organising the sales force. The employment of a sales person is an expensive business and it is the responsibility of the sales manager to ensure that he/she deploys his/her troops in a way that proves to take maximum advantage of opportunities being offered by the market place. For example, the sales force could quite easily consist of:

1   The main group selling the general range of products 'by territory' but each salesperson to be made responsible for his or her own distribution. All orders for those products, however gained, would be fed back to that distributor.
2   Another (smaller) specialist group would be responsible for selling direct to the end user one or two complex, high-tech products requiring a high degree of technical skill and knowledge. But still there would be a need to allocate a specific geographical territory to each of the specialists.
3   And in addition to 1 and 2, the manufacturer could employ a further one or two specialists whose intimate knowledge of the aerospace industry or the defence industry would make them an ideal candidate for selling to this large and lucrative market.

The modern sales manager must constantly be aware of the need for change – change in the economic circumstances and change in the needs of the customers and prospective customers. Having analysed the market needs, he/she now examines internal resources, personnel and facilities. And having chosen the correct structure to meet the new requirements, he/she must draw up the necessary plan to 'sell' the idea to his/her superiors and to the sales force. Proposing such a change and gaining acceptance is discussed in Part 7.

Designing the individual territories

Whether choosing the more sophisticated method of organising by product, by market and by customer, most companies allocate work by assigning a specific person to a specific geographical territory. If the organisation is large enough to warrant further grouping, a number of territories would be combined to form an area (in the charge of an area sales manager), and can be further grouped by forming a number of areas into regions (in the charge of a regional sales manager).

The regional sales manager(s) would then report direct to the sales manager.

When designing the individual territories, the sales manager generally attempts to provide the following ideal conditions:

1 Territories are easy to administer.
2 Sales potential is easy to estimate.
3 Travel time and expense are minimised.
4 Equal sales opportunity is provided
5 Equal workload is provided.

It is very difficult, if not impossible, to achieve all these ideal conditions. In order to provide equal sales opportunity, the sales manager must classify each potential account according to size of the potential business in each product category, the estimated share of that business from competitors, and the probability of achieving it. Then he/she must group such accounts until each territory has approximately the same volume.

The problem, in fact, is that in urban and industrial areas the total number of accounts that reach the desired potential are located close to each other. In larger, sparser areas, with the same potential, the accounts are spread out, requiring that much time be spent in travel. Clearly, the salesperson in the urban area can cover his or her accounts more quickly than the salesperson in the sparse area. Although the potential may be approximately the same, the workloads are not equal.

Compensation and motivation are discussed in detail in Part 6, but it should be noted that territory construction and the assignment of individuals to specific territories are fundamental to both of these problem areas. This is especially true when a highly productive salesperson can no longer handle a growing territory, and the sales manager wants to divide it into two or more territories. There are many possibilities of getting around the territory dilemma in utilising a hierarchy of salespersons, or 'specialisation'.

Summary

Moving from broad plans and encouraging innovation, this chapter delves into the short-term and day-to-day decisions of a sales manager. There is strong agreement on management principles for organising a sales force, which include the beliefs that activities should be coordinated, authority should be given along with responsibility, balance should be between units, span of control should be reasonable. The sales organisation should be stable in its foundation but flexible and adaptive to changing conditions.

Several examples of function dictating form or structure were considered, including:

1 A top management decision to limit production or to maximise production.
2 Electing to sell exclusively to original equipment manufacturers.
3 Selling service rather than the products themselves.
4 Conducting regular operations research to evaluate function and form.

Constructing territories is usually planning the lowest level of organisation chart.

In general, territories can be laid out on a geographical basis, by product, by groups or customers, or on some combination of all four. Individual territory construction, however, presents the dilemma of attempting to balance equal sales potential and equal workload.

14. *Importance of the Field Sales Manager*

Stages of growth and the Field Sales Manager

Let us assume that you are building a sales force from scratch, and that, as a process of success and natural growth, the need for a field sales manager emerges. Fig. 14.1 exemplifies a typical growth pattern in such a sales force, organised to sell 'by territory'.

The numbers game

At what stage should you move from Stage One to Stage Two? There is no definitive answer to that question but if you are carrying out the true role of the sales manager it is unlikely that you, personally, will be able to cater for the field training needs of more than six salespersons. So let us say that if you can anticipate continued growth, you should start looking hard at each member of the sales force well before the actual need arises; and then you can start a properly designed programme of advancement (for the candidate) well before the day you announce the position.

Defining the FSM

It would be sensible to agree a common definition for the job of, and name for, the person carrying out this highly important task. We would therefore suggest that in common with normal practice we call this first line manager a 'supervisor', and that the name applies to that person of junior management status who is in *direct* control of the day-to-day activities of the sales force or sales group.

The names already in use include field sales manager, area sales manager and area supervisor. Since a salesperson works what is called a territory and a number of territories grouped together for administrative and control purposes is called an area, the name area sales manager seems to be the most logical. However, since many sales people are given this title, we will use 'supervisor'.

The practice of some sales managers to call the salesperson 'area manager' is to be avoided. At best this is done to give the job status; at worst it is done to inflate the salesperson's ego and to fool the buyer into thinking the person is really not there to sell but to do something else. Neither of these reasons is sensible. They merely add to the widely held view that salespersons are almost ashamed of it being known that they sell for a living!

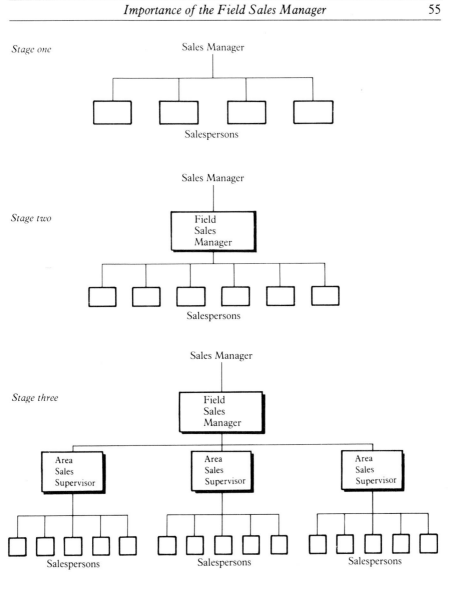

Fig. 14.1

Field sales management and supervision

Field sales management is an essential part of any sales organisation, however small. The function in smaller companies employing up to, say, four salespersons may well be carried out by the sales manager himself on a part-time basis. (In such a case it is vital that his other duties are arranged in a way to permit him to devote a considerable amount of uninterrupted time to this task.) In larger organisations a full-time field sales manager will be employed, and/or a number of field supervisors. Whoever carries out the task, the function is the same and for reasons of brevity the terms used will be supervisor and supervision in this section.

Purpose of supervision

The purpose of supervision is the motivation of the salespersons in the field. Whatever systems of control are employed, there is no substitute for human contact between the salesperson in the field and the company. Controls simply provide the data upon which action can be taken; they do not, of themselves, motivate. The supervisor is the link between the control and the salesperson, interpreting the control or assisting the salesperson to interpret it, and helping the salesperson to take appropriate action.

Supervision should never be confused with selling in a special fashion. Certainly the person supervising may handle special accounts or do prospecting, or even run the whole sales force, but these duties are quite outside that of motivating the salesperson in the field.

Number of supervisors

Quite clearly the number of salespersons per supervisor will depend very largely on the degree of responsibility assumed, the size of the organisation, economic considerations, geography, degree of complexity and uniformity of the selling operation, the ability of the salesperson and the other duties of those carrying out the supervisory function. A recent analysis of 400 companies produced the results shown in Table 14.1. It is clear that, in over three-quarters of cases, seven or more persons reported to the supervisor.

TABLE 14.1

Salespersons per supervisor	Per cent of firms	Cumulative per cent
Less than 3	3.1	3.1
3–6	22.3	25.4
7–10	24.7	50.1
11–15	22.0	72.1
16–20	7.6	79.7
21–30	10.2	89.9
over 30	10.0	100.0
	100.0*	

* Rounded off.

There is a considerable weight of evidence to show that the smaller number of men in the supervised unit, the more effective the sales organisation, but there is no guide on the break-even point between benefits and costs.

Qualities of a supervisor

A supervisor is first a 'man' manager and only secondarily a salesperson. Consequently the attributes of a good supervisor are not necessarily those of a salesperson. The most important qualities are probably the following, which may be used as a checklist when you are looking for a candidate:

(a) The supervisor must know the job to be done and must understand that 'leadership' in its best sense is expected of him/her. Ideas must be assimilated quickly and communicated effectively.
(b) The candidate must have integrity, honesty and sincerity.
(c) He or she should be frank, empathetic and understanding.
(d) Ability to lead and inspire and to give constructive help is important, as is enthusiasm.
(e) He or she should be able to sell, but not outsell!
(f) Lastly, the person chosen must have the ability to develop the salespersons to promotion standard.

It is in many cases desirable, when introducing the system of supervision for the first time, to promote from the field sales force to this post a person with the above qualities. The advantages of doing so may include the following:

(a) It establishes a promotion ladder from field selling to management.
(b) The person selected will be respected by other salespersons as having empathy with their problems from the start.
(c) He/she will be easy to motivate and will pass on the enthusiasm to other salespersons.
(d) Experience in selling the particular products will enable him/her to assimilate and communicate new ideas from management in language and with illustration the salespersons can understand.
(e) He/she will become more effective more quickly than one from outside the sales force.

Ideally, he/she should be promoted to supervise men/women with whom they did not work previously. When selected, the new supervisor must undergo a period of training for his new task. Since the number of trainee supervisors to be handled at any one time will be small, an 'in company' course will be out of place. The new supervisor should instead be sent on an 'open course' conducted by an established company with a reputation for conducting good field sales management courses.

Supervisor training

These are the items you should look for in the prospectus of a good training course:

1 Purpose of supervision.
2 Definition of duties and responsibilities.

3 Mechanics of supervision:
   (a) motivation by leadership,
   (b) communication of ideas.
4 A plan of action:
   (a) interpretation of controls,
   (b) assessment of salespersons,
   (c) supervision in action.
5 Reports and liaison with senior executives.

Purpose of supervision

The reasons leading up to the appointment of supervisors and the company's policy in this connection should be described in detail. Stress should be laid on the fact that it is not the supervisor's job to dash about getting big business, but that he/she must train and motivate the salespersons to do this themselves.

The importance of the job of supervision in ensuring that the company's future position is progressively improved will require detailed discussion, and the supervisor must be clear that he is an executive of the company and carries a big share of the responsibility for its successful operation in the sales field. (See 'Importance of the Supervisor as a Field Executive', p. 63.)

Definition of duties and responsibilities

The supervisor must be fully aware of the company's selling policies. Duties and responsibilities should be clearly laid down and verified in written form to the supervisor.

Mechanics of supervision

Motivation by leadership

This should cover all the appropriate items in Part 1 regarding morale and motivation. Particular stress should be laid on the bad effects on morale which result from the wanton exercise of disciplinary action and the use of naked authority. The newly promoted man may regard his position as one in which to exercise power and the idea must be suppressed from the outset.

Conversely, the easy-going person may have to be stimulated to take a firmer line in handling the salespersons, particularly if they have been until recently his/her close colleagues.

Communication of ideas

The effective communication of ideas leads to action. Communication comprises not just the presentation of ideas, but the enthusing of the recipient with a desire to put the ideas into action. Ideas have to be 'sold'. This 'selling' of ideas necessitates a desire on the part of the recipient to buy them. The analogy with selling a product is worth expanding.

Attention : Interest : Desire : Action.

A plan of action

Interpretation of controls
In training a supervisor in this aspect of the job it must be borne in mind that he/she is probably unfamiliar with the use of ratios, performance figures, percentages and so on in this context, and care has to be taken to ensure that he/she fully understands them before embarking on a detailed examination of what they imply. Of advantage in assisting the supervisor in this matter is a checklist or fault-finding chart showing what questions should be asked when the controls are examined. For example:

> Control figures for A show an upward trend.
>> This means that either x or y is happening.
>> Which is it?
>> Is it favourable or unfavourable?
>> If unfavourable, what do we do?
>> If favourable, what do we do?

Change in control data necessitates action. If the change is unfavourable, motivation, training etc. are demanded. If it is favourable, compliments, appreciation and rewards are called for. But in both cases action must result. This is the positive use of control information in the supervision of field salespersons.

Assessment of salespersons
The Supervisor must be trained to assess all the salespersons objectively. Such training helps the supervisor to appraise exactly at what points he can apply motivation to the best advantage.

Supervision in action
The following notes indicate very briefly the processes of supervision in action:

(i) *Appreciation of policy.* Before the supervisor can act effectively, he/she must know exactly what the company's sales policy implies in terms of action in the field. You, the sales manager, must make this absolutely clear at the outset.
(ii) *Appraisal of the problem.* The second task is the analysis of the situation as it affects each salesperson. The supervisor collates the assessment of the salesperson, the control information, and knowledge of local idiosyncrasies to form as full a picture as possible.
(iii) *Orientation of the salesperson.* Having a clear idea of the nature of the problems to be solved and the means of solving them so far as the salesperson is concerned, the Supervisor must set out deliberately to make the salesperson receptive to a suggested solution. By setting an example and by inviting criticism from the salesperson, the supervisor will create the atmosphere of mutual confidence so necessary in every selling situation.

The supervisor must be careful not to oversell with enthusiasm and to swamp the salesperson with bright ideas. It must be made clear that together they are a team with a common problem, not master and servant. This corresponds to the stage of 'creating attention' in the more usual selling operation. The supervisor needs to exercise all his tact and skill, carefully adapting his method to suit each salesperson, to carry out this process.

(iv) *Presenting the problem.* The supervisor presents the problem in such a way that the salesperson becomes aware of its importance to him/her. The abstract presentation unrelated to the person cannot succeed in stimulating action. The salesperson must be absolutely clear that he/she personally is involved and that prospects, earnings and status can be improved if this problem is solved. This is 'creating interest' in the problem.

(v) *Solving the problem.* If the problem has been defined and presented in the right way, then the solution can be found by the salesperson himself, guided by the supervisor. The way the problem has been presented will define the nature of the solution offered by the salesperson, so that care must be taken to ensure that it is only action by the salesperson himself which can solve it. In guiding the salesperson to the solution, the supervisor must be on guard lest this guidance is misconstrued as personal criticism.

Self-respect is one of the salesperson's basic assets. To damage it does more harm than good. This is not to say of course that the supervisor should subordinate his/her own personality to that of the salesperson, but he/she should be on constant guard against dominating the salesperson.

If this stage is carried out effectively, the salesperson should be inspired to carry out the necessary action to solve the problem. 'Desire' has been created.

(vi) *Action.* The salesperson, enthusiastic about the new idea, tries to put it into action. He/she may fail to attain the objective at the first attempt and becomes discouraged, losing self-confidence. The supervisor should observe these first efforts and give guidance to correct faults and improve the method used, before the feeling of failure asserts itself or the faults become habits.

The 'follow-up' is vital to the success of the process. It should stimulate the salesperson further because it shows that the supervisor's interest in the idea is sustained and that he/she also is anxious to make it succeed.

It is important that, when the new idea is perfected, a written record is made so that the salesperson can keep in front of him/her all the improvements which he/she has achieved. A copy of this record should be kept by the supervisor as a reminder to follow it up on subsequent occasions and to help to progress systematically to other problems with the salesperson.

It must be recognised that an individual's capacity to learn and to act on what he/she has learned is very limited. Consequently, only one major problem should be tackled at every meeting between supervisor and salesperson.

(vii) *Motivation by discipline.* Disciplinary action can be negative and repressive, but it can be used to provide stimulation. The complacent, satisfied, but ineffective salesperson who will not respond to leadership provided by the means above may require to be reminded that he/she is paid to do a fair day's work. The response to other forms of motivation may then be expected to improve. If motivation has to take this form, it is essential that an appraisal of the other methods used is made, because the possibility always exists that it is not the salesperson but the supervisor who is at fault.

Reports and liaison

It is important that the supervisory function is properly integrated with the management line between senior sales executive (you) and the salespersons. If the post of supervisor is a new one, difficulty may be experienced in weaning salespersons from direct contact with higher management. This can best be overcome by routing all salespersons' contact with the head office through the supervisor, or by keeping the supervisor informed on such items as expenses, reports, records, correspondence, complaints etc. Provision should be made for this in the organisation from the outset.

In all cases, however, communication between supervisor and senior sales executive should be made quick and easy. This is facilitated by using a pro forma weekly supervisor's report, which includes not only details of the subjects covered with individual salespersons in the week past, but also the programme for the coming week with contact addresses.

The information required by a supervisor to enable him/her to carry out his job effectively may include the following:

(a) Sales performance controls of each sales territory and of the whole supervisory area.
(b) Salesperson's salaries, expenses and bonus earnings.
(c) Salesperson's journey plans for future work.
(d) Details of new accounts, lapsed accounts and bad debts.
(e) Lists of prospects salespersons should call on.
(f) Exact definitions of salespersons' territories.
(g) All general sales directives, bulletins, conference programmes etc.
(h) Details of all sales promotion activities.
(i) Copies of letters to salespersons and customers.
(j) Field training programmes for salespersons.

It is advisable for the supervisor to be given assistance in setting up his/her own filing system and in compiling his/her own work programme. The work programme agreed with the senior sales executive should lay sufficient stress in the right proportion on the practical problems to be tackled in the correct order of importance. Typical lists might be as follows:

(a) Salesperson's effort not used to best effect:
  (i) Little or no selling on Friday afternoons or at certain hours.
  (ii) Late starting, early finishing, long meal breaks.
  (iii) Bad journey planning.
  (iv) Wasted time; waiting for buyers, idle conversation, broken interviews.
(b) Salesperson's skill not used to best effect:
  (i) Negative approach to selling; not creative.
  (ii) Pressure selling badly done; adverse customer reaction.
  (iii) Selling in but not out again; no display work.
  (iv) Sheer bad manners/dress/appearance.
(c) Salesperson's clerical work inefficient:
  (i) Untidy, sloppy and unsystematic; careless.

    (ii)   Too much paperwork.
    (iii) Follow-up on orders/accounts ineffective; complaints.

Such lists, coupled with a definition of function, training in management and adequate control data, should enable the supervisor to start his task in the most effective way. A short list of hints for supervisors is a useful reminder about minor points.

Supervisor's remuneration

The method of remuneration of supervisors depends almost entirely on the nature of their responsibilities. For example, if the supervisor's success is measured in terms of the increased sales volume obtained by his salespersons, it is appropriate that he/she should participate in the normal incentive scheme operating on those salespersons.

If, on the other hand, the supervisor is responsible for the economic operation of all the salespersons' territories, and if he/she has real authority over all the cost factors, it is appropriate to pay an incentive bonus based on the reduction in the cost/volume ratio. There are dangers in this, however, if a supervisor's attempts to reduce costs result in irrecoverable loss of business. A good supervisor is not necessarily a good business manager.

Because of the complexity of a supervisor's responsibilities, it may be unwise to direct his attention to only one factor in the situation over which he has control by applying incentives in these ways. It should be remembered that financial incentive is at best only one of very many ways of motivating supervisors.

An eight-point plan for the sales manager

Creating and building an effective sales organisation requires a very high degree of skill on the part of the sales manager – YOU! You may have only been recently promoted and may therefore have to learn a considerable number of skills in a comparatively short space of time. But it can be done and, indeed, the very fact that you are reading this book would indicate that you are intent on making the transition (from salesperson to manager) as painless and as successful as possible.

At the risk of this sounding like a recipe for instant success, (add water and you will be a sales manager!) here is a plan for transition:

Stage One. Study what has gone before. What did your predecessor do? If it went
    wrong, *how* did it go wrong? PRIME TASK TIME.
Stage Two. Get to know all those who will be instrumental in your success.
Stage Three. Visits with the sales force.
Stage Four. GO ON A SALES MANAGEMENT COURSE.
Stage Five. Get yourself a good secretary.
Stage Six. Announce your first sales meeting and tell them what they have been
    waiting to hear!
Stage Seven. Now carry out the plan, using a control system to monitor it.
Stage Eight. Start thinking about whom you will promote to your job!

Importance of the Supervisor as a Field Executive

Your company lives by sales. From managing director to customer there is a long chain of command. Weakness in any link must result in reduced effectiveness.

As a field executive you occupy an intermediate but key position between salespersons and senior executives. Your responsibilities in both directions daily demand a high standard of personal qualities and abilities if you are to succeed in your vital role. No matter how carefully your men are selected, trained in your products, and supported by Head Office, it is on the quality of their field supervision that success – or lack of it – will largely depend.

This means YOU.

Your work provides constant challenge as well as stimulus. It is in your power to solve many problems, clear up difficulties that puzzle your men/women, and help them develop their abilities to the full. This demands a readiness on your part to recognise each person's strengths and abilities as well as their personal limitations. You will then, through constant observation, be the better able to pass on acceptable ideas and methods which you know to be effective.

As a result, you will raise the level of individual achievement and, at the same time, help create a genuine team spirit. It is on the way you do this that your work as a field executive will be judged – by those above as well as below you.

PART THREE

Manning and Staffing your Organisation

Millions of words have been written upon this subject, proving the dictum that if you can find one bad theory to solve a problem, you can find twenty. In Part 3 we want to look at the practical methods of getting the best person to do an identified job, in the shortest possible time, at the least cost.

The word 'select' is defined by the dictionary as 'chosen for excellence; obtained by rejection or exclusion of what is inferior', which, if you go by the people that many companies choose, would suggest that those companies are not selecting but merely recruiting. A recruit is defined by the same dictionary as a 'newly enlisted and not yet trained soldier or beginner'. In many companies even recruiting is too strong a word for what happens and perhaps a better description of what they do would be 'finding bodies'.

There is a current delusion that with a high level of unemployment it is easy to find the right person. In fact it is likely to be more difficult now than it was previously.

If we look at sales people and sales managers in this context, we find that in days gone by, when it was relatively easy to change jobs and find a better one, there was a mobility which caused good people to be available. They were available because they knew that they would not be available for long. This is no longer the case and the good sales person or manager tends to stay where he is rather than sample the greener pastures elsewhere. So, while there are a lot of people available, it is doubtful whether there are as many of the right people as in days gone by.

The positive side of this argument is the fact that, once the right people have been selected, they are likely to give longer service to your organisation than in the past, providing they are properly managed.

It has been said that, when faced with someone leaving, managers should ask themselves:

Who hired this person?
Who trained this person?
Who motivated this person?
Who controlled this person?
Who failed this person?

The latter questions are dealt with in different sections of the handbook, but the first has to be answered in its widest sense in Part 3.

While we do not subscribe to the theory that sales people are born not made, it is true that only some people can become productive sales personnel and even less (and sometimes not the same people) can become good sales managers. So long as a manager's success is judged by the results which come from the calibre of the members of his/her sales team, the importance of a professional approach to the function of recruitment and selection cannot be over-stressed.

This professional approach includes:

1 Deciding that there is a *real* job to be filled.
2 Analysing that job to prepare a practical job description.
3 Extending that job description into a profile of the person needed.
4 Reviewing the various sources and picking the one or ones that are appropriate in any particular case.
5 Constant improvement of interviewing skills.
6 Making decisions based on fact and experience and not just gut-feeling.
7 Following through with positive action to ensure that the person selected actually starts.
8 Constant review after selection to measure the success of the recruitment activity.

In these chapters these areas are investigated and the available alternatives are analysed to enable the modern sales manager to choose the appropriate method.

15. *Job Analysis and Description*

Many sales managers faced with the prospect or the fact of a vacancy immediately leap into action and either place an advertisement, call their favoured selection consultant or contact their company's personnel department for an 'immediate' replacement, thereby ignoring the golden rule of engaging the brain before getting things to happen.

The 'engaging the brain' action that should occur is firstly to investigate why there is a vacancy at all.

1 Is it because someone has left the sales force? If this is the case, then the reasons have to be thoroughly investigated to ensure wherever possible that the next person is not just being recruited to be lost.

Sales staff normally leave a company for one of the following reasons:

(a)   They are being seriously mismanaged.
(b)   They have become completely frustrated either by (a) or by the nature of the organisation.
(c)   They are not enjoying enough success (particularly true of sales people).
(d)   They have been offered a better job elsewhere.
(e)   They are bored by what they are doing.
(f)   External pressures (family problems etc.).

Whatever the reason, now is the time (or even past the time – but better late than never) to investigate and take whatever positive steps are within your power to improve the situation and prevent the future loss of productive staff.

2 Is it because actual or required growth dictates the need for improved territory coverage? In this case the sales manager has to ask him/herself, 'Will recruiting an extra sales person or persons achieve my objective or are there other more cost-effective ways that I should investigate?'
3 Is it because a sales person has been promoted to another position? Here sales managers have to decide whether they need a replacement or whether it is feasible to operate as successfully with one fewer salespersons. In other words, by looking very carefully at why that vacancy exists it can be decided whether there is a real vacancy, since the only acceptable criteria for recruiting someone new is that there is a *real job to do*.

If there is a real job to be done, then it must be feasible to analyse and write a proper job description. The emphasis here is on 'proper', since many job descriptions bear little or no relation to the actual job or are written in such verbose, woolly terms as to be meaningless.

Every person in a company should have an accurate job description for the direction of their day-to-day activity. It is also impossible for the sales manager to move to the next step in the professional selection process without such a job description.

Specimen job description

The job description should contain the following:

1   Job title.
2   Purpose and primary objective.
3   Supplementary objectives.
4   Responsible to.
5   Responsible for.
6   Other relationships.
7   Duties.
8   Authority levels.
9   Performance standards.
10 Remuneration.

Fig. 15.1 gives a specimen job specification for a salesman, and Fig. 15.2 a job definition.

SPECIMEN JOB SPECIFICATION
SALESMAN

A salesman is responsible for:

1   Achieving the quota allocated to him by the company on a monthly as well as annual basis.
2   Selling the company's products in accordance with the company's policies within the area assigned to him.
3   Having a thorough knowledge of:

   (a) Professional sales techniques.
   (b) The company's products.
   (c) The application of them.
   (d) His sales territory.
   (e) The market and potential in it.
   (f) His customer's business.

4   Having a thorough understanding of the company's policies.
5   Creating, developing and maintaining the company's image in his territory.
6   Expanding the company's position in his area by developing both new and existing accounts.
7   Selling equipment to the company's and the customer's advantage.
8   Employing the sales methods imparted by the company.
9   Providing adequate information about competitors' activity in his territory.
10 Presenting other information as required with clarity, brevity and precision.
11 Maintaining comprehensive records as required.
12 Maintaining in first-class condition the company's property issued to him.
13 Carrying out from time to time such duties as shall be required of him by the company's management.

Fig. 15.1

Job title

This is the official and actual name of the job. It has to be accurate or the wrong people will be attracted. It should avoid the trap, into which many companies have been falling, of giving high-blown titles for the sake of boosting the ego of either their customers or their staff. If the true definition of the job is that of sales person or sales engineer, that is what it should be called, not area manager or customer relations supervisor!

Purpose and primary objective

This is the reason why the job exists. It is a brief and specific statement which quantifies the method by which success will be evaluated. Getting this part right is not easy – too long and we run the risk of clouding the specifics, too short and we will almost certainly miss out some of those specifics. Perhaps the most significant omission in most job descriptions is in the area of how success will be evaluated. If profitable new business is the key area, for example, then the amount of increase per annum should be given as a guideline. 'To increase profitable new business by 10 per cent per annum' is more specific than just 'to increase new business'.

Supplementary objectives

These describe other priorities within the job function.

Responsible to

This states the one to whom the person reports – there are almost no excuses for this to be more than one person. If there is more than one person, it normally suggests a fault in the organisational structure.

Responsible for

This lays down, by job title, those persons who report to the job holder.

Other relationships

These comprise those persons with whom the job holder will have normal direct contact outside the vertical line structure, and includes those outside the company.

Duties

The primary functions of the job holder will obviously relate directly to the 'purpose and primary objective' and 'supplementary objectives' mentioned above.

Authority levels

These comprise the financial and other levels of responsibility and authority.

Performance standards

These lay down the basic quantitive and qualitative standards which have been decided on as necessary for the objectives to be achieved.

Remuneration

This should have been decided upon in relation to the job's objectives and responsibilities and should include all tangible rewards included in the package, i.e. commission/bonus, car, holidays, fringe benefits, etc.

Once an effective and efficient job description has been compiled (Figs 15.1 and 15.2), a person profile/specification can be defined.

JOB DEFINITION

JOB TITLE:	Sales Representative
RESPONSIBLE TO:	Sales Manager

MAIN FUNCTIONS: (a) To promote the sale of company's merchandise to existing customers, accurately recording and processing related documents and records.

(b) To obtain new business in line with company policy.

RESPONSIBILITIES AND TASKS   **MEASURE OF PERFORMANCE**

ACTIVITY AREA 1:
Product and Technical Knowledge

1 To acquire and maintain complete knowledge concerning the firm's range of products and services.
2 To apply the above knowledge in relation to customers' requirements and problems.
3 To acquire and maintain up-to-date information concerning competitors' products and services and related pricing policies.
4 To acquire and maintain up-to-date information concerning the technology of our industry and particularly to keep up with all developments which in turn affect our product range.

ACTIVITY AREA 2
Planning and Organisation

1 To optimise the time available by effective planning.

(a) The operation of the territory on a fortnightly basis, with allowance for exigencies.
(b) Individual interviews, with particular detailed reference to major prospects and customers.
(c) The sequence and nature of calls, making appointments for a hard core of interviews and visits around which to build the day's activity.

2 To maintain an up-to-date record and information system covering in detail all customers and prospects, and the current negotiation situations.
3 To maintain a financial record system of business obtained.
4 To maintain an up-to-date working file containing relevant memoranda, sales bulletins and general information, including sales, sales areas and personnel.
5 To maintain up-to-date literature, sales aids,

samples and price lists.

6   To maintain an up-to-date working file on competition regarding their personnel, products, service and activities.

7   To complete and return the paperwork required by firm, including expense sheets, enquiry/quotation requests, action reports and market intelligence reports.

8   To analyse activities continually, making use of such ratios as:

(a)   approaches to enquiries obtained,
(b)   numbers to value of orders obtained,
(c)   presentations to orders obtained,
(d)   miles covered per call per order.

9   To ensure car is properly serviced and maintained.

ACTIVITY AREA 3
Selling Skills

1   To locate every prospective customer on the territory.

2   To obtain enquiries from existing customers and new prospects by:

(a)   Conducting an approach or opening in the interview that obtains the opportunity to present the firm's merchandise to meet prospect's needs.
(b)   Providing a satisfactory presentation combined with demonstration as appropriate.

3   To meet the set quotas for orders and types of orders by:

(a)   Providing a satisfactory presentation, with a positive close to the negotiation.
(b)   Answering to the satisfaction of the customer such objections or questions as are raised.

4   Continually to sharpen selling skills and activity by:

(a)   Preparing beforehand the sequence of selling activity required for each type of interview encountered.
(b)   Analysing past interviews and selling performances with an analytical approach designed to learn from both mistakes and good points made.

5   To ensure customer satisfaction by providing liaison with the relevant departments of the firm, and following up by checking the service provided by those departments.

6   To obtain payment against outstanding accounts
    and where applicable to clear queries or
    misunderstandings which have held up such
    payment.

ACTIVITY AREA 4
Market Research

1   To provide continual feedback through
    completion of formal reports concerning:

    (a)   The image of the firm held by customers,
          competitors, distributors and the trade in
          general.
    (b)   The acceptance of products, prices and
          service in general.
    (c)   The existence of product sales opportunities
          not being exploited by the firm regarding:

          ● existing range – new markets
          ● modified range – existing markets.
          ● modified range – new markets.
          ● new range – existing markets.
          ● new range – new markets.

    (d)   Such technological factors in the industry
          which will influence the firm currently or in
          the future.
2   To provide continual commentary on customers'
    businesses, developments and marketing
    activities, particularly where their needs are, and
    our existing range of products is, concerned.
3   To provide continual sales audits relating to
    competitors.
4   To provide feedback concerning competitors'
    total marketing activity.
5   To complete individual project reports within the
    time, and in the detail, specified.

Fig. 15.2

16. *The Person Profile*

The National Institute of Industrial Psychology has given us a good framework for constructing a practical person profile under the following seven headings:

1 Physical make-up.
2 Attainments.
3 General intelligence.
4 Special aptitudes.
5 Interests.
6 Disposition.
7 Circumstances.

We can use these seven headings to list those things that are (a) essential and (b) desirable in the successful candidate. Let us look at those headings in slightly more detail.

Physical make-up

From the job description we can decide the acceptable standards of age, health, appearance, manner and speech. The relative importance of these things can be emphasised when we look at them individually.

Age

In looking for sales people many companies seem to be locked-in to the 25–30 age group, presumably because they think that maturity has been reached, senility has not and that this age group will show a high activity factor. Yet there are countless immature 35-year-olds, and many 50-year-olds are more active than most of those aged 18. The important thing is to consider the job this person has to do, eg in many cases a 30-year-old will not have had sufficient technical experience, in others a great deal of lifting of heavy goods is required, which may debar those in the higher age group.

Health

Many people underestimate the need for not just good health in sales and sales management personnel but fitness as well. A doctor told me that a day spent driving and communicating with customers probably takes more out of a person than two days' hard physical labour on a building site. The other health factor to note is physical defects, such as back trouble. This ailment causes more time off in the UK than any other physical problem. One company that sold photocopiers recruited, in one twelve-month period, five sales people who had permanent back problems! It goes without saying that most of their time was spent in lifting demonstration machines into and out of prospect's premises. So again decide on the minimum health requirement in terms of the job description.

Appearance, manner and speech

While first impressions are not the only important criteria, it is true that they are important, particularly in the one-off, no repeat, sales area. The persons recruited have to be *acceptable* to the people with whom they are going to come into contact, so again the job description will provide the standards required.

Attainments

Here we need to consider three areas.

(a) What educational qualifications do we need?
(b) Do we need someone with a successful track record in their occupation?
(c) How desirable is it that the person has had occupational training?

Educational qualifications

Companies still continue to ask for educational standards in excess of the educational needs of the job, and then wonder why those recruited leave because they are bored. The type of education received may well in many jobs be more important than the qualifications achieved. The sign often seen in the Indian sub-continent – BA Oxford (failed) – may be less of a joke than many people think, since it is often more important to have done the course than to have got the piece of paper at the end of it.

Track record

Just because someone was successful with another company or in another occupation does not necessarily mean they will succeed in the future. It depends heavily on the differences between the two companies or two occupations.

Question of occupational training

Many sales managers would prefer to take on someone who has not been trained by another, since it may be better to start from scratch rather than take on not just some other organisation's good habits but also their bad ones.

General intelligence

A more difficult area to assess, but what we will need to establish in each candidate is not only how much general intelligence they *can* display but also how much they will *ordinarily* display. In the profile we will need to show that the candidate must have sufficient general intelligence to perform in certain defined ways and situations.

Special aptitudes

Are there any needed for this job? Such aptitudes as mechanical, manual or physical dexterity or a particular facility with words, figures, music, drawing? One or more of these may be vital.

Interests

A person's interests are certainly an indication of his/her character, activity level and sometimes intelligence, but are there any particular interests that would help the person doing this job? Incidentally, approach with caution anyone who is *too* good at something. For example, someone applying for a sales job who is a low-handicap golfer may spend more time on the golf course than selling.

Disposition

Here we can consider and define the degree of needs for the person to be reliable, self-reliant, an influencer, dependable, industrious, etc.

Circumstances

It is often impossible, and many would say undesirable, to separate a person's business life from his home life. It is important, therefore, to consider the circumstances under which the job will be done and the necessary personal circumstances of the candidate, eg a job that is going to require a person spending months away from home may indicate that either a single person or someone with a very settled marriage would be desirable.

By defining the required person under the seven headings, it is feasible to arrive at the word portrait of a candidate who will meet the essential requirements of the job. Remember, however, that supermen or gods rarely apply for jobs in selling, so do not start out by looking for one. Make sure the profile is practical by listing only those things that are (a) essential and (b) desirable, as does the example in Fig. 16.1.

So once we know that there is a job to do, that we have a description of it and a profile of the person desired, then we can go on to look at the sources we can use to find our candidate.

EXAMPLE OF PERSON PROFILE – SALESMAN

FACTORS TO BE CONSIDERED	ESSENTIAL	DESIRABLE
1 *Physical*		
Age	Maturity	28–35
Health	No physical disability	
Appearance (including manner and speech)	Businesslike, formal dress, articulate	Confident but pleasant
2 *Attainments*		
Education	'A' Levels (or equivalent) in maths, physics	Degree standard – science-based
Experience	Minimum two years industrial selling	Has dealt with large petro-chemical companies
Professional qualifications	—	M.Inst. Physics
Training		Has had some formal training in selling skills
3 *General intelligence*	Ability to apply logical thought to technical problems	Has broad range of intelligence to be able to communicate with senior scientists
4 *Special aptitudes*	Able to compile comprehensive technical reports	Some experience in using computers for evaluation of projects
5 *Interests*		
(a) Work-related		Active member of technical association
(b) Social (are these related to group activities or alone?)		Group-related, eg social club/drama group
6 *Disposition*		
Stability	Not more than two jobs in last five years	
Reliability		Self-reliant. Able to make decisions
Industry		Show evidence of willingness to work
Perseverance	Can obtain new business	Evidence of finishing task started
Motivation factors: – money – status – security – competitiveness – recognition – growth, advancement		
7 *Circumstances*		
Home		Married and buying own home
Area	Willing to relocate	Lives in area
Mobility		Will accept long and irregular hours
Driving licence	Clean	

Fig. 16.1

17. *Sources for Staff*

The intensive search programme

The major sources for new sales/management staff are: (Joes of the world take note.)

1 Internal applicants.
2 Advertising:

    (a) National newspapers,
    (b) Local newspapers,
    (c) Trade journals,
    (d) Commercial television,
    (e) Commercial radio.

3 Selection consultants.
4 Headhunters.
5 Employment agencies.
6 Educational establishments:

    (a) Universities,
    (b) Technical colleges.

7 The armed forces.
8 Professional bodies.
9 Government job centres.

While not every country has all these sources, most countries have most of them, so let us take a closer look at each one.

Internal applicants

Enlightened self-interest suggests that the modern sales manager should always look first within his/her own organisation for sales and management staff before looking externally, for the following reasons:

(i) Selecting from within ensures that there is a career path to follow for all staff.
(ii) The time between selection and taking up the new job will normally be shorter and the time from then to operating profitably should be reduced, since important elements of knowledge about such things as basic company facts, procedure, and products will probably already be known by the applicant.
(iii) Recruitment externally is an expensive process.

Many companies have, in fact, made it a policy that all opportunities are advertised internally first.

However, a word of warning here. Some companies have taken the good principle of 'looking within' too far. It must be remembered that we are looking for a practical, efficient sales person or area manager, and just because Joe in the accounts department is good at his job, is a helpful person, and has applied, does not necessarily give him the appropriate abilities to become a good salesman or sales manager.

Advertising

While the majority of sales positions are still being filled through the medium of advertising, the rapidly escalating costs have caused many sales managers to re-think their attitudes about where and how they advertise. There has been a strong movement away from national towards local papers.

National newspapers

In most countries there would appear to be a salespersons' newspaper such as our own *Daily Telegraph* which most sales people tend to read when job-hunting. The advantages to the advertiser are obvious, since he/she knows that a fairly high proportion of those looking will read that particular newspaper. However, the advertising rates are very high and the advertiser is competing against a great many other companies, which are all trying to attract the right individual's attention.

Local newspapers

The movement towards this medium has been caused by its lower costs; the fact that the individual reading the advertisement is likely to be already living in the area, thus saving the company relocation expenses; and the local paper's greater tractability about such matters as the positioning of the advertisement. However, the other side of the coin is that the response from local press is likely to be smaller and may, if you are unlucky, be non-existent. In any case, a daily paper, whether local or national, will always get a better response than a weekly publication.

To find the suitable local paper, sales managers in the UK only have to consult BRAD (*British Rate and Data*), which lists every national, local and specialist daily weekly and monthly journal, with details of rates, publication and final copy dates, audited circulation, area covered and a host of other useful information. Many other countries have similar publications, such as *Standard Rate and Data* in the USA, *Tariff Media* in France and *Media Daten* in Germany.

Trade journals

While we have never had very much success through this medium, many sales managers have told us that all their jobs are filled this way. It is likely that this depends entirely on the individual journal; certainly the weekly will have a better response and less waiting time than a monthly journal. It might also be that the sales manager may not want the competitors to know that there is a vacancy and, short of telephoning to tell them, there cannot be much more chance of them knowing than a job advertisement in a trade journal.

Advertising copy and layout

Whether the sales manager uses national/local newspapers or trade journals to attract candidates, it is still going to cost money, and far too many people waste this money by not thinking sufficiently about either the wording or the layout of their advertisement or both. In fact many advertisements not only do not attract applicants, they positively turn off the right people.

Job advertisements go through cycles, and one cycle that has been completed in terms of its attraction power is the brash and startling: the sort, for example, that starts 'Do you want to fly your own aeroplane?' Salespeople have become cynical about this style of advertisement and sales managers should really stop using it. Good clear factual details laid out in an attractive manner will always have the best chance of success.

So what information should a job advertisement contain? See the following checklist:

1   Name of firm (avoid box numbers like the plague).
2   Nature of organisation (eg major products).
3   Job title.
4   Salary or salary range.
5   Job location or area.
6   Major duties and responsibilities.
7   Prospects (be honest, if there are none, do not waffle).

In addition, if there are any unattractive features of the job – wanting the person to spend six months out of every year away from home, for example – say so.

At all costs avoid overselling the job.

One last point about the wording of the advertisement. Many firms ask applicants to telephone for an application form, still others ask for complete details to be written out and sent. Many applicants dislike 'phone-ins', while others ignore 'write-ins'. Why cut down the number of applicants unnecessarily when your advertisement can say 'Write or telephone for an application form to ………' Regarding the last method of application, that of sending in full details, if you are going to adopt this method, *please* do not write back immediately asking people to complete an application form. This is an unnecessary waste of your time and the applicants'.

It may seem to be stating the obvious but we have to remember that the reason for placing the advertisement is to attract the right candidate(s), which means that the advertisement has got to leap out of the paper and catch the candidate's eye. Yet many job advertisements seem to be designed with the intention of both avoiding the candidate's attention and, if by the remotest chance he or she does find it, of boring them to tears.

To both attract and be attractive the advertisement has to be positioned in the paper correctly. One that is in the centre of the right-hand facing page will always get the most attention, and you will recall that there is more chance of influencing the position with local papers than with nationals.

It also has to look attractive. Advertisements where the space is completely covered with words have little chance of fulfilling this criteria. On the other hand, an advertisement that:

(i)   is correctly positioned,
(ii)   has a good strong border,
(iii)   uses space properly, and
(iv)   has sufficient detail without being fussy,

has the best possible chance of success. Another good way of ensuring that your advertisement is seen is to use an appropriate picture.

Commercial television and radio

While many jobs are certainly advertised and filled through this medium, those companies that have tried it for sales vacancies have in the main reported that they received a large quantity of replies, but the candidates concerned did not qualify for interviews because they were either too youthful or too inexperienced, or both. This comment may not, of course, be valid in countries other than the UK.

Selection consultants

Qualified selection consultants are certainly playing an increasing role in the recruitment procedures of many companies. The reasons for this are numerous but include:

(a)   Many small to medium-sized companies have realised that they lack the necessary expertise to select properly.
(b)   The good selection consultants are unbiased professionals, which means that they bring both clear heads and considerable expertise to the aid of their client.
(c)   Many candidates prefer to deal through a consultant rather than submit themselves to the boredom of writing out countless application forms, which so often are not even acknowledged.
(d)   Quite often the consultant can speed up the process of recruitment.

However, consultants are expensive – normally 10–12 per cent of the first year's salary, including any commission or bonus guarantees (in the computer industry this fee can be 15–17½ per cent) – so it is important to know what you can expect from a consultant and how to achieve that aim.

The consultant should provide you with a shortlist of qualified applicants all of whom should have been interviewed and approved by them.

Selection consultants can only be as good as the briefing you give them. Just as advertising agencies need to be given the time and effort in order to understand your needs and problems, so do selection consultants. They need to have the job description and person profile, and preferably should be given a day's outing with one of your existing better sales people to ensure that they thoroughly understand what they are looking for. Consultants should preferably come from a sales background and ideally have sold similar products to your own.

If you are choosing a consultant, do not just rely on someone else's experience but have them come and make a presentation to you. If they cannot make a good selling presentation to you, they are unlikely to be good enough to find the right people for you.

Most consultants will try to sell you the idea of their advertising at your expense. Try to resist this if you can, certainly in the early stages. Send them away to search their existing files to see if they can come up with some suitable candidates. This achieves two purposes: firstly, it could save you money and, secondly, by evaluating those candidates you can ensure that the consultants have understood what you are looking for. If they have not, you can rebrief them.

Headhunters

Headhunting is a specialised division of selection consultancy and can only be used when you know the names of the persons you want to recruit but do not want to approach them direct. The headhunter's function is to act as a go-between, to sell the person on the idea of the job and get their approval to a meeting prior to giving them full details of the company concerned.

Employment agencies

If we are talking about recruiting sales and sales management personnel, forget about the idea of using employment agencies. By definition, employment agencies' primary activity is finding work for part-time or temporary staff, and they are, therefore, completely unqualified to solve your needs.

Educational establishments

Universities and technical colleges usually have career guidance sections and can be extremely useful in the recruitment process, providing, of course, you wish to recruit someone direct and are prepared to train them from the ground up as sales people. Most companies, however, prefer to recruit people who have had at least some business experience.

Armed forces

All branches of the armed forces in the UK offer very good guidance in future careers to those who are approaching the end of their service, some even going so far as to give initial training in subjects like selling. While they will have little, if any, direct experience in selling, these personnel do have the advantage over university and technical college of having experienced life, and many companies have a very good record of selling success in using ex-service personnel.

Professional bodies

The institute or association covering your particular discipline may well keep a register of qualified personnel who are looking for new opportunities, and it is worthwhile to check this out.

Government job centres

It is hardly worth looking for sales/management applicants in job centres, since they do not appear to attract suitable candidates. However, they will provide use of interview space and facilities free of charge when you want to interview away from your base as an alternative to hiring expensive hotel interviewing facilities.

Those then are the major resources available for finding applicants. Now let us look at the activity which needs to take place before the interview.

18. *Pre-interview Activity*

Once the media for finding the suitable applicants have been selected, a number of things have to be done before the interview:

1 Preparing the application form.
2 Dealing with 'phone ins'.
3 Writing to candidates.
4 Dealing with the paperwork.
5 Spending the vital five minutes before the interview correctly.

Application form

It should be clear, concise and able to achieve its objectives. It should give sufficient information to enable us to:

(a) Judge whether the candidate merits an interview.
(b) Decide the major areas for investigation during the interview.
(c) Plan the interview.

The example in Fig. 18.1 does this.

Dealing with 'phone ins'

It is a matter of constant surprise that, in spite of the high cost of advertising, companies still fail to plan how they are going to deal with candidates when they phone in. One of the prime requirements of anyone in selling is the ability to communicate verbally. Ideally, therefore, the sales manager should screen applicants when they telephone and thus reduce time and administrative costs. It is unlikely, however, that they would have the time to devote to this activity, and should delegate this job to a responsible, well-trained person.

If the job advertised is for a telesales person in the sales office, then, obviously, the first priority must be telephone ability, and phone-ins should be the rule and not the exception. An example is given in Fig. 18.2. In all cases, a list of pertinent questions to be asked should be compiled. These should include:

(a) why they are applying,
(b) what their present job is,
(c) age and present salary (if relevant),

as well as the more obvious ones of name, address etc. Even though the purpose of the telephone call is to ask for an application form, this telephone screening will reduce the cost of sending them to obviously unsuitable applicants.

PERSONNEL DIVISION

APPLICATION FOR EMPLOYMENT

Ref...............................

PERSONAL PARTICULARS

Surname (BLOCK LETTERS):	Forenames:
Mr./Mrs./Miss	Maiden Name:
Permanent Address:	Temporary Address (if applicable):
Tel. No.	Tel. No.:
Tel. No. (work):	Age: / Sex:
Position applied for:	Salary expected:
Date of birth:	Place of birth:
Marital Status: single/married/engaged divorced/separated/widowed:	No. and ages of children:
Nationality:	When would you be free to take up new appointment?
Next of kin—name, address, and Tel. No.:	

EDUCATION (since age 13)

Dates From	Dates To	Secondary Education—schools attended:	Subjects and examination results (mention any special achievements, positions of responsibility):
		University, Technical College (state whether full-time, part-time, or evening classes):	Subjects studied (specify qualifications obtained):

Fig. 18.1

EMPLOYMENT HISTORY (include service in H.M. Forces)

No approach will be made to your present employers without your prior permission

Please start with your present employment and work backwards:

Dates		Name and address of Employer and type of business:	Position(s) held	Salary:	
From	To			Starting	Leaving
				Other benefits	
				Other benefits	
				Other benefits	
				Other benefits	
				Other benefits	

Professional or other qualifications, membership of Professional Institutions, and any other further training:

Foreign languages (please indicate proficiency):

Location preferred....................... Why?...

If necessary, to what areas would you be willing to transfer?...

How much time per month could you spend travelling away from home?...

Do you own a car? Yes/No   Have a Company car? Yes/No   Make, model and year of car.................................

What car insurance do you carry!   Type..

Fig 18.1 continued

It is our normal practice to contact some of your previous employers prior to short-list interviews.
Please indicate any of the following employers you do not wish us to contact.

To whom responsible— Name and position:	Duties and responsibilities:	Reason for leaving:

OUTSIDE INTERESTS

Please indicate any hobbies, sporting, or other outside interests:

MEDICAL

Detail any illnesses, physical or mental, that have necessitated hospital or specialist medical care:

Registered Disabled Person No. (if any):   Expiry Date:

Fig 18.1 continued

DESCRIPTION OF CAREER

Give a brief description, in your own handwriting, of your career since leaving school. Mention the things you have most and least enjoyed doing, any strong likes or dislikes, give strong and weak points. Explain why you believe you are qualified for the position you are applying for and what your future plans and ambitions are.

REFERENCES. Please give details of two referees. (Personal, not business):

Name ....   Name ....

Address ....   Address ....

....

....

....

Tel. no ....   Tel No....................................

The information I have given on this form is correct and may be used as a basis for any offer of employment you may make to me. I understand that any such offer is also subject to receipt of satisfactory references.

Date..............................   Signed ....

Fig. 18.1 continued

1 **Job applied for**	**Telesales operator**
2 May I have your name?	
3 And your address?	
4 Have you a telephone number where you can be contacted during normal working hours?	
5 Could I have your date of birth?	
6 What kind of job are you looking for?	
7 What is your present job?	
8 Who do you work for?	
9 How long for? (If less than 12 months ask for previous employment.)	
10 How much do you expect to earn?	£
11 How much are you earning now?	£
12 Are you married? If Yes have you any children?	Boys: no.____ ages____ Girls: no.____ ages____
13 When could you start?	
14 Will you describe yourself?	

Fig. 18.2 *Phone-in questionnaire.*

Selling the company

Far too many sales managers fail to realise that it is as important to sell their company to applicants as it is to allow applicants to sell themselves into an interview. First impressions count on both sides. Good managers try to ensure that their side is not at fault by planning what has to be done once the advertisement has been placed.

There are two areas to be considered, telephone calls and letters, and the people concerned need to be briefed. As for telephones, it is not the job of the switchboard operator to screen or question applicants. If the advertisement carries a contact reference, the operator should be briefed to connect the caller to that reference or explain if there will be a delay.

The contact reference (usually the secretary) should be briefed to deal effectively with the applicant, using the 'phone-in' form (Fig. 18.2). Experience has shown that for two or three days after the advertisement has appeared, the activity of telephone calls is extremely high. It may be advisable, therefore, to delegate someone to this activity exclusively for this period.

Writing to candidates

If someone takes the trouble to write to you, they deserve the courtesy of a prompt reply. There are three possible replies to be considered:

Sending an application form

Many companies send an application form with a compliments slip. While the volume of forms to be sent is often used as an excuse for this, it must be remembered that it does nothing to sell the company. With the ever-increasing use of word-processors it does not require much effort to produce a simple letter to cover the application form. Something like, 'Thank you for applying for the position of ——— with our company. As the first stage may I ask you to complete the enclosed application form. Once this has been returned to us we will consider it carefully and let you know as soon as possible whether we would like you to attend for an initial interview'. The objective is, of course, to promote the company as an efficient organisation and also, wherever possible, to give an applicant some idea of the time scale.

Immediate rejection letters

If an applicant's letter indicates an unsuitability for the job, do not prevaricate. Write and tell him/her but make sure the rejection letter also sells. For example, 'Thank you for your letter of the —— regarding the appointment of ——— with this company. The response has been considerable and whilst your application has been carefully considered, I feel I should let you know straight away that in this instance we have decided not to proceed with it any further. My sincere thanks for your interest and my best wishes for your search for a suitable position to match your experience and ability.'

Double-edged, perhaps, but certainly nice to read and certainly indicative of a 'caring' company.

Interview invitation letters

This is the opportunity of a lifetime for a manager to be pompous, benevolent, condescending, or a mixture of all three. The truth is that the applicant only really needs to know the good news or the bad news – interview or no interview.

If you are going to invite the applicant to your offices for the interview, there are basic points to remember:

1 Salesmen, especially good ones, will have planned appointments for two or more weeks ahead.
2 If you are not in their area, they will appreciate directions on how to find you.
3 They need a direct, telephone contact name to confirm the appointment.

An example of an invitation letter is:

> Thank you for returning the completed application form. I would now like to discuss your experience and general background in more detail and have arranged an interview for (time) on (date) at our offices.
> Directions for finding us are enclosed and I would be gratful if you would telephone my secretary, (name), to confirm that you can keep this appointment.

It might be thought that offering alternative times/dates may be a better selling proposition but the administration problems become quite enormous. Management by exception works much better in this instance.

Dealing with the paperwork

Whether responses have been initiated by telephone calls or by letters, the end result is the same – a wealth of paper begins to accumulate. The organisation of this paperwork marks the difference between an efficient organisation and one that just muddles along. Imagine the thoughts in a salesman's mind if he needs to telephone to change an appointment and is met by, 'I'm sure we've got your details here somewhere' or 'Hang on, I'll try to find your file'.

You know you are going to generate the paper, so you should have organised a system to deal with all the responses. Basically, all that is required are two forms (a) an on-going situation form (Fig. 18.3), and an interview booking form (Fig. 18.4). Having set the system and organised the filing and cross-referencing, we can now go ahead and plan how the interviews will be conducted.

The vital five minutes before the interview

Recruiting and interviewing applicants is both time-consuming and expensive, no matter which method is employed. There is no valid excuse, therefore, for not preparing for the interviews.

Assuming that the dates, times and venue have now been organised, re-check to ensure there are no last-minute snags. Make a particular check on the setting of the interview room. There is no golden rule as to whether the interview should be

SITUATION REPORT   VACANCY REFERENCE ....

No.	Name and Initials	Location	Date of first contact	Type of contact T-telephone L-letter	Application form sent (date)	Application form received (date)	1st screening I-interview R-reject H-hold	Interview date	2nd screening I2-2nd interview R-reject	Date of 2nd Interview	Result
1											
2											
3											
4											
5											
6											
7											
8											
9											
10											
11											

Fig. 18.3 Situation report.

		INTERVIEW BOOKING FORM. VACANCY			
Date	Time	Ref. No. (from Situation form)	Applicant Name	Interviewer	Result (Go forward) (Hold) (Reject)
20/7	0930 1030 1130				
22/7	0930 1030 1130 1400 1500 1600				

Fig. 18.4 *Interview booking form.*

formal from behind a desk or more relaxed over a coffee table. There are, however, several rules that should be observed regarding the conduct of the interview:

1   For at least five minutes before you see the applicant, go through the application form again. Check you have all the relevant papers you need. Make notes of any particular areas you need to probe.
2   Make sure you have arranged that there will be no interruptions during the interview.
3   Check that your secretary has sufficient expenses claim forms *and the cash* to settle each applicant's travelling expenses immediately after the interview. Many sales managers leave it to the applicant to ask, or ask the applicant to send in his expenses claim. The cost of paperwork for this simple exercise alone is enormous.
4   Trying to organise interviews so that you have time for a tea or coffee break is very difficult. Much simpler to arrange for the necessary refreshments to be brought in when due, with the applicant automatically included in the service.
5   If there is to be more than one interviewer, have a dress rehearsal, emphasising who does what and stressing the importance of general control.
6   Allow time after each interview to write up your notes on the applicant.
7   Finally, clear the desk/table of all previous papers before seeing the next applicant.

19. *The Selection Interview*

Like many other aspects of selling, preparation calls for the greatest amount of work. No one should ever dream of 'playing it by ear' – that method is fraught with dangers, from making the wrong opening remark to making the wrong decision.

Once all the preparatory moves have been completed, the interview itself should run in a logical way, with plenty of two-way communication. Before we go into the structure of the interview it may be as well to consider what the purpose of the interview is.

Aims

To get the facts straight
The facts set out in the application form are only black and white. For example, 'Head Prefect during last year at grammar school'. Get the applicant to fill in the shades of grey details by asking, 'How do you think being Head Prefect helped you in your subsequent career?' Merely confirming that he/she was head prefect does nothing for either interviewer or applicant.

To obtain the applicant's opinions
Keep to matters relevant to the job and the type of people with whom the applicant will be working.

To judge the quickness of the applicant's responses
Mental alertness is a very necessary attribute of anyone in selling. As an interview for a new job is a milestone in anyone's career, they should at least come to the interview prepared to think.

To get an immediate impression
If you were a customer, would you react favourably to the applicant. This is not simply a question of personal hygiene but more of a personable impact.

To find out the applicant's likes and dislikes
It is pointless selecting someone for a job if you then discover they do not particularly like doing it or that they will not fit in with the rest of the team because of any pet dislikes.

To establish a trend in achievements, thinking and reactions
This is, without doubt, one of the most important aims of the selection interview. Movement in jobs in itself is not a true indication of an applicant's progression in

his/her chosen career. What is important is *why* that movement was chosen. What was the purpose behind it?

To attract the applicant to the job
We have already mentioned earlier the importance of 'selling' the company to an applicant, and this *is* a very important aspect in the selection interview. A word of warning, however! Not all applicants, even if called for an interview, are going to be found suitable for second interviewing. It is necessary, therefore, to set out the parameters of the job to be done and the framework for doing it, but 'selling' the job to the right applicant might well be left to a later interview. Nevertheless the concept of two-way sales process must be borne in mind the whole time.

Structure

Stage 1   The beginning

The objective is to establish as relaxed a situation as possible. Considering the aims outlined above and taking five minutes to read the applicant's papers again should help to relax you. After all, interviewing is a test for both sides.

Step 1   Make it clear where the applicant will sit, put coats etc.
Step 2   Explain how the interview will basically be conducted.
Step 3   Give background of company and go through the job description.
Step 4   Invite applicant to ask questions at any time but suggest that at the end may be more appropriate.
Step 5   Make sure applicant is aware you will be making notes, and invite him/her to do the same.

Stage 2   The main part

A simple way of leading into the business discussion and at the same time relaxing the atmosphere is to use any of the following approaches:

(a)   the 'common link' approach – 'I see we both attended the same college', 'I see we were both born in Hertfordshire'.
(b)   The 'off-balance' approach. Note that this can only be carried off successfully at a 'one-to-one' interview. The interviewer starts off with a casual greeting and then talks briefly about something totally irrelevant to the interview but which requires a response, eg 'What do you think about this new photograph I've got on the wall?' It is not the sort of cross-examination style the applicant was expecting and usually evokes a more relaxed atmosphere.
(c)   A mixture of (a) and (b).

Step 1
Go through the information in the application form in detail. There is no need, in fact it is often undesirable, to have a set order of questioning. You know from your preparation which parts of his/her career you want to probe more deeply, so be an opportunist. However, make sure there is a defined connecting thread

between the groups of subjects you want to discuss. Keep a checklist to make sure you cover all the points you want to discuss.

Step 2
Put the right questions to the applicant.

(a)   Those which require more than a yes/no answer.
(b)   Those which help you to assess the qualities you are looking for.
(c)   Those which probe for the truth, not only about unexplained gaps in a work history but also to qualify. For instance, 'Do you feel you will fit in to a rapidly expanding sales operation?' will invariably produce a 'Yes' because that is what the applicant thinks is the answer you are looking for. Far better to ask, 'Why do you feel you will fit into a rapidly expanding operation like ours?' Whatever the answers, follow up opinions with more probing to check that the answers are not just platitudes paying lip-service to a stereotyped interview session.

Step 3
Avoid trick questions. Questions like 'Do you drink?' or 'Do you tell lies?' do nothing to help an applicant's morale. The object of the exercise is to keep him talking, not embarrass him into silence.

Step 4
Tell the applicant more about the job and the conditions attached to it. Encourage him/her to ask questions about it. This step is vital, since if the applicant cannot ask you questions about the organisation and job he/she is considering for his/her future career, he/she is unlikely to be able to probe your customers to find out their wants and needs.

Stage 3   The ending

Step 1
Tell the applicant when he or she can expect to have an answer one way or the other. Be absolutely clear on this and make sure you carry out your undertaking.

Step 2
Thank the applicant for attending.

Just because you have prepared a plan for the interview does not mean you have to pursue it to the bitter end. If, at any time, it becomes clear that the applicant will not suit you or the company, then terminate the interview there and then. Be diplomatic. Remember also that not every applicant will want the job after discussing it in more detail, so be prepared to give him the opportunity of finishing the session.

Stage 4   Decision time

If the interviews are initial ones, the only decision perhaps to be made is hold, reject or advance to second interview. Whatever the decision, the steps are the same:

Step 1
Consider the evidence relative to the key qualities/factors you are looking for.

Step 2
Add your own impressions. This is not a licence to 'play hunches'. Rather, you should be comparing factual evidence against interpersonal relationships. Certainly your hunches come into it, but where you feel there is an element of doubt, go back and check the facts. Long, long ago, a philosopher said, 'The best indicator of what a person will do in the future, is what he or she has done in the past'.

Step 3
Make up your mind. No help is offered for this undoubtedly painful process. Be guided by facts and not emotions. The interview report shown in Fig. 19.1 will help.

The seven deadly sins of interviewing

Even professional interviewers have weaknesses. Here are seven you should certainly guard against.

1 Lack of preparation.
2 Jumping to conclusions on insufficient evidence.
3 Not listening.
4 Talking too much.
5 Harassing the applicant with trick or irrelevant questions.
6 Giving way to bias or prejudice.
7 Getting side-tracked.

Testing and checking

Running concurrently with the main subject of the selection interview are the subsidiary, but none the less important, considerations which have to be dealt with.

Psychological testing

There may well be a case for psychological testing in some jobs but in selling no one has yet found a test which will necessarily pick out the right applicant. Selling is a 'people' business. The sort of qualities required of a salesman are:

(a) Industry and perseverance.
(b) Empathy and ego drive (on the one hand, understanding the customers' points of view and, on the other, having the courage to attempt to change those points of view).

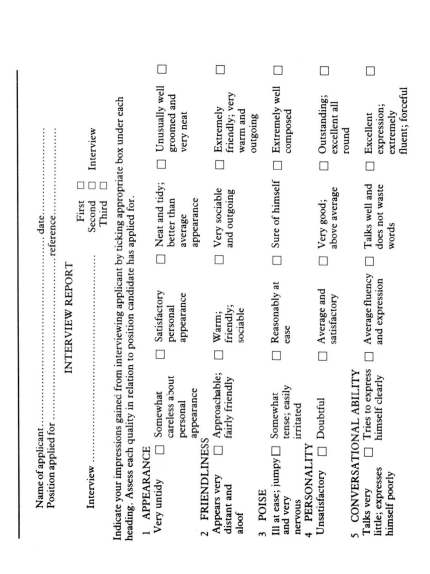

Name of applicant...date..................
Position applied for...reference..................

INTERVIEW REPORT

Interview ....

First ☐
Second ☐   Interview
Third ☐

Indicate your impressions gained from interviewing applicant by ticking appropriate box under each heading. Assess each quality in relation to position candidate has applied for.

1 APPEARANCE

| Very untidy | Somewhat careless about personal appearance ☐ | Satisfactory personal appearance ☐ | Neat and tidy; better than average appearance ☐ | Unusually well groomed and very neat ☐ |

2 FRIENDLINESS

| Appears very distant and aloof | Approachable; fairly friendly ☐ | Warm; friendly; sociable ☐ | Very sociable and outgoing ☐ | Extremely friendly; very warm and outgoing ☐ |

3 POISE

| Ill at ease; jumpy and very nervous ☐ | Somewhat tense; easily irritated | Reasonably at ease ☐ | Sure of himself ☐ | Extremely well composed ☐ |

4 PERSONALITY

| Unsatisfactory ☐ | Doubtful | Average and satisfactory ☐ | Very good; above average ☐ | Outstanding; excellent all round ☐ |

5 CONVERSATIONAL ABILITY

| Talks very little; expresses himself poorly | Tries to express himself clearly ☐ | Average fluency and expression ☐ | Talks well and does not waste words ☐ | Excellent expression; extremely fluent; forceful ☐ |

6 ALERTNESS

☐ Very slow to grasp ideas

☐ Rather slow; requires more than average explanation

☐ Grasps ideas with average speed

☐ Quick to understand; perceives well

☐ Exceptionally alert; understands new ideas instantly

7 KNOWLEDGE OF WORK FIELD

☐ Poor; no appropriate knowledge at all

☐ Limited knowledge covering some areas

☐ Average knowledge not covering all areas fully

☐ Well informed; knowledge covers all areas

☐ Excellent knowledge with faultless coverage

8 QUALIFICATIONS

☐ Not relevant to job

☐ Some relevance to job

☐ Satisfactory; as good as might be expected

☐ Very suitable for job

☐ Ideal for job; perfect match

9 SKILL

☐ None appropriate

☐ Some skill in job area

☐ Reasonable amount; average for job

☐ Well skilled in job area

☐ Excellent skills; ideal for job

10 EXPERIENCE

☐ No relation between background and job requirements

☐ Some experience in relevant area

☐ Average; background covers job area

☐ Very good and relevant experience

☐ Excellent and ideal background

11 DRIVE AND INITIATIVE

☐ Poorly defined goals; acts without purpose

☐ Makes little effort to achieve goals

☐ Average effort; some initiative

☐ High desire to achieve; strives hard

☐ Sets high goals; always takes initiative

Fig. 19.1

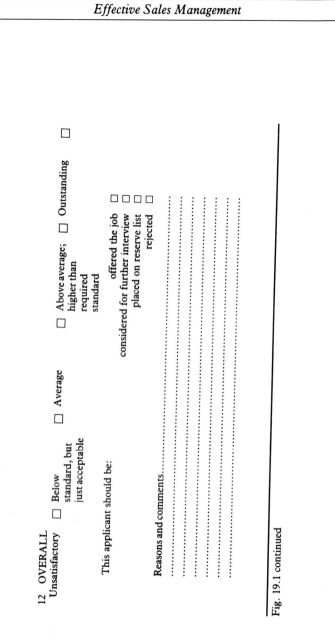

12 OVERALL

Unsatisfactory ☐   Below ☐   Average ☐   Above average; ☐   Outstanding ☐
                     standard, but   higher than
                     just acceptable   required
                                                standard

This applicant should be:

                             offered the job ☐
     considered for further interview ☐
            placed on reserve list ☐
                               rejected ☐

Reasons and comments...

....

....

....

....

....

....

Fig. 19.1 continued

(c) Self-reliance.
(d) Energy, enthusiasm and abundant drive.
(e) Business judgement.

Psychological testing only measures unitary activity, not relative relationships. Incidentally, in the USA, traditionally considered to be the spawning-ground of such tests, including graphology (handwriting to the uninitiated), psychological testing has been declared to be discriminatory and is not allowed to be used in recruitment and selection of any staff.

Checking references

This is an area of considerable controversy. Some sales managers consider reference-checking to be a waste of time. Others think it vital. The true answer probably lies somewhere in between.

One of the most effective ways is to check by telephone. Most previous employers are only too happy to give information on the telephone but baulk at committing their comments to paper. Using a telephone checklist similar to that shown in Fig 19.2 may often, if used *before* an interview, give some pertinent discussion points.

EMPLOYER REFERENCE CHECK (Telephone)

Applicant's name:...Date of check......................
Previous employer: Company ....
                    Contact... Position.......................

1. Mr X is an applicant for the position of .... with this Company. The purpose of this call is to verify information regarding his employment with you.	
a) What were the dates he was with you?	From: To:
b) What position? –Starting –Finishing	
c) Salary – Basic Start	£
Finish	£
Commission Start	£
Finish	£
2. How were his sales results?	
3. Why did he leave?	
4. Would you re-employ him? – if no, what reason?	Yes ☐ No ☐
5. What were his strengths?	
6. Were there any weaknesses – please detail.	
7. Any general comments?	

Fig. 19.2

However, in fairness to any applicant, you should never take up a reference from a current employer except when you (a) make the job offer to the applicant, or (b) have his permission to contact his present employer.

Group selection techniques

The question 'How many people should interview an applicant?' is often asked. As usual, there is no one finite answer – the number depends on the type of company, the job and whether the applicants are being interviewed singly or as a group.

There are, basically, four interview situations:

The two-to-one interview
Probably the most widely used and the most effective for general sales positions. It is important that the interviewer is trained in interviewing techniques, and if it is necessary for another manager to see the applicant, this should also be a one-to-one situation.

The one-to-two interview
There is obviously a danger here of over-stressing the applicant. The greater danger, however, lies in the fact that if either or both interviewers are unskilled in interviewing, questions will be duplicated, the logical sequence of the interview may be thrown out of balance and the applicant become even more stressed. If two-to-one is practised, it is vital that the roles, control and areas to be covered by each interviewer are pre-planned.

Group selection board with group tasks/problems for applicants
For assessing qualities of leadership and decision-making this could be said to be a good method of interviewing. It is widely used by the armed forces and some major industrial groups. For selecting salesmen, the technique is really a 'non-starter', particularly when other, more effective, methods can be used.

Selection panels
Not to be confused with the old concept of selection board, the panel interview situation is growing in the UK, particularly where up-gradings to levels of management are concerned. Many companies have decided that internal promotions are so vital to their future success that the results cannot be left to any one person and are therefore using a panel of between two and four people in order to improve the process. They will often invite the applicants to prepare in advance a presentation about a particular aspect of the activity that will be part of the person's duties if promoted, and/or will often give some form of written test as well.

20. *The Final Decision and Action*

Making the right choice is not easy. Everything said so far is designed to help sales management recruit the right calibre of applicants and select the most suitable of those for interview.

Initial interviews, basically a condensed version of the selection interview process, will reduce your list of suitable candidates to a mere handful. The second interviews of these are much more detailed and exhaustive and will lead you to the point we are now writing about – making the final decision.

Perhaps it is as well to consider that only two basic principles need to be applied in selection:

1 *Facts*. Be guided only by facts and preferably proven facts. Avoid letting your judgement be clouded by such prejudices as:
(a) limp handshake equals weak personality,
(b) applicants who look you straight in the eye are confident,
(c) you do not like the Welsh/Scots/Irish/English.

2 *Performance*. The best guide to future performance is past performance. Here we do have the facts – the application form and the results of your interviewing.

Using these two principles, compare the interview results of your final shortlist. Decide on your first, second and third choices. It should be obvious, of course, that your second and third choices are reserves just in case choice No. 1 declines your offer.

That offer needs to be made in writing and must specify a date for acceptance (or rejection). Remember that the job offer, the letter of appointment, is a contractual document. It must be formal and should be checked by personnel or legal departments. An example of a letter of appointment is given in Fig. 20.1.

EXAMPLE – LETTER OF APPOINTMENT

Mr A N Other
1 Upper Street
Lower Wallop
Leics   23 July 19..

Dear Mr Other
    Further to your application and our discussions, I am pleased to offer you an appointment as .... for the .... area. This appointment is subject to receiving satisfactory references from your present employer and to you passing the medical examination.

The terms and conditions of your employment are set out below. Would you please sign the duplicate copy of this offer and return it to me by .... 19...

Fig. 20.1

Terms

1 *Salary* Your starting salary will be £A p.a. payable in arrears on the .... of each month. Salaries are reviewed annually each June.

2 *Commission* You will earn commission on all sales made in your area at the rate of X%. In addition, new business introduced by you will qualify for Y% bonus, paid half-yearly.

3 *Expenses*

4 *Company Car*

5 *Company Pension Scheme*

6 *Holidays*

7 *Sickness*

8 *Termination*

Yours sincerely,

Fig. 20.1 continued

There are several points to note:

(a) *References.* The offer should be conditional on the checking of current references proving satisfactory.

(b) *Medical.* The offer should also be conditional on the applicant passing a medical examination. (The company nominates the doctor and also pays the fee.)

(c) *Source of Income.* The applicant must provide an undertaking to work only for you on a full-time basis.

(d) *Legislation.* The laws relating to hiring and firing, unfair dismissal, restraint of trade and so on do not get easier. There are four Acts governing the recruitment and selection of personnel in the UK:

   (i)   The Employment Protection Act 1975.
   (ii)   The Employment Protection (Consolidation) Act 1976.
   (iii) The Sex Discrimination Act 1975.
   (iv)   The Race Relations Act 1976.

Contract of Employment

In 1972 the Contract of Employment Act laid down that every employer must issue to every employee a written statement setting out the terms and conditions of employment. Amendments were made by the Employment Protection Act 1975 and the Employment Protection (Consolidation) Act 1976.

A statement must be issued to everyone working more than sixteen hours a week and new employees must be given the statement by the end of the thirteenth week of employment. This statement must contain:

1 Name and location of employer.
2 Name of employee.
3 Job title and location.
4 Date of employment.
5 Date of issue of statement.
6 Details of terms:
   – pay,
   – hours,
   – holidays,

    – cars,
    – sick pay/absence,
    – pension scheme,
    – periods of notice.
7 Trade union requirements.
8 Disciplinary procedures.
9 Grievance procedures.

Provided it complies with the requirements of the above, a letter of appointment is, in fact, a written statement as required by law.

Conclusion

Customers, the life-blood of any company, are becoming more sophisticated in their tastes and more knowledgeable about what they buy. On that basis, therefore, they tend to take a far more critical look at the salesmen who sell those products or services. So salesmen have to be better than ever before, which means management must recruit and select better salesmen than they did before.

Buyers are trained to buy.

Salesmen are trained to sell.

Who trains managers to select the right salesmen?

If this part of the handbook realises just a 1 per cent improvement in selection results, it will be worth it:

(a) to the company,
(b) to the manager,
(c) to the new salesman,

as all of them will benefit from greater professionalism.

Keep one thing in mind: The best that any interviewer can hope to do is gradually little by little, cut down the number of times he/she is *wrong*.

The action checklist on page 106 should increase your odds on success.

Action checklist

	YES	NO	ACTION

1 Is there a reviewing procedure to analyse job vacancies?
2 Is there a job description?
3 Is there an employee profile?
4 Is there an existing method of recruitment?

    – Is it successful?
    – Have we examined other ways?
5 Are our application forms good enough?
6 Do we have forms for:

    – dealing with 'phone-ins'?
    – interview situation reports?
    – interview booking?
    – telephone reference checks?
7 Have we an interview report form?

    – does it cover all requirements?
8 Are interviewers briefed fully?
9 Do we have booklets on the company to give to applicants?

    – if not, would it be helpful?
10 Have we a control mechanism to measure recruitment and selection effectiveness?

PART FOUR

Training and Developing the Sales Force

Training is one of the most vital functions any manager has to perform, since not only does it provide the skills to enable a person to perform well but it is also one of the most important motivators available. Yet even now, when management thought has expanded so rapidly, in some companies induction training has not moved forward very much from the typical activity of twenty years ago. It was quite normal then for a person to be welcomed to the company, given two bags (one with samples, one with paperwork), the keys to a car and instructed to 'keep in touch'.

In many companies very little systematic thought is given to the design and implementation of a regular programme of (a) induction training, (b) skills improvement, (c) development training. Very often the following invalid arguments are still put forward.

Sales people are born not made
Of course, certain sales people do have more natural talent than others, but in the vast majority of cases good sales people have been developed by training and experience rather than having been created fully fledged by some sort of 'magic dust' sprinkled on them at birth. If this argument were true, it would mean that the selection process becomes the only way of ensuring we get the right person. Here we would remind the reader of the comment we made at the end of Part 3 – 'The best that any interviewer can hope to do is gradually, little by little, cut down the number of times he/she is wrong'. It would indeed paint a bleak picture for the future of most sales forces if this argument was valid.

You only need to know everything about the product to be successful
This attitude, which is more usually encountered in industrial and technical companies, is equally invalid. Where this view is held, all the training is centred on this one area of knowledge, and the normal result is a product specialist who cannot talk to customers! While it may have been possible for companies to sell on the basis of product specialists in the past, it certainly is not true today. To be successful now, sales people need both complete product knowledge and the selling skills to present that knowledge effectively.

While discussing this point, let us also discount the opposite view, which is that as long as the salesperson has got all the sales skills, product knowledge is unimportant. This is equally invalid in today's market place.

'Learning from Nellie'

This expression came originally from factory training, where the idea was to sit a trainee next to an experienced operator to learn from her. It has been applied to sales training by sending out the new sales person with an experienced one to learn the techniques.

This method is invalid on three counts:

(a) Usually the person acting as trainer has not been taught how to train, and the amount of knowledge that will be imparted is therefore suspect.
(b) Since the 'trainer' will have both good and bad habits, the trainee is likely to pick up equal amounts of both.
(c) As a method of learning, observation is at the very least suspect, since watching someone else do something is never the same as doing it.

While these three invalid views are bad enough, most training organisations would report that they still receive requests from organisations that have some money left in the budget, and they have decided to spend it on training! What a meaningless reason for training that is.

In these chapters we are going to consider the following major aspects:

1 Formal (classroom) training.
2 Field training.
3 How and by whom these forms of training should be carried out.
4 Management training.

Also a number of subsidiary issues which will ensure that the training is effective.

21. *The Need for Training*

If persons are to operate successfully, they will need to be totally trained in all aspects of the job. As someone once said, 'We work with average people but we require above average results'.

One aspect of being average is that there is only so much we can take in at one time, so that a properly designed training programme will need to be planned over a period of months or years rather than days. We are therefore discussing a high and continuous cost element, and the temptation may be to say 'Let us give them a few days initial induction, then let them get on with it. Those that do well, we will keep. Those that do not, we will replace'.

When one considers the following aspects, the absolute necessity of planned training becomes clear:

1 The cost of keeping a salesperson on the road continues to escalate rapidly, and the majority of that cost is there whether the person is successful or not.
2 Recruiting replacement staff is expensive, time-consuming and, as discussed in Part 3, becoming more difficult.
3 Almost every type of selling is becoming more competitive, so that, to succeed, sales people need to be far more professional now than ever before.
4 The sales force carries on its shoulders the burden of success for the whole company, since it matters little if the product is right, the service is right and all other departments are successful. If sales are not made, the company will not survive.

In Fig. 21.1 the main elements of performance for any salesperson are listed. While individual companies may require further functions, it is likely that all companies will require their sales personnel to perform the items shown, since successful sales will depend on them.

The problem is that many companies train in only one or two of these elements. Few companies continuously update their staff in all elements.

There are a variety of different ways that this knowledge can be imparted, refreshed and extended, such as:

1 Formal training programmes
   (a) In-company schemes run for the sales staff by the sales manager or other in-company personnel.
   (b) In-company schemes run by external trainers.
   (c) Open courses run for delegates from different companies by external trainers.
2 Field training.

3 Sales meetings.
4 Sales bulletins.

Let us look first of all at formal training.

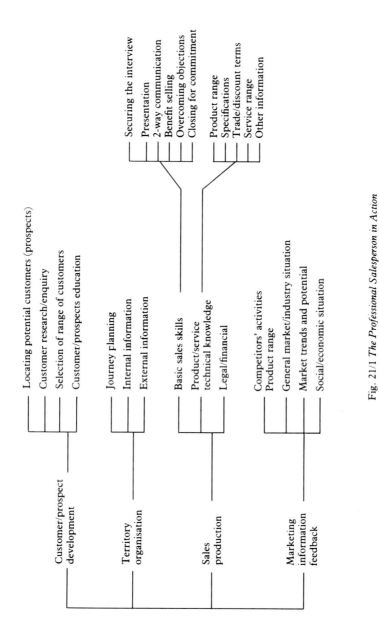

Fig. 21/1 *The Professional Salesperson in Action*

22. Formal Training

If a successful training programme is to be developed, a number of basic but vital questions have to be considered and answered.

Defining programme objectives

You may say that the answer is simple – to get better results – but a properly designed programme has many practical benefits. For example:

(a) Increased sales.
(b) Reduced individual selling costs.
(c) Increased individual earnings.
(d) Reduced personnel turnover.
(e) Reduced need for supervision.
(f) Improved employee morale.
(g) Better customer relations.

But if we are to be able to measure the results of that programme the objectives have to be meaningful. In other words, they need to be measurable in order for us to judge if the programme has been successful.

To have an objective of increasing sales may well be laudable, but how do you decide afterwards that the programme has worked, since so many different factors could lead to an increase in sales. For example, a company that makes flags runs a programme with this objective and shortly afterwards a special event like a royal wedding takes place. What caused the increase in sales?

However, an objective which, for example, states that increased sales are required by reducing the ratio of calls to orders from 5:1 to 3:1 is much more likely to be meaningful and is certainly more measurable. Therefore, the objectives have to be formulated in these terms, ie turning the company's investment in personnel into an asset producing an increased return.

In addition, of course, specific objectives should be formulated, depending upon the job specifications: eg if the job includes dealing with trade conferences, then the training objectives would include the need for developing the trainees in public speaking techniques. In other words, although the training programme is usually designated a 'sales training programme', the number of skills covered by the term 'salesmen' will differ from company to company and even from job to job within a company.

The pupils

Once the objectives have been decided, the question of the pupils may well be answered in one word – everyone. However, the choice does depend on both the objectives and the individual's current abilities and previous training.

Ideally there should be an individual training plan for each member of the sales force, in which case the question is *who* would be dealt with before the objectives are set. There would be a case for reviewing the plans, seeing that a number of individuals require training in knowledge areas A, B and C, and building the objectives round those needs.

The syllabus

An examination of Fig. 21.1 will show that there are basically four prime areas of knowledge which must be imparted to the sales force:

(a) Product knowledge, including product range, competitors, place in market, uses, benefits, etc.
(b) Sales skills, including the role of salesmanship, product analysis, prospecting, preparation, approach, presentation, objection handling, closing, and customer servicing.
(c) Company knowledge, including history, growth, organisation structure, and administrative procedures (expense claims, commission system, etc.).
(d) Work organisation, including journey planning, call planning, time saving methods, etc.

As we have already stated, quite often not all these elements are imparted, and sometimes they are taught in a way that limits their use. For example, product training is often taught as a list of features, but unless the sales force is shown what those features mean in application terms to the customer, salesmen will find it difficult to link those features in terms of benefits.

Primarily, the decision as to what will be taught in any programme will be based on the objectives that have been designated, since the criterion for choice has to be 'What will enable us to reach our objectives?'

The teachers

The answer to this question is that the salesperson should always be taught by his/her immediate manager, since the training of staff is the manager's primary responsibility. Furthermore, if the manager is the trainer, the following benefits result:

(a) It helps to build the relationship between manager and staff.
(b) It ensures that what is taught is what that manager wants taught in the way that he/she wants it taught.

So the manager must not and cannot give away that responsibility to the training department or to outside consultants.

But is the manager competent to train? If he is not, an important aspect of management training comes into play – training the trainer. However, the manager can delegate certain aspects of training either in the interests of time or because other people may have more expertise. We will discuss in Chapter 23 how to select and use these people.

If other people do the formal training, it is vital for the manager *immediately* to follow up with field training, both to ensure that the training was effective and to ensure that the skills learnt are used. Among the areas that can be delegated are:

(a) Initial training – on company knowledge to various specialists (eg personnel).
(b) Initial training – on product and basic sales techniques to sales training manager or consultants.
(c) Refresher and continuation training to sales training manager or consultants.
(d) 'Broadening' training (ie management development) to consultants or external courses.

The methods

Many traditional training techniques, such as the lecture method or 'Learning from Nellie', are at best suspect, since they tend to employ only two of the trainee's five senses – listening and watching. The decision on method has to be based on the question 'How am I going to ensure the total participation of the trainee?' The more participation there is, the more likely it is that learning will take place.

There are numerous different aids that a trainer can use to help participation. Among them, the following are likely to be familiar to readers:

1 Flip charts/blackboards.
2 Overhead projectors.
3 Slide projectors.
4 Films.
5 Case study discussion.
6 Syndicate group discussion.
7 Role play.
8 Closed circuit television role plays (CCTV).

Of these, perhaps only the last two require amplification.

Since selling is a social skill and its success often depends on the interaction between two people, role play, whether with or without CCTV, is an obvious technique to enhance training. However, many managers and sales staff have become doubtful about the value of role play on the grounds that they feel that it is unreal and/or it puts too much pressure on the participants. While there is both an element of unreality and pressure in the use of role play, we would suggest that it arises more from the way the medium is used than from the medium itself. We would suggest the following 'Do's' and 'Don'ts'.

1 *Don't* make two people play out full-scale interviews in front of a room full of people.
2 *Don't* set up situations which the sales force would not encounter in real life.
3 *Don't* have the camera so close to the participants that they cannot fail to be

constantly aware of it.

4 *Don't* keep them sitting around for ages waiting to perform. Make sure they have another task to do while waiting to go on and waiting for the rest of the group to be recorded.

As for the 'Do's':

1 Have the role play take place in a separate room, preferably with only the participants there, and record it for later review.
2 Take a lot of trouble to set up a situation for the role play, and make it so real that participants will recognise it from previous experience.
3 Keep the camera as far away as possible – if it can be in a different room looking through a glass hatch, so much the better.
4 Most people will do better if they have the time to prepare properly for the role play.
5 Ideally, the review of the playback should take place between the participants and trainer only, with selected highlights being shown to the whole group.

CCTV can be an extremely helpful medium for reinforcing people's good techniques and acquainting them with things that need improvement – but only if it is used well.

One new technique that is now being developed is interactive video. This medium uses the linking of a computer and a video recorder. The trainee sits at the computer keyboard and watches an action sequence on TV. Questions are then asked, and the trainee uses the keyboard to answer. The result of that answer is then shown by a follow-up action sequence. This can be a very useful additional aid to reinforcing learning that has taken place in the formal session.

Length of training

While the duration of the formal training programme is dependent upon the objective, content and method, there is a limit on how many days we can usefully keep people confined to the training room absorbing knowledge. More and more training programmes are now being built on a regular modular basis. Each module tends to last one to three days. The advantages of this idea, which is particularly appropriate for in-company training, are:

1 It is easier to keep the learning curve at a high level for two to three days than for five or more.
2 Since the modules are regular, eg monthly, each module can start by reinforcing the previous one.
3 The gap between allows the skills to be tried out, so that the succeeding programme can solve application problems.
4 Delegates are not away from their jobs for so long, and this makes territory coverage easier.

The other time consideration is, when should it be held? The first point to make is that there are always good reasons for not holding a training programme and there is rarely a good time for it. So the best answer to the time question is to base it on the needs and objectives decision while obviously avoiding peak business periods.

Locations

There are three primary places where formal training programmes can be held: on company premises, in hotels, or in training centres.

Company premises

The two big advantages here are that whatever is needed in terms of sales aids, sales literature, typing facilities etc. is readily available, and there is nothing to pay out.

Company premises, however, do have one major disadvantage: everything and everyone are *too* available. The temptation for senior managers to need delegates just for a few minutes to answer a customer's query and for delegates themselves to be diverted into areas that have nothing to do with training is almost overpowering. So much so, that we cannot recall ever running a training programme on behalf of a client at their premises without losing at least one of the delegates for part of the programme. That may at face value not seem so desperate, but if one person is missing for even half an hour, the delicate rhythm of a programme starts to be affected. In addition, the trainee has lost part of his training.

At its worst, it can play havoc with a programme. One of our training colleagues talks of a recent assignment comprising three days' training for three different groups of ten people – a total of ninety training days – over 20 per cent of which was lost through people being unavailable for anything from fifteen minutes to a whole day.

We would only recommend holding a formal training programme on company premises if it was an induction programme. Even then strict care will need to be taken.

Hotels

Hotels have the great advantage of making it much more difficult for interruptions to take place. Another major advantage, if the course is to be residential, lies in the growth of the team spirit that arises through the after-hours discussions among delegates.

Care needs to be taken to choose the hotel that has the right atmosphere and the right facilities, but even more care needs to be taken to ensure that the hotel has the experience to cater for the special needs of training programmes. It may seem a minor thing, but serving coffee/tea on time is vital if time is not to be lost and delegates are not going to become disgruntled. There are a large number of hotels who find it impossible to serve a meal within an hour.

However, many hotels now earn a large part of their income from conferences and training programmes so the situation is improving. But do not take their word for it – ask previous users.

Training centres

Many large companies have their own training centres that have all the advantages of hotels at less or no direct cost, and, since they are housed in a separate building, have the additional advantage that trainees are not available to their offices or superiors. A further advantage is that the whole environment is built around training, which aids the whole process. Even the small company can benefit from the advantages that pertain to training centres, since there are now a number of commercial training centres providing facilities at a 'per head' cost.

Motivation and measurement

The manager has now gone a long way to ensure that successful formal training will take place. But two more questions need to be answered to make certain of success:

1 How am I going to ensure that delegates start the programme with the right attitude?
2 How am I going to measure the success of the programme?

The more the delegate looks forward to being trained, and the more positive that he/she is at the start of the programme, the more successful will be the result. But the delegate will need to be sold on the training, which means selling the personal benefits of it to that individual. To ensure that delegates really want to attend, they should be *individually briefed* and the benefits to them highlighted.

			ACTION PLAN	

OBJECTIVE	HOW DO I ACHIEVE IT? (The Plan)	HELP FROM (If required)	ACTION DATE	
			START	FINISH

Fig. 22.1 *Action planning* An action plan is a statement of objective which in turn is a collection of words or symbols describing one or more of your *intents*. To achieve the objective you should describe what you will be *doing*, how to demonstrate your achievement and how you will know when you are doing it. Write a separate statement for each objective – the more statements you have, the better chance you have of making your intention clear. The purpose of completing an action plan is to make a firm personal commitment of the plans you intend to put into action as a result of the course. Remember, objective-setting should become a way of life. Once you are on the way to achieving these targets, new ones will have come to take their place. Treat these in the same way.

Course Assessment Form

COURSE TITLE: _____

FROM (NAME) _____

COMPANY _____

DATES _____

HOW COURSE DETAILS RECEIVED?

☐ Brochure ☐ Via my company ☐ Recommendation ☐ Previous attendance ☐ Personal enquiry

REASON FOR ATTENDANCE

Were you requested to attend by your employer   YES ☐   NO ☐

Did you yourself specifically ask to attend   YES ☐   NO ☐

EVALUATION OF WHOLE COURSE

5	4	3	2	1
○	○	○	○	○

Excellent   Poor

RELEVANCE

PRESENT JOB

5	4	3	2	1
○	○	○	○	○

Very   Not at all

FUTURE JOB/ CAREER DEVELOPMENT

5	4	3	2	1
○	○	○	○	○

Very   Not at all

CONTENT LEVEL OF THE COURSE

5	4	3	2	1
○	○	○	○	○

Too advanced   Too elementary

TEACHING EFFECTIVENESS

Lecturer's Name	Lecture Content Value				Method of Lecturing			
	Covered subject matter very well	Covered subject matter well	Covered subject matter not very well	Did not cover subject matter	Put subject matter over very well	Put subject matter over well	Put subject matter over not very well	Did not put subject matter over

Fig. 22.2

GENERAL ANALYSIS

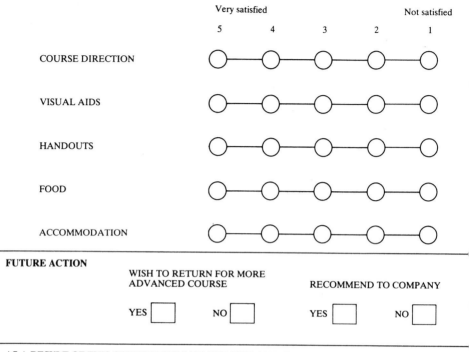

FUTURE ACTION

WISH TO RETURN FOR MORE
ADVANCED COURSE   RECOMMEND TO COMPANY

YES [ ]   NO [ ]   YES [ ]   NO [ ]

AS A RESULT OF THIS COURSE I WILL DO THE FOLLOWING

COURSE DELEGATES REMARKS

Fig. 19.1 continued

The success of the programme should be measured in five ways:

1 At the end of the programme delegates should always set personal action plans. A formula for this is shown in Fig. 22.1.
2 Before leaving the programme, delegates should also complete a course assessment form. Figure 22.2 shows an example of such a form.
3 The delegate should have a debriefing interview with the manager. This is vital if others have done the training.
4 Formal sales training sessions *must* always be followed by field training, both to assess changes and ensure that the skills are starting to be used.
5 In the longer term, results must be monitored both to ensure that the objectives have been reached and to evaluate future training requirements.

Induction training

Our definition of induction training is perhaps slightly different to most. We believe that it is that training which takes place between the first day the new salesperson joins the company and the time when that individual is capable of conducting his job with only normal field training supervision. The length of this period will obviously depend on the individual's previous knowledge of the industry, the products/services and selling in general and on the complexity of the products/services that individual is going to sell. The quality of this induction will in a major way decide the future attitude of that individual to the company and will also decide how soon he/she starts to contribute to the success of the company. Yet many companies even now think that a morning with the sales manager, an afternoon with personnel, a walk round the factory and a day or so for familiarisation with the products/services are sufficient to ensure success.

It is impossible to set out in these pages a formula for induction which will apply to every reader's company but we would suggest the following guidelines.

Any managers inducting new staff have to ask themselves two questions:

1 What information does this member of staff need to know immediately?
2 What information does this member of staff need to know to be able to do this job properly?

Immediate information

The following list includes most of this necessary information:

(a) *The important places* – For external staff details about head and branch offices, factories, etc. and their territories.
   – For internal staff their work station, the rest rooms etc.
(b) *The important people* – With whom they work and those people's job functions, to whom they report, for whom they are responsible.
(c) *The important papers* – Collect their P45 and confirm they have been entered on payroll.
   – Obtain any necessary signatures e.g. pension form.
   – Check that contract has been completed.

(d) *Explain – terms of contract*
Disciplinary procedures.
Grievance procedures.
Holiday and sickness entitlements.
Methods of salary payment, salary reviews.
Hours of work.
Probationary period.
Training to which they are entitled and will receive.
Development and career prospects.
Perks (e.g. pension plan, etc.).
Office/staff rules (e.g. clothing, smoking).
Security procedures
Health and safety at work procedures.
Office rotas.

(e) *Paint the picture*   –Tell them about the company, where it stands in the market place, about its history and about some of the important people.
– Tell them about the products.
– Explain that each and every member of staff has a responsibility to be part of the sales function.

(f) *Explain what is expected of them* – Immediately.
                                    – Later.

Long-term information

The induction process does not finish until that person is completely able to perform their job properly. A programme must be designed or followed that will give the new employee that ability.

This means that, for a sales person for example, induction will not be completed until they have sufficient knowledge of:

(a) The company and its administration.
(b) The products/services.
(c) Sales techniques.
(d) The territory.
(e) The customers.

In fact, sufficient knowledge to be successful.

23. *The Use and Selection of Training Consultants*

We have already stated that the ideal person to train the sales force is the sales manager, but equally we accept that the sales manager may lack the time or the expertise and therefore may need help from outside to perform this function. This help may be available from an internal training department, but in many companies these are either not directed towards sales training or perhaps may not even exist. Let us consider, therefore, the case where the sales manager needs to choose external training consultants.

The first consideration is whether he/she should have an internal programme for the sales force run by a consultant or should delegates be sent on open programmes where they will mix with people from other companies? Both have specific advantages.

The internal programme can be designed to meet the specific needs of that sales force and that company in their marketplace. An additional major advantage is the growth in team morale and team spirit which will occur as a result of a good programme.

The open course will allow delegates to take advantage of the opportunity to look through other people's eyes at mutual problems and gain insight into how other organisations are tackling these problems. An additional advantage is that, as the learning is not taking place in front of colleagues, inhibitions are lessened or removed.

The number of people requiring training also has relevance to this choice. It is difficult to run an internal programme for less than six people (many trainers would put five as an absolute minimum), so if the manager has less than this number of people to be trained in a given area of knowledge and he/she wants that knowedge imparted by external trainers, then it will have to be on an open course.

On the other hand, most companies running external courses limit the number of delegates they allow to attend from any one company to two or three as a maximum. If there are a larger number of people, therefore, and the training requirement is urgent, then an internal programme would be the obvious choice.

While talking about numbers of people, a comment is appropriate about maximums. In Chapter 2 we said that if practical learning is to occur a high degree of participation is vital. It is difficult to achieve this with too many people, so whether the manager is considering a self-run or a consultant-run internal programme or an open course, he should ideally look for an upper limit of twelve delegates on that course.

Choosing the consultant

It would sometimes appear that there are more firms of training consultants than there are companies to be trained! Certainly the choice is made more difficult by the sheer numbers to choose from, so how can the manager make the right choice? We would suggest the following set of actions:

1 First of all, be absolutely certain of your own objectives. Having clear-cut meaningful objectives is *even* more vital when approaching consultants than when running your own programme.

2 Ask around. Talk to other sales managers, other people in your own industry, and your own training manager and prepare a list of recommended consultants. Other countries may well have an equivalent to our National Training Index, where members report to the Index the result of using external trainers and that information is collated and distributed to members.

3 Examine the mail shots arriving on your desk, for most of the more active training companies use this method of promotion.

4 Having got together a list of likely consultants, start the sifting process by asking to sit-in on one of their programmes. It is vital that these consultants approach training in the way that is right for your objectives and your delegates, and one of the easiest ways to check this is to go and spend half a day to a day watching them operate. If the consultant refuses this request, there is at the very least a question mark about whether that is the training organisation for you.

5 Invite the consultants to visit you to discuss your needs. If the consultant spends the majority of the interview telling you how wonderful his/her company is, cross him off your list, because he does not know how to sell. The consultants worth further consideration are those that spend the majority of the available time finding out about you, your company, your staff and their needs.

6 If your requirement is for open courses, the consultant should, by the end of the interview, be able to recommend the specific courses to satisfy the needs. Providing you have already sat-in, the decision can then be made as to which course from which organisation most closely matches your needs. So send one delegate as a trial. If that is successful, continue to send delegates.

7 If you are looking for an internal course, the next step will be to have the consultants prepare a proposal. It will probably not be possible for them to give you a detailed programme at this stage, since no research has been done (in fact beware if they do want to give you a detailed programme, since it means that you will be getting a pre-packaged programme, not one built round your specific needs), but the proposal should contain the message about how they intend to approach your training.

8 On receipt of the two or three proposals (if your sifting process was correct, there should not be more than this) evaluate these proposals against your objectives, and against each other, giving due weight to the results of your sitting-in.

9 Make your decision, but not before you have met the person who is actually going to carry out the training.

10 Having made your choice, ensure that the research the consultants will want

to do enables them to establish the needs of the staff to be trained and includes sufficient time with yourself and other managers to ensure that they know what you want done. You are going to be paying for this research, so make sure it is properly organised.

11 The consultant will then submit a detailed agenda for the programme(s). Check it against your objectives to make sure they are compatible. If you are not completely happy, ask the consultant to come for further discussions. It may be that his expertise proves that the programme is correct, but do not just accept this. Remember, it is your staff and your investment.

12 Keep an eye on the training. At the very least, have lunch or dinner with the group, at best sit-in for a while. It will probably be better if this sitting-in is not done on Day 1 – give the consultant time to get the group together and working well without the stress of your presence.

13 After the programme debrief the delegates and the consultant.

14 Follow up the programme with immediate field training both to monitor immediate results and ensure that the skills discussed are being used.

This process may seem both elaborate and protracted, but it is vital if your investment in training is to be both protected and worthwhile. Training is not an end, it is a means to an end – improved results – and as such is a control operation that must be controlled.

24. *Field Training*

Give a man a fish and you feed him for a day –
Teach a man to fish and you feed him for a lifetime.

Line one of the above saying epitomises so much of what has and is being done in field training today. That is, sales people often see their sales managers sell for them but rarely get training to sell themselves. Yet, of all the training that can be done, probably the most vital is field training, since the easiest time to improve someone's performance is when they are performing.

Providing an individual has been given the skills through formal induction, development and advanced programmes, then they need regular attention to (a) hone those skills, (b) develop them and (c) ensure they acquire good not bad work habits. The best way to do this is by field training.

Aims

The primary aims of the field training are:

(a) To assess performance in the field against the background of an existing and agreed job description and standards.
(b) To determine current strengths and reinforce them.
(c) To determine current areas of need and secure recognition of these.
(d) To coach in skills and techniques to overcome the recognised areas of need and impart other knowledge to the extent that this can be done effectively in the field.
(e) To foster the attitudes of professionalism in selling by example, encouragement and instruction.
(f) To give specific help in the process of self-training, which must occur in the absence of the field trainer.
(g) To determine training requirements that may not be fully tackled in the field, assessing and reporting on appropriate means of meeting them.
(h) To evaluate improvements of performance, the effect and methods of training given.
(i) To increase the confidence in the ability of the person being trained.
(j) To motivate.

Trainer's role

Thus the prime function of the trainer/supervisor in the field is that of *control*.

In the process of fostering a complex skill like selling, the manager must:

(a) Analyse the task in which skills are deficient into units within the intellectual grasp of the person being trained, and ensure that they are understood.
(b) Set the goal or standard of performance by demonstration (NB: demonstration does not in itself *teach* a complex skill).
(c) Initiate trial of the demonstrated skill.
(d) Indicate success and failure in specific terms.
(e) Suggest specific improvements.
(f) Maintain morale during the periods of poor progress, which will naturally occur.
(g) Distribute training time as far as possible in the light of learning patterns revealed by the individual.

To help achieve this the manager will need a carefully designed appraisal form, based upon a detailed breakdown of all the tasks listed in the job description. A number of alternatives will be shown and discussed later in the chapter.
    However, the field trainer also requires:

(a) Considerable selling skill and experience.
(b) Analytical ability.
(c) The sense of priorities which will allow him/her to concentrate upon the real and most serious needs of each individual.
(d) Managerial attitudes enabling him/her to judge all that is observed in the field in the light of the company's commercial purposes.
(e) An extraordinary degree of professionalism, integrity, self-discipline, and empathy, allowing the trainer both to establish a close bond between trainer and trainee and at the same time to typify the responsible, disciplined behaviour required by management.
(f) Creative ability and the imagination to experiment with method.
(g) The system, tenacity, and general understanding of training, which allows the trainer to see and conduct his field visit within the context of a long-term development programme for the individual salesman.

    One of the most important skills the manager has to learn is that of using the praise sandwich. So many field trainers positively encourage their sales staff *not* to do better because their whole approach is one of criticism. No one but a masochist enjoys being criticised, and the natural response to being criticised is to fight back.
    The properly used praise sandwich makes people *want* to improve. It consists of the following:
1 *Praise*
    Tell people all the things they did well. Be specific.
2 *Ask*
    Ask them how they thought the performance went. The natural inclination, having heard all the good points, will be for them to pick out the improvement areas.
3 *Encourage them*
    If they miss a vital improvement area, encourage them to recognise it by probing, but if they still fail to see it, then, and only then, tell them.

4 *Improve*
   If possible, get them to tell you how that improvement can be brought about, but if they cannot do so, give them specific guidance to achieve success.
5 *Demonstrate*
   Show them how this specific guidance works, either by role play activity or by making a demonstration presentation.
6 *Praise*
   Conclude by praising them again for the good parts of their performance.

Content of field training day

Let us now look at what a good field training day should contain:

(a) *Pre-meeting*
     The things the trainer has to do before meeting the salesperson.
(b) *Start of day*
     The things that have to be achieved on meeting the salesperson at the start of the day.
(c) *Pre-call*
     The things that have to be done before each call.
(d) *Call*
     The things that the trainer should do during a call.
(e) *Post-call*
     The things that should happen after each call.
(f) *Lunch*
     The things that should occur during the lunch break. For those people who will be having business lunches, many of the things listed here will have to occur straight after lunch.
(g) *End of day*
     The things that need to occur at the end of the working day.

Before looking at these seven areas in more detail, we should report the finding of a number of surveys we have completed over the last two years of field management activity. While they showed nothing we did not expect to see, they did show how far we have still to go in improving management activity.

The term field managers in this context can be defined as those managers who have direct control of field sales personnel without help from subsidiary managers or supervisors.

1 The majority of field managers still spend less than 50 per cent of their time in field training activity.
2 The majority of managers spend most, if not all, of their field time with either the inexperienced or 'problem' sales personnel.

While these two categories require help, so do the experienced or successful sales personnel. In fact 1 per cent improvement in an experienced salesperson can be much more valuable than a 10 per cent improvement in a 'problem' salesperson.

3 Most field training was not actually field training but 'double calling', where the trainer had made the call as either a higher level negotiator or more experienced salesperson.

We are not suggesting that double calling cannot be worthwhile, only that it is not field training and should not be classed as such.

4 Many field training days were not days but half-days. There can at best be only limited value in half-day training.

Each and every salesperson requires and deserves a minimum of one day's field training per month. The inexperienced require even more.

5 Usually the same salesperson always had training on the same day and it was always the person who lived closest to the manager, the day was always a Friday – and it usually finished by lunchtime!

We have this jaundiced view of most field sales training days. They so often consist of the following:

(a) Manager meets salesperson at 10.30 or 11 am.
(b) They go for coffee.
(c) A couple of calls are then made before lunch.
(d) Lunch is highly 'liquid' and is taken at a pub (half an hour) or at a top class restaurant (two and a half hours).
(e) One call is made after lunch.
(f) Then the manager thanks the salesperson for a good day and says he/she would like to stay longer but has got to get to the office/home to complete an 'urgent report'.

This view may be cynical or exaggerated, but is not too far from the truth in too many cases.

This is not field training, this is mutual therapy; what is worse is that it is teaching bad work habits. Professionalism was item (e) in the primary aims of the field trainer (p. 125) and is mainly taught by good example.

A good field training day consists of good activity in the seven areas already listed, which we shall now elaborate.

Pre-meeting

A good training day starts not with that day but with the work that has been done already in preparation for that day. This will have consisted of:

1 Reviewing the previous field training report and action plans it contained.
2 Review of sales reports and figures since that day and a comparison with previous periods.
3 Review of journey plan to see where the individual has decided to be on the day in question.

4 As a result of 1, 2 and 3 the manager will set his/her objectives for this specific day.

5 He/she will, of course, have arranged a time and place to meet the salesperson. This time will be at least 45 minutes before it is intended the first call will take place. Irrespective of the travel time of the manager, it is vital that the first call starts at its usual time. This promotes professionalism by example.

6 The manager will have checked his personal sales kit to ensure that it is both complete and up-to-date. The only way to ensure that the salesperson will have everything needed is to have your kit with you!

7 The manager has to be highly motivated and totally ready for an exciting and fulfilling day; therefore he/she needs to get ready for it.

Pre-day

Before making any calls the following things have to be done:

1 Review the salesperson's journey plan and objectives for the day.
2 Discuss training objectives for the day.
3 Bring the salesperson up-to-date with any 'hot' news, especially if it is good news.
4 If this is an inexperienced salesperson, check that he/she has *all* the equipment-sales aids, etc., that are going to be needed. If an experienced salesperson, equipment will still need to be checked but more subtly under each pre-call discussion.
5 Discuss the role that the trainer will adopt during the calls. We will review this in more depth under 'Pre-call' below, but the salesperson needs to know under what circumstances the trainer will participate. This is vital, particularly when an inexperienced manager is training an experienced salesperson, since if this is not done, the latter may well try to catch the former out by suddenly passing the call over when it is least expected.
6 If the salesperson signifies by word or action that he/she has a problem, it is probably better to bring it out in the open than to leave it festering under the surface. Having brought it out, the trainer then has either to deal with it, if it can be dealt with rapidly, particularly if it is non-contentious, or put it firmly but pleasantly aside to deal with at the end of the day.
7 Get the salesperson 'charged up' for a good day. There is often a degree of tension on the salesperson's side at the start of a training day. This must be removed as rapidly as possible and replaced with or overcome by excitement about the good day that is in store. Partly this will be achieved by the trainer's own enthusiasm which is why it is so important that the trainer is charged up himself.

Pre-call

This activity will take place before the first and all successive calls. It consists of the following phases:

1 Reviewing existing data on both the person and the company being called on:

for example, previous purchasing pattern (if any), previous call results, and all other relevant data.

2 Discussing salesperson's objectives for the call.

3 Discussing how it is planned to reach those objectives. The process of open-ended questioning is vital in this context. We can ensure that the salesperson is thinking in terms of the customer's problems by asking:

'What are these customer's needs/problems?' (record card should be analysed and discussed).
'What is the potential here?'
'What is the turnover currently?'
'What competition does the company face?'

These questions ensure that the salesman is aware that while the aim is to sell the company's product, the prime objective of the sales call is to '*Sell answers to problems and satisfy needs*'.

Having established the prime objective, the manager now needs to check that the salesperson is properly equipped to achieve them. Further questioning should establish:

'How will the call be opened?'
'What objections are likely to arise?'
'What questions are going to be asked to ascertain needs?'
'What benefits will we stress, and how?'
'What sales aids will be necessary?'
'How are we to ask for the order?'

During these questions, the manager should be making a note of any variance in procedure or noting points that have been omitted by the salesperson. The manager must then ensure that the salesperson fully understands and agrees the call plan.

4 As regards role play, it may be necessary to rehearse or reinforce certain aspects of the call at this stage if there is an indication of doubt or uncertainty on the part of the salesperson.

5 Decide how the manager is to be introduced. Providing the customer does not already know the manager, it may not be necessary or even desirable for his/her title to be mentioned, since that automatically involves a hierarchy problem. By that we mean the customer sees the manager in a different light and starts to react differently. It is to be remembered that this is not a customer relations visit – the trainers are there to train, so if the introduction can be 'This is my colleague, Jim Jones', so much the better.

6 Decide what role the manager will take and under what circumstances (if any) he/she will play a part in the call itself. The desirable role (as we shall discuss later) is a background one, but there will always be certain circumstances in which the trainer will be drawn in. These must be pre-set if the training is to be successful.

To jump in, in order to save the sale, almost guarantees the training will fail, because it is a no-win situation for the manager. Either the salesperson will insist (even to him/herself) that if the manager had not interrupted 'I would have got there in the end' or will say 'When I've got as much experience as you,

I'll expect to get those sales equally *easily*'. Whichever of these or other similar comments is made, training is lost. The roles must be agreed in advance and stuck to rigidly.

7 Get the salesperson charged-up for the call.

Call

During the call ideally the manager will become the fly-on-the-wall; as we said earlier the trainer should remain in the background. This will usually happen in the following circumstances:

(a) If the trainer is introduced in the right way, as discussed under the previous heading. When the manager does have to be introduced by title, there is still often an opportunity to put the power where it should be – with the salesperson. The customer will often say 'I am glad you have come, I have been wanting to discuss X'. If the manager immediately indicates that the salesperson can solve that particular matter, that salesperson has then been given the power.

(b) If the trainer adopts the correct position to sit (or stand). The trainer should tactfully adopt a sidelines position out of the direct line between customer and salesperson.

(c) If the trainer uses eye contact properly. There are two forces of the eyes. The first is the magnetic compelling force. If the trainer concentrates all his/her eye contact on the customer, that person will be bound to start looking at the trainer, so the trainer should distribute eye contact liberally between both parties, changing the point of contact often.

   The second force is the directing force. If the customer does start looking at the trainer, all he/she has to do is look at the salesperson and the customer's eyes will automatically be directed that way. Similarly, the first time that the customer directs a question at the trainer, if the trainer looks at the sales person, who then answers the question, it is unlikely that the customer will again try to deal direct with the trainer.

What the trainer should actually be doing during the interview is:

(i) Observing and listening to all that is happening in the light of the objective and plan that was previously set.

(ii) Assessing the reasons for and effect of any deviations from that plan.

(iii) Noting for later discussion both the good points and the primary points for improvement.

(iv) Assessing this call against previous calls, whether on that day or the last field training day.

   Incidentally, if the salesperson is taking notes on the call (and he should be if only to show the customer that they are interested), then there is no reason why the trainer should not be unobtrusively doing the same. However, the trainer is noting the points for later discussion. A useful form for this is shown in Fig. 24.1.

PREPARATION
   Was he prepared to do business?
   Advance knowledge – sales aids – product knowledge – prices – trading terms –
   relevant proposition.
APPROACH
   Was it businesslike – friendly – confident?
   Was the customer's ATTENTION obtained?
   Was his INTEREST obtained?
PRESENTATION
   Was it clear – simple – convincing? ☐
   Were sales aids used effectively? ☐
   Was it enthusiastically presented? ☐
   Were there any positive speech and other mannerisms? ☐
   Was it conversational? ☐
   Were objections located and dealt with? ☐
   Were buying signals noticed and acted upon? ☐
   Was it positive? ☐
   Was the right product being sold? ☐
   Was enough information obtained? ☐
   Was he a good listener? ☐
   Did he invite, and attempt to obtain, agreement on points made? ☐
   Was the proposition adequately summarised? ☐
   Did he ask for the order? ☐
   Did he ask for the order properly? ☐
   Did he explain (a) delivery (b) discounts (c) credit terms etc? ☐
   Did he thank the customer for the order? ☐
OTHER COMMENTS

(Award marks out of 10 for each question)   TOTAL ☐

Fig. 24.1 *Field training checklist.*

(v)   Keeping out of the limelight wherever possible – any book or training programme on 'Training the Trainer' will say categorically: 'Do not get involved even if it means losing the sale'. While we agree with this statement, we only know one trainer in a hundred who can do so, so our advice would be do not get involved unless it is absolutely imperative, eg the sale is absolutely getting away or the Trade Description Act is being contravened. If you do have to step in, do so not by taking over the sale but by trying to help the salesperson into the right path by using such phrases as:

'It might help if you were to show Mr X (the customer) the figures on . . .'
or
'Perhaps if you were to explain the results of our research to . . .', or (to the customer)
'John can show you, Mr X, how we overcame that problem with another customer by . . .'

Thus the trainer can step in and out again in one easy stage. Of course, the more professional the pre-call procedure has been, the less likelihood there is of the trainer *having* to help out during the call.

Post-call

Many trainers believe that an in-depth 'kerbside conference' should take place after each call. We disagree. In fact, providing the trainer is in a situation where a minimum of three or four calls will be done during the day, we would suggest that for assessment purposes the first call should be virtually ignored, since it is most unlikely that the person being trained will have acted normally during the call. They will either have been better than normal or worse than normal because of the pressure of being accompanied.

Those trainers who will only be able to see one or two calls in a day should ignore the first half an hour or so of that first call. After the first call the trainer should, therefore, simply offer praise and encouragement and move on to the pre-call procedure for the next call. Gradually, as calls progress, a pattern of activity which will highlight the training needs will develop, and at that point the post-call discussions will become more valid.

All post-call discussions will follow the 'praise sandwich' principle, which we have already discussed. Pre-call, call, post-call will continue until lunch.

Lunch

Many trainers are now using the lunch break as the first in-depth post-call discussion. The timing of the break will have been decided by and signalled by the person being trained. It is very important, however, that the trainer decides on the *venue* for lunch, since it is vital that the place has the right atmosphere for a business discussion. A 'greasy-spoon' cafe or 'grotty' pub are not conducive to the right atmosphere, and we would strongly suggest that alcohol is avoided.

So what should occur once the right venue has been achieved?

(a)   A full review of the morning's activity, using the praise sandwich method.
(b)   In line with item 4 of the sandwich – improve training – set objectives for the afternoon activity.
(c)   Introduce role play to help the effect of the training if necessary.
(d)   Eat and have a 'relax' period where anything can be talked about *but* business.
(e)   Get the salesperson charged up for the afternoon.

A word here about demonstration calls, which are those calls in which the trainer acts as the salesperson in order to demonstrate a particular point. This can help to reinforce the training but must only be done when the trainer is certain that he/she *can* demonstrate that point. While it is not vital that a sale is made on the 'demo' call, it *is* vital that the point to be demonstrated is well done. If the trainer is not absolutely certain that he/she can demonstrate it effectively, he/she should use role play instead. Pre-call, call, post-call will now continue to the end of the day.

End of day

When the final call has been made, the trainer again needs to find the right venue for a post-day discussion, which comprises:

(i) A full review of the day's activity, using the praise sandwich method.

(ii) The setting of objectives for attainment between today and the next field training day.

(iii) The completion of the field training report. Many people would suggest that this should be signed by both parties, and we do not disagree, but it is vital that both parties have a copy of the report. A number of different examples are shown in Figs. 24.2 to 24.4.

(iv) Arrangements should be made where possible for the next field accompaniment day.

(v) The trainer should end the day by both praising the salesperson specifically for all the good events of the day and thanking the salesperson properly.

One final point for the inexperienced manager to watch out for is that any experienced salesperson worth his salt can set up a good day. If you find yourself in this situation, use a simple technique that will ensure it does not happen again. Simply say, 'I have had such a good day, let's spend tomorrow together as well!' The word will go round the sales force so fast that the problem is unlikely to occur again.

The field training day we have outlined will not only achieve the aims we noted at the beginning of the chapter, it will also ensure that 'your sales staff look forward to the next time. This 'look forward' will enhance the experience for both trainer and trained.

Field training assessment forms

The first of the field training assessment forms, Fig. 24.2, looks at both quantitative and qualitative factors, the latter being placed under the headings Organisation, Skills and Personal attributes. One of the benefits of this short form is its capacity to measure on the one form up to fourteen different field training days for comparison purposes.

The second form, Fig. 24.3, is the first of two in-depth assessment forms that we include. It looks at every aspect of the salesperson's performance, and one of its most important assets is the final page, which requires the trainer to give his or her conclusions and recommendations and to outline a programme to carry out the latter.

The third and final example, Fig. 24.4, enables the trainer both to note the time facts at the beginning, and, if he/she wishes, to note the calls made for later reference.

We include all three forms for you to compare with your existing form, or, if you do not have one, to choose the one that you find most appropriate. Incidentally, these are just three among the hundreds we have seen, and we have selected them because of their usefulness. If one of our readers was instrumental in helping to write one of them, we thank him for his contribution.

FIELD TRAINING ASSESSMENT FORM

Salesman.. Manager ....
Period ....

Dates of assessment

A. Quantitative

Average call rate for period
Turnover for period
Conversion ratio for period

B. Qualitative
1 Organisation
Knowledge of
    Competition
    Products
    Customers
    Prospects
    Company
    Potential
Reports/correspondence
State of records and use
Territory planning
Call planning
Customer follow up
Call objectives

2 Skills
Introduction
Use of questions
Establishing requirements
Benefits/investment
Closing
Overcoming objections
Range selling

3 Personal attributes
Interest and enthusiasm
Co-operation
Honesty/loyalty
General attitudes
Time keeping
Grooming, dress, car
Human relations
Communications
Self-expression
Receptiveness

Fig 24.2

FIELD SELLING PERFORMANCE
EVALUATION

Code — Name_____
1 Knowledge — Company_____
2 Skill — Date of appraisal_____
3 Attitude — Rated by_____

Code	Preparation	Poor	Fair	Good	Excellent
1	Knowledge of company policies				
1	Knowledge of products				
2	Knowledge of buyers as individuals				
2	Knowledge of customer application				
1	Knowledge of competition				
1	Knowledge of trade practices				
1	Knowledge of marketing trends				
3	Questioning attitude				
3	Evidence of willingness to learn				
2	Analytical skills				
1–2–3	Does he plan ahead and organise work?				

Fig. 24.3

	Opening the sale				
2	Ability to gain entrance	___	___	___	___
2	Ability to obtain prospect's attention	___	___	___	___
2	Alertness in sizing up buying situations	___	___	___	___
2	Penetration (getting story across)	___	___	___	___
1–2	Selection of proper benefits to stress	___	___	___	___
3	Diplomacy, tactfulness	___	___	___	___
3	Personal appearance	___	___	___	___
3	Friendliness, sociability	___	___	___	___
	Arouse interest				
2	Skill in arousing prospect's interest	___	___	___	___
2	Sensitivity to prospect's buying motives	___	___	___	___
2	Appealing to buying motives – pride – profit – convenience	___	___	___	___
2	Speech effectiveness – delivery – vocabulary	___	___	___	___
1	Proper use of samples	___	___	___	___
2	Skill in getting buyer into the act	___	___	___	___
2	Skill in talking 'buyer's language'	___	___	___	___
	Tell the facts				
1–2	Use of facts which support benefits	___	___	___	___
2	Answering questions promptly and thoroughly	___	___	___	___
1–2	Gearing facts to individual buying situations	___	___	___	___
	Code preparation				
1–2–3	Conviction in presenting facts	___	___	___	___
1	Accuracy in presenting facts	___	___	___	___
	Overcoming objections				
2	Skill in recognising retardants	___	___	___	___
2	Listening ability – understanding	___	___	___	___
1–2	Handling price	___	___	___	___
1–2	Handling prejudice (quality – appearance – performance – reputation - delivery – service etc.)	___	___	___	___
2–3	Handling procrastination	___	___	___	___
2	Skill with visual presenter	___	___	___	___
	Closing the sale				
3	Attitude of confidence – conviction	___	___	___	___
2–3	Possession of control over buying situations	___	___	___	___
2	Prudence in timing closes	___	___	___	___
2	Proper use of feelers to secure buying action	___	___	___	___
2–3	Persistence in requesting action	___	___	___	___
	Other working relationships				
1–3	Thoroughness in preparing orders – reports – expenses	___	___	___	___
1–2–3	Amount of supervision required	___	___	___	___
3	Co-operation with other salesmen and departments	___	___	___	___
1–3	Bringing in information on customers – competition – markets	___	___	___	___
1–3	Maintaining territory records on customers – prospects	___	___	___	___
1–3	Keeping informed on prices – stocks – advertising	___	___	___	___
1–2–3	Customer relations – explaining shortages – delivery – or other temporary difficulties	___	___	___	___

Conclusions _____

_____

_____

Recommendations _____

_____

_____

Programme _____

_____

_____

Fig. 24.3 continued

FIELD VISIT REPORT

Representative's Name:
Date of Visit:
Number of Calls: Existing Accounts: ....Effective   ....Non-Effective
                 Prospective Accounts: ....Effective   ....Non-Effective

Time Started   ....Hrs.
Time Finished   ....Hrs.
      Total: ....Hrs.
Of this Total
Travelling:
Meals & Breaks:
Face to Face:
Waiting:
Other:
Area Covered:
Accompanied By:

ORGANISATION		BENEFITS	
Personal Appearance		Company Benefits (Knowledge of)	
Customer Records		Product Benefits (Knowledge of)	
Prospecting Records		Technical Knowledge	
Territory Planning		Timing of Visuals	
Visual Aids/Samples		Control of Visuals	
Use of Time		Third Party Testimony	
Punctuality		Summary	
Overall		Overall	
PLANNING		INVESTMENT MERIT	
Getting Appointments (Quantity)		Selling Investment Merits	
Getting Appointments (Quality)		Showing Savings	
Seeing Right People		Selling 'Quality' versus 'Price'	
Consulting Records		Check Back Questions	
Anticipating Needs		Comparison & Summary	
Anticipating Objections		Overall	
Setting Objectives		OVERCOMING OBJECTIONS	
Preparing Visuals		Listening to Objections	
Overall		Questioning	
INTRODUCTION		Finding an Opening	
Company Image		Restating Benefits	
Stating Objectives		Restating Investment Merits	
Creating Confidence		Closing on an Objection	
Relaxing Buyer		Overall	
Overall		CLOSING	
REQUIREMENTS		Perception of Signals	
Logical Questioning		Trial Closes	
Establishing Needs		Use of Closing Methods	
Customer Participation		Action (By whom, by when)	
Establishing Problems		Summary	
Product Knowledge		Terminating Interview	
Knowledge of Competitors		Overall	
Switching Objectives		CONVICTION	
Range Selling		Knowledge	
Summary		Skills	
Overall		Attitudes	
		Overall	

Fig. 24.4

VERBAL FACILITY		ATTITUDES	
Emphasis & Modulation		To Company	
Persuasive use of language		To Products	
Speed		To Higher Management	
Overall		To Immediate Superior	
PERSONAL ATTRIBUTES		To Colleagues	
Interest & Enthusiasm		To Salary & Incentives	
Courtesy		To Car (including upkeep)	
Self Analysis		To Promotion Prospects	
Persistence		To Advertising	
Positiveness		To Selling	
Co-operation		To Training	
Receptiveness			

Marking Code 10 V. Good   E = Effective
          8 Good   N/E = Non-effective
          6 Acceptable
          4 Poor
      NEA No Evidence Available

ALL CALLS MADE

Name   Location   Contact   E or N/E
                                                   & Status

Fig. 24.4 continued

25. Training the Trainer/Training the Manager

We have indicated in earlier chapters the vital role that training has to play in achieving results. We have also discussed in Part 6 Herzberg's idea that motivation is a function of ability and the opportunity to use that ability, which indicates how important training is in the process of motivation since ability can only be increased by training. Yet in many companies very little attention is given to training the trainer.

Many a newly appointed manager is told that a vital part of his/her job is to train the staff but very few are shown how to do it. Developing a good manager should be given just as much, if not more attention, than developing good sales staff since the second will occur if the first has been done properly.

Ideally, line managers (those in direct control of the sales staff) should be developed from within the organization since this ensures that there is a career structure within the company which aids the motivation process.

So how do we develop effective line managers.

1 The senior manager (sales manager/sales director) should be constantly assessing the sales force to pinpoint those who display the skills and personal qualities mentioned in earlier sections of this book.

2 When someone is found, and providing there is an opportunity for promotion within the company, their skills should be gradually assessed and honed by a series of increasingly important short-term tasks.

    It is vital that in the earlier tasks it is made very difficult for them to *fail* and that when they do win they are properly praised for their success.

3 At the time when the individual has both proved his/her potential and the opportunity is available, their appointment should be either preceded by or accompanied after three to six months by the opportunity to attend a field sales management training programme.

The advantages of the training programme preceding the appointment are:

(a) The programme will enable them to avoid many of the pitfalls into which they would otherwise fall.

(b) Their confidence that they can cope will be tremendously increased.

Alternatively the advantages of allowing them to attend the training programme three to six months after appointment are:

(a) They will be far more aware of the problems and challenges having experienced them at first hand and will be more aware of their own areas for improvement;

Fig. 25.1   *Field sales management training programme*

	DAY 1	DAY 2	DAY 3	DAY 4	DAY 5
1	Marketing and the role of the field sales manager	Syndicate activity discussion	Running effective sales meetings Film: 'Meetings, Bloody Meetings'	*BUDGETING* Purpose, principles and practice	Syndicate presentations
2	Leadership The qualities and action-centred approach	The motivation of salesmen in the 80s Film: 'Jumping for Jelly Beans'	Recruiting and selecting sales people Film: 'Manhunt'	*FORECASTING* – Principles and practice – Market demand – Statistical method	*TIME* The greatest restraint Film: 'Time to Think' course review
3	The major function of the F.S.M. Film: 'Training Salesmen on the Job'	Motivation-syndicate and discussions	Recruiting – practical CCTV	*SALES AND CUSTOMER ANALYSIS* – Small orders – Variance analysis – Cash flow forecasting	
4	Field Training Continued . . .	The F.S.M.'s personnel role Film: 'How am I Doing'	Review of practical interviews	*CONTROL SYSTEMS & RATIOS* – Use of information – Fixed and variable costs – Break-even analysis	
5	Syndicate and individual activity	Pair and individual activity	Review CCTV and syndicate activity	Syndicate activity	

(b) Their self-confidence will be greatly increased as they realise that many of the things that they have done instinctively were the right things to do.

These programmes are normally of four to five days duration and Fig. 25.1 shows a typical four and a half day programme. Many training organisations run such programmes. When choosing which one to send your managers on the reader should have as a major criteria those programmes which emphasise participation and practical involvement.

Whichever option is chosen we recommend that they re-attend the same or a similar programme about eighteen months later both to revise all the skills learnt and overcome problem areas.

4 Many companys would now consider their manager as having been trained. They could not be more wrong. The training has just begun on two grounds:

(a) No one programme can ever be complete. The idea that any programme can turn a person completely into a manager is erroneous just as no one programme can turn a person into a salesman;

(b) The role of a manager as discussed in earlier sections of the book is far too complex to be learnt in a programme, however long.

Every manager should spend at least a few days each year away from the job learning new skills or revising existing skills. A brief re-look at some of the skills needed to be an effective manager (see Fig. 25.2) should prove, if proof be needed, the necessity of on-going management training.

The abilities to:
1 Structure the team properly.
2 Plan.
3 Provide effective leadership.
4 Control.
5 Motivate self and others.
6 Recruit.
7 Train.
8 Manage time.
9 Assess.
10 Set objectives, standards and targets.
11 Forecast future results.
12 Conduct formal appraisal and counselling interviews.
13 Sell ideas and negotiate.
14 Delegate.

Fig. 25.2 *The skills required of an effective manager*

PART FIVE

Controlling Your Sales Operation

Planning and controlling are commonly known as the 'management twins'. It is obviously true to say that with no plan there is nothing to control and with no control even the most comprehensive plan is useless.

Planning is concerned with making certain that all those involved are quite clear as to what you are seeking to accomplish. Planning indicates action that must be taken to reach objectives and it identifies the skills required to attain the ultimate goals.

Controlling is measuring and regulating action to ensure that what you *want* done *gets* done. There are two specific areas in controlling:

(a) Organising – establishing structure and authority, the most efficient means of working etc.
(b) Supervising – developing competent people who know what needs doing, providing help and information, developing indicators to determine what is happening, and providing means for adjusting plans and organisation to meet changing needs.

These principles should be applied to the control of a sales force in just the same way as in other areas. Putting a salesperson in a car, with brochures, and pointing him/her in the general direction of a prospect is good planning. But how do we ensure that the person stays on course and that the plan is right?

26. *Concept of control*

In many companies sales reports seem to be used as a form of discipline and the information on them is never used. Likewise, no real control is exercised over the field force, because, although there is a record of what has actually happened, there is no clear idea of what should have happened. In other words, no clear objectives have been set for either of these two important areas.

Nature of control

If control is to be exercised, it implies the setting of standards, comparison of actual against standard and the analysis of the variance.

As far as possible, quantitative standards should be set, as this gives us a measurable and objective view. Without standards we have no control, and without variance analysis there is no point in having a control procedure.

Control must be preceded by planning, and planning must be followed by control, if either is to be of real value.

Standards

There are three basically different types of standard, and we must be careful which we use.

Fixed standards. For example, annual sales targets. These have the drawbacks that normally any comparison against them is too late for action to be taken, and, in any case, they are descriptive standards, so although it may be clear something is wrong, we do not know *what* is wrong.

Variable standards. For example, monthly or weekly targets. These have the advantage that variance is indicated earlier and, therefore, corrective action can be taken earlier, when the degree of variance warrants it. However, they still do not reveal why.

Analytical standards. These are attempts to define why there is a variance and can be derived from one basic question:

What is the cause of success in selling?

Here we are concerned with those standards within the salesperson's control, of which there are basically four.

(i)   The people visited (who), which is based on customer list, prospect list, and customer profile.
(ii)   The number of those people (how many), depends on the call rate and the prospecting rate.
(iii)   The frequency of call required.
(iv)   The content of the call, which is checked by the call report and the field appraisal.

If we set these analytical standards, we can control performance before the event, and prevent adverse variances resulting from wrongly directed sales effort.

Other standards can also be set in terms of expenses, average gross profitability, and order to calls ratio.

Collecting the information

Information will come from sales results, call reports, and field visits. Sales results, although important, may give a misleading picture of the sales effort, owing to factors beyond the salesperson's control.

Call reports are very important if correctly designed: They should contain the following information:

(a)   Contact's name.
(b)   Dates of this visit and previous visit.
(c)   Buying record to date.
(d)   Objective of call.
(e)   Description of call.
(f)   Results obtained.
(g)   Action to be taken by saleserson.
(h)   Action to be taken by office.

Field visits should be made regularly by field managers to assess and train the sales people – minimum one day per man per month. The information gained should be recorded on a field appraisal form.

Analysis of variances

It is often insufficient just to compare monthly budgeted figures against actual, as variations may be high. Therefore, some form of averaging is required, eg quarterly moving average, moving annual total, or Z Chart.

Averages need not, of course, be used over time, but can be plotted across the sales force, thus giving comparisons of one man against another – very useful for expenses, for example – and discovering better selling methods.

Other ratios can be useful as control systems. For example:
Expenses : sales
Expenses : calls
Selling calls : courtesy calls

Cold canvass calls : total calls
Call time : sales
Total turnover : length of experience

It is worthwhile deciding (based on experience) the variances that can be permitted: e.g. if call rate should be ten a day there is probably no point in taking action if it varies between eight and twelve.

Corrective action

This may mean either an alteration of the plan, if it is obviously unrealistic, or corrective action to ensure the pre-set plan will be met. The virtue of planning and control in this way is to ensure forewarning of future problems.

If the problem lies in the structure of the plan, obviously this will have to be re-thought out. If it lies in the execution of the plan, it is probably a sales force problem. If the latter, it can only be solved by training the salesperson or changing the salesperson.

If training is needed, controls should be established to ensure the plan is met. Specific objectives should be established from research into the situation, eg the person may need training on 'closing' or on 'gaining an entry', but otherwise is a good salesperson. The training can, therefore, be directed exactly at the problem area.

Designing and implementing an effective reporting system

Most sales reporting systems suffer from a major problem: They do not measure sales activity.

There are three main characteristics of 'traditional' sales reporting systems:

1 They have been imposed on the sales management.
2 They are actually a 'spin off' of an accounting or a sales/inventory system.
3 They are cumbersome and of no use as a tool to help manage the sales team.

The result is often a system that has a low level of commitment from the sales team. Returns are completed only under duress and never early enough to be an accurate representation of what has happened. Even when accurate, the reports from the system rarely allow you to analyse, compare or recommend action.

In the design of any system, keep it simple. Ask if your 'ideal' report will be capable of immediate use without ten minutes 're-training' time? Never initiate a new report just by sketching out the headings; try to use the information. See what systems are available 'off the shelf' – starting from a blank piece of paper could 'seriously damage your wealth!'

Test the report layouts

There are a number of simple tests you should apply to the design of all computer or manual systems:

1 Can the reports be easily completed by secretarial or administrative staff?
2 Will the reports still work and be meaningful if someone fails to complete a return or report?
3 Are deviations from plan highlighted?
4 Are important percentages calculated for you?
5 Can sales people, teams and divisions be easily compared?
6 Will the system 'survive' the transfer of a salesperson or a reorganisation?

Four basic objectives

There are four basic objectives central to the development of a professional sales reporting system:

(a) To monitor sales activities. This might be regarded as the lowest level of report. It is intended to measure just how busy is the salesperson/team and how effective are the activities being completed.
(b) To identify the problems and opportunities. Problems may include the poor conversion rate of new prospects or insufficient quotations in the pipeline. Particularly good performances are identified for further development and application across the company.
(c) A diagnostic approach, which is best seen as preparation for your field accompaniment or counselling, and should identify individual strengths and weaknesses.
(d) 'Automatic' forecasting, where the results produced from your reporting system can be directly applied to produce an accurate forecasting base.

Designing the reports the salespeople complete

The forms or returns that your salespeople will need to complete will need to be simple and as easy to complete as is practicable – or they won't be completed!

Where an existing reporting system exists, change will be obviously easier if 'grafted' on to that system. The minimum information to be recorded would be:

(i) The call (separated into existing and new customers).
(ii) Products discussed.
(iii) Results of the call, sales/orders and action needed.
(iv) Source of the customer or prospect.
(v) Time spent face to face.
(vi) Mileage.

The easier the information is to record, the more likely it is to be done at the time. The obvious benefit to the sales manager is that the information will reflect what happened and not what was remembered.

Designing your reports

Much depends upon whether your system will be produced on a computer or from a regular clerical exercise. The principles of a good reporting system are the same for both, but a computer system should be easier to prepare.

Donnelly's 4th law
'If there isn't a column on the right side of a report to add notes and action points it wasn't designed to be used. . . . Poor paper quality and a low absorbency factor may inhibit the only alternative application!'

Check the report works
Before you draft a report, complete a sample with actual data and try to use the results, asking these questions:

1 What are you actually going to do with this report (is it a good idea in search of an application)?
2 Is the information in the right sequence?
3 Would the automatic highlighting of exceptions or variations be useful?
4 Could percentages and positions be automatically calculated?
5 What further information could usefully be included?
6 What information could be omitted?
7 Is the form so complex that only you understand it?
8 After two weeks' holiday, would it still make sense to you?

Monitoring the sales activity

The reports should be capable of interpretation at individual salesperson and team level, and provide company totals.

(a) How 'busy' were the sales team? The reports should show simple measures of activity, such as the number of calls, mileage and the time spent with customers.
(b) What sales activities were completed? Analyses of such factors as the ratio of new calls to service calls, the level of quotations and proposals.
(c) What was achieved? This is where we start to analyse the results and achievements such as:

    (i)   Calls per order.
    (ii)   Prospect to order conversion.
    (iii) Average order value.
    (iv)   Level of repeat business.
    (v)   Effectiveness of demonstrations.
    (vi)   Effectiveness of proposals/quotations.

Identifying the problems and opportunities

This is the natural follow-up to the monitoring stage, where you use and develop the information on a more 'tactical' level.

1 There are a number of problems which you should be able to identify and investigate further. These might include:
    (i)   What is the pattern behind worsening conversion rates?

(ii) Where are excessive calls, demonstrations, proposals per order significant?

(iii) Where is there an imbalance between existing and new customer activity?

(iv) Which products and personnel problems are the worst and deserve immediate action?

(v) Is insufficient customer contact time a problem?

(vi) Insufficient pipeline of proposals, prospects, quotes and demonstrations.

2 Without a professional reporting system the day-to-day pressures on sales management may prevent them analysing and 'chasing' opportunities. The examples below give an indication of the way in which a reporting system could help:

(i) Particularly good individual performance can be recognised, analysed and adopted across the company.

(ii) Identify/analyse exceptional product performance.

(iii) Plan territory changes on a sound and 'scientific' basis.

(iv) Early identification of changes in established sales patterns.

The diagnostic approach

A good reporting system should enable you to analyse and quantify individual strengths and weaknesses. This activity should be seen as vital preparation and support for field accompaniment or review/counselling. By comparing performances you can identify the particular problem areas, not just 'a failure to get the business'.

The analysis will differ from business to business but your system should be capable of answering such questions as the following:

(a) Is the salesperson 'busy' at the cost of effectiveness?

(b) Is the appointment to call ratio low?

(c) Is the proportion of orders to quote/demonstration or proposal too low?

(d) Have too many/insufficient products been discussed?

(e) Is the balance right between new and existing customers?

(f) Is there a weakness in certain product areas?

(g) Are insufficient appointments being made?

'Automatic' forecasting

So often forecasts are based on guesswork, and made even less accurate by the compulsory application of a dose of corporate optimism. The analysis of 'pipeline' activities should provide the basis for early and more accurate forecasting. Even bad news is more palatable if delivered in time for action to be taken and defences prepared.

Apply the current pipeline of prospects, appointments, demonstrations and quotations/proposals to the known historical conversion level achieved. The forecast can be built up from the individual salesperson's figures, from region/

area/branch totals or from company level totals.

The Repstats* System

As management consultants and trainers we spent a long time looking for a reporting system which we could recommend to our clients.
In every system we reviewed there were fundamental drawbacks:

(a) They were so complicated that a science degree was necessary to be able to complete and another degree necessary to understand the results; or
(b) They took ages to complete by the sales force and/or they took hours if not days of management time to quantify the results; or
(c) They asked for the wrong information, i.e. information that was not going to be used; or
(d) They failed to obtain the information which was needed to manage the business and so on. . . .

In every system, that is until we found the Repstats Reporting System, which contains most of the facilities and features already described. Repstats runs on a desk top computer and the thing which really caused us to decide to sell the system through InTech Sales Dynamics Limited is that it does not tell the sales managers what to measure. It asks the manager what he/she wants to measure and then the software is built round those needs.

Relation between planning and control

(a) Planning is necessary to ensure company policy is achieved and to give purposeful direction to the activities of the sales force at minimum cost.
(b) Control is complementary but necessary to any plan, for it ensures the plan is being achieved or, if not, what needs to be done to ensure achievement. It also provides data for future planning and decision-making.
(c) Plans are nothing, planning is everything. But there is little point in planning without instituting control mechanisms.

*Repstats is the copyright (1983) and registered trademark of Target Achievement Ltd.

27. Setting Goals

In whatever field of human activity you choose there will be a striving to achieve. There will be an objective or goal on the one hand and an intention to reach that objective on the other.

Controlling a sales organisation is a highly skilled business. It requires a clear vision on the part of the person in control and it requires the ability to motivate those being controlled in such a manner as to achieve the goals set by the controller.

The setting of the ultimate goal should be:

(a) realistic, so that even the most cynical salesperson will see it as feasible;
(b) achievable, so that even the poorest performer can imagine it possible to reach his/her target;
(c) fair, so that even the 'grumbler' in the group has to admit that he/she is being treated justly.

Step by step

It is unwise to set the 'ultimate goal' too far ahead without setting at the same time a series of smaller 'step goals'. These are stepping stones that are planned in such a way as to encourage even the fainthearted to believe it possible to achieve the final target, the ultimate goal. An example of this might be a sales incentive competition, where the objective is to produce the salesperson of the year (SOTY). It is well known that long competitions are not as effective as the shorter ones, but this could be overcome by running the SOTY competition as a series of *monthly* competitions. Each month the objective would be different, e.g.

Jan.	Greater per cent over target for month,
Feb.	Largest number of new accounts,
March	Highest sales of a designated product,
April	The best quotation/order ratio,
May	Greatest number of orders taken in the hand,

and so on each month for the whole year.

Each month carries a pre-determined number of points, the SOTY being the person who achieves the highest score over the 12 months. Thus the ultimate objective (to produce the best all-round salesperson) is achieved by providing a series of monthly 'step goals', which in turn maintains a high level of activity and motivation.

Goals are a must

Many sales managers have been known to question the need for goals, or objectives, or even targets, which in turn means that such people would question the value of incentives, bonuses, competitions, prizes, etc. These managers usually belong to the old school, and are rash enough to believe that their product or service does not have to be sold. With a slightly patronising, even pained expression, these people have been heard to say 'Our product/service sells itself!'

Unless you have a monopoly of the market and people *have* to buy *your* product/service (to survive), *you have to sell it*. You only need *one* competitor and you have to *sell*. And if you have to 'sell' your product or service, you, your sales force, your company and all those who work for it, and all your customers, will benefit from the superior edge given to a product by accepting the pressure of competition.

With such acceptance comes the need to be better, and to be better you must set standards and targets. These are goals. Do you want to be better? Then you must set goals.

Sales activity equals sales results

The purpose of setting goals is to provide motivation, which in turn is designed to produce a high degree of profitable activity. Profitable activity stems from meaningful activity, which, if planned, controlled and monitored in a professional manner, will give the sales results required by the organisation.

However, not all sales activity is meaningful and not all sales results are profitable. This is particularly true where the sales manager has been promoted because of his outstanding personal sales performance by a singularly un-enlightened senior executive who believes that such a promotion will instantly provide the answer to the company's current sales problem! Such a sales manager feels obliged to adopt the role of super salesperson and promptly does his best to justify his promotion by performing even more incredible sales feats, rather than learning how best to fit into the new role of 'manager'.

If the newly promoted sales manager will follow our previous suggestions (see Chapter 12), he/she will resist the urge to achieve short-term kudos and go instead for the more profitable long-term gain. This can best be done by following the advice of Peter Drucker and 'manage by objective'. Here are a few guidelines.

Management by objectives

Management by objectives is a dynamic system which seeks to integrate the company's need to clarify and achieve its profit and growth goals with the employee's need to contribute and develop himself. It is a demanding and rewarding style of managing a business. See Figure 27.1.

When a worthwhile system of management by objectives is operating in a company; there is a continuous process of:

(a) Reviewing critically and restating the company's strategic and tactical plans.
(b) Clarifying with each employee the key results and performance standards he must achieve, in line with unit and company objectives, and gaining his

contribution and commitment to these.

(c) Agreeing with each manager a job improvement plan which makes a measurable and realistic contribution to the unit and company plans for better performance.

(d) Providing conditions in which it is possible to achieve the key results and improvement plans, notably:

    (i) an organisational structure which gives a manager maximum freedom and flexibility in operation,

    (ii) management control information in a form and at a frequency which makes for more effective self-control and better and quicker decisions.

(e) Using systematic performance review to measure and discuss progress towards results and potential review to identify people with potential for advancement.

(f) Developing company training plans to help each employee to overcome weaknesses, build on strengths and to accept a responsibility for self-development.

(g) Strengthening employee's motivation by effective selection, salary and succession plans.

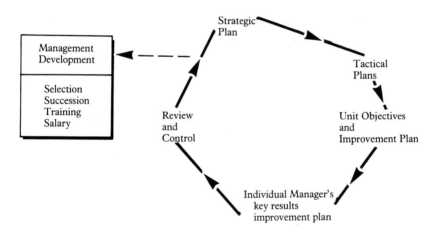

Fig. 27.1

Two things follow:

First:
MBO is essentially the distillation into a practical system of the best practice followed already by managers. It is not something 'fashionable' or 'new'.
Second:
The development of people, which is a matter of vital importance to every company, only makes sense if it is integrated with the purpose of the business. Looked at in this way, management development is a valuable by-product of running a business efficiently.

Benefits

The benefits to the company include:

(a) Concentration, individually, and as a team, on the really important profit influencing tasks instead of dissipating energy on tasks which even if done superbly well could have little impact on overall results and growth.
(b) The identification of problems which prevent high performance, and improvement plans to solve them.
(c) A demonstrable improvement in morale and sense of purpose arising from the involvement of managers, eg labour turnover amongst key staff, which arose mainly from frustration was reduced in a multiple retail concern within a year of introducing management by objectives.
(d) The identification of people with potential so that reliable management succession plans can be built up.
(e) Better management training at a lower cost. A critical study of management training in a consumer durable manufacturing group showed that its content was mainly what the personnel department thought necessary and not the real needs, shown by performance review. A group of managers were being trained in 'report writing and communications' when the urgent priority was for them to understand and use a new method of statistical quality control. People were sent on outside training courses by rota with little consideration of individual special problems and with no provision for follow-up action on return.
(f) Improvements in management controls and management performance standards. For example, it may be much more meaningful to express control data in tons/man hour rather than money, or to provide crude evidence of trends quickly rather than wait for more precise information. These points, to which lip service is often given, emerge vividly when controls are related to specific results which a manager agrees to achieve at a specific standard in a specific time.
(g) Sounder organisation structure with more effective delegation of responsibilities and accountability.

From the individual manager's view, typical benefits include:

(a) A greater opportunity to make a personal contribution and to accept more responsibility.
(b) Less frustration as the 'framework' of company objectives and the limits on his authority are clarified.
(c) Better, more purposeful communication about things that matter with his boss, colleagues and subordinates.
(d) Increased opportunity for personal growth, strengthened by the knowledge that the company is systematically planning training and succession.
(e) Recognition of achievement by himself and his boss through clearer performance standards and sharper management controls.
(f) More equitable material rewards and promotion plans.

28. *The Sales Process*

It is not our intention at this stage to teach you how to sell, but it might be helpful if we outline the number of relevant factors concerning sales and selling. For example, the assumption that all sales managers are necessarily ex-salesmen and therefore know all about selling is untrue. They may not be ex-salesmen, and even if they are, they may never have been taught how to sell. They may have been thrown in at the deep end on the principle of sink or swim.

It might therefore be prudent to run over some of the components of the selling sequence.

Since the modern salesperson costs the company so much money (about £25,000 ($35,000) per annum in 1984), it is essential that every call, every interview be of maximum time value. It is, therefore, important that the salesperson be trained to appreciate the need for each interview to be seen as an investment of his/her time and of the company's money. The best way to ensure this happens is to see that your sales people act as follows:

1 Plan their territory so as to get the maximum number of calls from it.
2 Research each prospect to ensure that the call is worthwhile and potentially profitable. And find out who the decision-maker is.
3 Think about the presentation before arriving at the prospect's desk so as to:

    (a) match his problem to their solution,
    (b) show that they know about his business,
    (c) maximise face-to-face interview time.

4 Conduct a thorough businesslike interview, based on *his* (not their) needs. Sell benefits.
5 Ask plenty of open-ended questions, get maximum information for writing the proposal or quotation. This stage is called the survey.
6 Are prepared for the inevitable objections, which should be welcomed and answered sensibly and honestly. This can be the real test of product knowledge.
7 Above all, *ask for the order*, fearlessly and naturally. It is the logical conclusion to everything that has gone before.
8 Realise that the ability to communicate does not mean having the 'gift of the gab'! It means having the ability to get the prospect talking about his problems while the salesperson listens and seeks the solution. To communicate properly means ensuring that it is a two-way process.

For the benefit of the reader we have included in this chapter a number of appendices which outline the sales process. These appendices are printed by kind permission of InTech Training Ltd, the College of Marketing and Joe Windsor.

Before going into the sales process, however, we shall look at two specific areas of the selling activity which are often misunderstood or ignored by sales managers. These two areas are merchandising and average values. The former is not just of concern to those companies in the FMCG/retailing operation but can be applied in some form or another to most industries. The latter shows how a grasp of finance can be used to make a sales manager's job both more interesting and simpler.

Merchandising

The term 'merchandising' rarely means more than a point of sale display to most sales managers. As a result, they fail to capitalise on the benefits that expanding their understanding of this term would mean. It has been defined as 'The right product in the right place at the right time'.

Main techniques

The main techniques necessary to make sure that this deceptively simple statement is achieved are outlined below:

1 *The range plan.* This planning technique is intended to produce a range of products/services, and should achieve the best possible balance between price/facilities and an acceptable level of stockholding.
2 *The intake controls.* This implementation control technique provides delivery schedules and controls to achieve the planned balance developed in the range plan.
3 *Merchandise reporting system.* This monitoring and reporting system enables you to correct imbalances and pursue opportunities in time to take action.

Changes in product performance need to be identified early if they are to affect your marketing and promotional decisions constructively.

Changes in the sales pattern

All too often the underlying change in a sales pattern is masked by a change in sales pattern for which you are responsible!

1 Reduction in sales buoyancy. A natural decline which should be corrected by executive action could be hidden by the application of 'excessive' additional sales effort:

    (a) Your reaction: 'An all-out effort on Product A, we are well down on plan'.
    (b) The immediate result: resources diverted from more buoyant products and a 'you get back on plan'.
    (c) The final result: you return to plan and the cost of this effort is 'hidden'.
    (d) The future: 'next year's plan will be this year's actual plus 10 per cent!'
2 Increased sales from a buoyant product/service. So often 'hitting target'

means switching off, and the transfer of effort to other areas. The company may even encourage this where sales have embarrassed supply or production.

(a) Your reaction: 'Well done, we have sold all our quota'.
(b) The immediate result: resources are switched or momentum slows and relatively easy additional sales are sacrificed.
(c) The final result: the real potential is not appreciated and supply drives the company, not sales opportunity.
(d) The future: 'Next year's plan for this area will be this year's actual plus 15 per cent'.

Increasing the 'debit' through add-on sales

Little extra sales cost and effort comes into the sale of 'add-ons' if they are made at the same time as the original sale. Too often the sale of additional services or equipment is seen only as a follow-up activity.

1 Fixed price maintenance contract. If you are selling capital equipment, then the sale of maintenance should be included. Even if you provide twelve months' free servicing, sell the service for the ongoing period as early as possible.
2 Supply consumables. An agreement to provide any necessary consumables on a contract price will be seen as a customer service activity and should ensure that you control quality.
3 Complementary equipment/services. The provision of complementary equipment or services can be arranged, possibly on a franchise or concession arrangement.

None of the three activities above should be allowed to detract from the main business, however, they all give you a number of advantages:

(i)   The customer has to take positive action to terminate the recurring sale.
(ii) You have an 'excuse' to return and check supply, which may produce further major sales opportunities.

Measure/evaluate change and innovation

As a nation we are criticised for being slow to innovate and even slower to capitalise on successful innovation. However, change should be planned, controlled and monitored if it is to be ultimately successful. The real dilemma is how to achieve this activity within an acceptable time-scale.

When new products/services are launched, there are two key areas, which are rarely measured but which impact directly on to the sales manager:

1 What proportion of effort is needed? The organisation, training and sales effort needed in any new launch should be planned and monitored. Any serious deviation from plan could be the first quantifiable indication of impending trouble!

2   What is the cost to your other business? The cost to your other products/ services will be significant and you should ensure that you recognise *all* those costs:

   (i)   Salespersons' time.
   (ii)   Lost opportunity for other products.
   (iii)   A sales switch to the new product.

From careful monitoring we can establish what improvements are needed, particularly in the sales area. This may mean changes in product training, point of sale material, pricing and advertising.

Merchandising benefits

The real benefits of adopting a merchandising approach to analysing product/ service performance are the following:

1 Early feedback. For a successful product additional supplies can be organised against a quantified demand. When there is a serious shortfall, early action can be taken to cancel, divert, discount or replace. Only unsuccessful products are available at short notice, only orders for successful ones can be easily cancelled!
2 Balancing the sales effort. If excessive sales effort and cost are necessary to move a product, this can be recognised; conversely, a relatively low sales effort per product can be identified.
3 Identifying the real potential. The real potential for a product can be significantly different from the sales plan.
4 Products in balance. Good range planning should provide a range that is in balance for all the factors that affect sales, such as price, facilities, colour and size.

Two daft questions

There are two loaded questions which should emphasise the importance of merchandising:

Q1   How many failed products are kept on the market for a period that embarrasses even the vested interests of the originators?
Q2   How often has the sales planning of a successful product (based on a 'restricted' sales history) completely ignored the size of the market?

Average values

Improving the average sales value can be

1 The simplest route to raising sales and reducing costs.
2 A way of controlling your company's manufacturing or supply policy.
3 A route to making the finance function work for you.

A 'typical' sales plan

Most companies make up the total sales plan to reflect supply and not the demand that you recognise at the sharp end. The statement below reflects a typical approach to providing the sales manager with a breakdown of the company sales plan:

> Next year's sales will reflect a 10 per cent increase in money terms and a 5 per cent increase in units. The sales plan is broken down as follows:
>
> – at least 600 units of Model A
> – at least 400 units of Model B
> – at least 50 units of Model C

To criticise and constructively change this plan you need to identify the effort needed to sell the different models, which is frequently 'hidden' in the company accounts. The information you need to know and apply to the company plan is the average cost of selling each product.

Let the accountant do the work

The following information should be requested from those who perhaps spend time normally chasing you for data!

(a) Average sales visit cost. If possible, this should include all direct and indirect costs, such as salary, bonus, motoring costs and expenses. An element of company central overheads should be included if they are easily available.
(b) Average discount per product sold. What is the average discount for each product type.
(c) Average promotional cost per product. The best estimate of the promotional and advertising spent for each product type.

To this information you need to provide your best estimate of the average number of calls needed to sell each product.

TABLE 28.1 *How to calculate the cost of sales*

	Selling price (£)	Sales visits × cost	Average discount (£)	Promotional cost (£)	Total sales cost (£)	Costs/selling price (%)
Product A	1,000	3 × £45	20	5	160.00	16
Product B	1,300	4 × £45	45	25	250.00	19
Product C	2,000	2 × £45	nil	50	140.00	7

If the profit varies considerably by product, then you might need to replace selling price with gross profit.

When multiple sales of a product are the norm, then the figures should be expressed for the average number of units that make up the sale.

The sales cost per product

With the information collected above we can now prepare a simple table which will quantify the differences in cost (and effort) in selling different products. See Table 28.1. From this table we can prepare and identify the changes that the sales manager would want to make in the plan, *and quantify the reasons for the changes.*

There are a number of implications that can be drawn from Table 28.1:

1   The total cost of selling Product A seems high in view of the relatively low selling price.
2   The effort of selling Product B is apparently excessive, and still requires a high level of discounting.
3   Product C may be capable of increased unit sales if the resources are available. That no discount has been used to sell this product adds weight to the argument.

Table 28.1 will not give you all the answers to help you create the best product mix for your sales plan, but it will help you quantify the effort needed to sell each product type.

The other product implications

Preparing a table similar to Table 28.1 will also provide you with an action plan which will help you tackle the other product problems. Table 28.2 shows some of the further implications, together with the suggested remedial action.

TABLE 28.2   *How to interpret sales cost – what to do*

	High cost of sales	Low cost of sales
Pricing implications	Is price too low? Is discount effective?	Is price too high? Is discount needed?
Quantity implications	Sell more per customer Sell service and extras Reduce dependency on this product	Are the sales targets too low? Is apparent potential correct?
Promotional implications	Advertising might reduce sales effort 'Three for the price of two' promotions	Will more promotion sell more units?
Other implications	Why so many visits? Better demonstration/quotations etc? Quality of current promotion?	More emphasis of this product? Is this coming from repeat business?
General	Obviously this is a problem area and the solutions will lie in more areas than those under the control of the sales manager	Few problems with this product other than how to maximise the potential of this product. However, if this product is being phased out, in short supply or a low profit generator, then you will need to act.

The cost of sales is normally a very high proportion of a company's total costs. It is rarely analysed in a way which helps the sales manager, but Table 28.2 will help you fill that gap.

from medicine, dentistry, engineering, law, music and so forth? It isn't really. The only difference perhaps is that the other professionals *expect* it to be hard in the early days, whereas many salespeople expect instant riches and a minimum of 'hassle' to go with it.

If selling is to be truly rewarding, it must be taken seriously and treated like any other profession in the early days, ie like an apprenticeship. There must be a plan and there must be consistent practice until the person is note or word-perfect in the techniques. Such a plan is shown in Fig. 28.1.

Many so-called professional salespeople say they are afraid of a good presentation sounding like a parrot script. Rubbish! Does a good actor sound like a parrot with his lines? Of course not! He realises that being word-perfect enables him to concentrate on technique.

Appendix 1
Planning

Sales people and managers often receive their target figures from their boss – or they work them out themselves and agree them with their boss. The moment they have agreed their targets they can start planning to achieve them. For a sales plan see Fig. 28.1.

Some principles for planning are the following:

1 Planning cannot be left to chance. It must be made to happen, and time found for it.
2 Planning must start at the top, but there should be an 'upward push' as well.
3 Planning must be organised. Planning and doing cannot be separated. Decision-making is central to the planning process.
4 Planning must be definite. Break down general plans into a series of definite and interrelated parts.
5 Planning and controlling go hand in hand. Decide how you will control your progress as you make your plans.
6 Plans must be flexible. Planning must include awareness and acceptance of change.

Appendix 2

INTANGIBLE REASONS FOR BUYING

The intangible reasons why a customer places an order can be very powerful. Here are some of the specific aspects under the headings of:

The customer – and his needs.
The salesman – and ways in which he can help.
The supplier – and how he must appear.
The equipment – and particular attributes.

Note these lists exclude tangible influences such as whether the equipment is right for the job! These are more easily identified and more often given consideration.

CUSTOMER
Loyalty, habit, historical relationship.
Prejudice, sentiment.
Apathy, laziness, reluctance to change.
Fear of change.
Pride, ego, flattery, attention to personal needs.
Personal relationship, trust, rapport, attitude.
Surplus money in budget.
Convenience.
Confidence – in equipment and supplier.
Means of gaining esteem with his company.
Pride of possession, prestige value.
Apparent value for money.
Feeling of 'a good deal' – gain.
Ease of justification of purchase.
Personal pressures at time of decision.
Impulse.
Demonstration of decision-making power.
Security, peace of mind.
Satisfaction of emotion.
Company policy.
Politics, national attitudes.
Local loyalty.
Spreading risk.
Speculation, anticipation.
Relative status compared with other customers.
Social implications of purchase.
Recommendation from others.

SALESMAN
Personal presentation and acceptability.
Personality.
Credibility and reliability.
Enthusiasm.
Personal relationship, trust, rapport, attitude.
Empathy.
Identification with customers' needs.
Communications, ease of dealing.
Timing.
'Technical' competence.
Integrity, trust.

SUPPLIER
Image, reputation, prestige, stability.
Politics, national attitudes.
Company policy.
Location.
Identification with customers' needs.
Resources.
Record as an employer, social acceptability.
'Technical' competence.
Back-up facilities.

EQUIPMENT
Product presentation.
Quality, reliability.
Image.
Implications of design.
Identification with suppliers' needs.
Manufacturer's resources.
Technology.
Safety.

Appendix 3

PROSPECTING AND THE PRE-APPROACH

Prospecting may be defined as selecting for a call the company/companies most likely to do business. Prospecting is making a positive decision about *where to go, when to go, how to go*. The route to an order begins with prospecting.

Prospecting is creative and necessary – it needs to be done to provide tomorrow's business. It is also important to offset losses caused by bankruptcy, change of ownership, new buyer, or movement of company.

There are two methods:

Primary method: family, friends, suppliers, acquaintances, existing customers.
Secondary method: endless chain, centre of influence, personal observation, cold canvassing, mailing shot.

Start as near the top of the tree as possible. This increases your chance of (a) getting a decision, (b) raising maximum interest, (c) being told the truth, and (d) being outside the political arena.

SOURCES OF INFORMATION
Town hall, police station, fire station, public library, chamber of commerce. Trade directories/ magazines, Kompass, Yellow Pages, Dunn & Bradstreet, press advertisements, news items. Non-competitive salesmen, social contacts, trade exhibitions, etc. Build up a *prospect file* and keep it topped up. Replace 'customers' with prospects and replace ordinary prospects with better prospects. When you stop prospecting, you are beginning to rely entirely on your present customers for all your business – a dangerous practice, owing to *competitor activity*.

SALES ACTIVITY FLOWCHART
Stage 1   Prospecting, ie where unknown potential is surveyed.
Stage 2   Prime prospect selection, where a need has been established.
Stage 3   'Hot' prospect selection, where there is a need to buy *now*.
Stage 4   Customer acquisition, where a sale is made.

To be successful at prospecting, you need to keep up a flow through all four stages.

PRE-APPROACH
This may be defined as selecting the *right* person/persons to discuss your products with. For the

salesman who is aiming to make every selling hour yield full time value, it is important to test each prospect for his potential as a customer.

Use this three-point test to determine prime prospects:

(a) Does this prospect have the necessary *money*? Although a prospect has a definite need for your service and is authorised to purchase it, you are wasting your time if he cannot afford to pay the price.

(b) Does the prospect have the *authority* to buy? You may successfully 'sell' a prospect who needs your service, but if he lacks the authority to buy, your presentation is wasted.

(c) Does this prospect have a significant *need* for your service?

IDENTIFYING THE 'HOT' PROSPECT

As a corollary to qualifying a prospect as 'prime', remember that a prime prospect becomes a 'hot' prospect, if:

(i)   He has a strong reason to buy *now*, ie an immediate need.

(ii) The time is ripe to follow up, eg a let-down by a competitor.

Appendix 4

A PROFESSIONAL APPROACH TO SELLING

Every professional salesman knows the importance of first impressions. The following gives you a chance to check your standards.

1 Prepare yourself as follows:
  (a) Develop the right kind of personality: confident – courteous – helpful – cheerful. Be a professional in everything you do. Self-expression. People must be able to understand you.
  (b) Be careful of your appearance. What sort of first impression do you make? Does your appearance immediately command interest – respect? Plan your clothes – clean and pressed. Your hygiene – hair – hands – breath.
  (c) Make sure your property is in good shape. The things you own and use are extensions of your own personality – so be careful. Your car – it must be clean (inside and out). Your briefcase – a credit to you and your company. Your literature – in mint condition.

  No real professional would ever overlook these elementary points.
2 Prepare your knowledge of products, service and procedure. Know your service inside out and backwards. Know your literature – read it thoroughly yourself. The prospect does not care how good your products or service are from your point of view – relate them in terms of benefit to him.
3 Do your homework – know the potential of your area. Make your call reports mean something. Don't exaggerate – be punctual.
4 Prepare your plan for selling. Every call you make is different, so plan every one carefully – the prospect – his needs – his desires – his ambitions – all different. Find out all you can about him – be observant. Every small piece of information will help you to make your plan and help you to present the facts more clearly – overcome objections – make more calls – obtain more business.
      Enjoy your work and meet the challenge of selling with enthusiasm and confidence. If you cannot, do something else.
5 Be a professional and command respect by your presence – knowledge – enthusiasm – sincerity – loyalty to your company and your colleagues – integrity in all your dealings.
  Behave like a professional and you will be treated as one.

Appendix 5

BUYING AND THE PURCHASER

Buying may be classified as follows:

Irrational – impulse or spur of the moment buying over which the seller has little influence.

Rational – logical and reasoned purchasing, where the pros and cons are evaluated and the need is satisfied. The seller can help the buyer to reach the right decision.

What do you buy? Whatever the product or service, you buy what you are going to get from it – ie the benefits. Thus as a seller you must sell what the buyer is going to get from your product – the *benefits to him*.

People who buy do so to solve problems and to satisfy needs. A good buyer relies upon reason to reach his decision. He expects a good salesman to help him. His criteria are objective, his objectives are logical and sincere.

The purchaser's problems are the following:

(i)   basic problems,
(ii) product problems,
(iii) price problems,
(iv) source problems, and
(v)   time problems.

Decision-makers are the persons who have the means and the ability to buy. It is up to you to convince them that they have a need.

The decision-making unit (DMU), usually a board or committee, makes decisions to buy. Often the link between you and the DMU is the *influencer*. Although he cannot make decisions, he can influence those that do. The *specifier* is similar to the influencer, but is often an agent for the purchaser, such as an architect or consultant.

All the above need to be motivated into deciding in your favour. It is essential, therefore, to discover what are their 'buying motives' in order to be in a position to emphasise the *right* benefits.

One or more of the following 'Buying Motives' apply to your product/service:

Profit.
Cost-saving.
Increased efficiency.
Time saving.
Simplicity.
Security.
Safety.

There are many personal 'buying motives', which should be taken into account:

Health.	Prestige.
Fear.	Popularity.
Sentiment.	Pleasure.
Tradition.	Greed.
Status.	Affection.
Convenience.	Cupidity.

It is essential to create the *desire to buy*.

Remember, to display true empathy the professional salesman must ask himself the question WIIFH? (What's in it for him? How will he benefit from ownership?).

Appendix 6

VISUAL AIDS IN PRESENTATION

The value of using visual aids in presentations is well illustrated by the following:

	Recall	
	3 hrs later (%)	*3 days later* (%)
Telling	70	10
Showing	72	20
Telling and showing	85	65

This also indicates that visual aids should not be used in isolation, but must be complementary to the spoken word.

There are numerous forms of visual aid that can be employed. Some are more appropriate to certain products than others.

LITERATURE

Brochure. One of the basic forms of visual aid, as most companies produce a brochure of some sort. Usually contains pictures and words, which can be distracting. However, failing all else, use the company brochures, with which it is essential that you are fully conversant, for the prospect may already have read it.

Catalogue. An extended form of brochure that normally lists and illustrates the whole range of company products.

Photographs. Used to illustrate the company premises, your products in use, exhibition stands, etc.

Graphs. Used to show performance, comparisons etc.

Charts. Another way of illustrating the above.

Drawings. Usually technical, and used to indicate, in diagrammatic form, component parts, how a product will operate, flowcharts.

Specification. A technical back-up to the illustrations.

Journals. Articles from trade journals may give a good account of your products and may show them being used by a customer. Can be used as proof.

Letters. Those from satisfied customers may be shown as proof of good service, solving of a problem, etc.

Binder. Useful, with polythene envelopes, to hold all of the above.

PROJECTIONS

35mm slides. Slides can be used to illustrate the product in action, diagrams, graphs etc. This method has good visual impact. They can be shown either on 'viewers', some of which are contained within a briefcase, or to a larger audience, projected on to a screen. Used in conjunction with pre-recorded cassette tapes, a good presentation can be devised.

Overhead slides. Portable overhead projectors are available and are ideal for showing charts, graphs etc., to a number of people at the same time.

Video tapes. A number of video cassette viewers are available, and some of them can fit into a briefcase for neatness. Used with suitable soundtrack, they are good for showing the product in operation and do in fact bring the demonstration into the prospect's office. May also be used to show current or future TV commercials for the products.

Films. Not so practical, as a large projector and screen are required.

THREE-DIMENSIONAL

Samples. Where practical, samples can be the best possible visual aid as to the actual product. When used properly, samples can prompt several buying signals. Specially constructed cases are produced to hold samples in a convenient and practical manner.

Models. When the product is large, models may take the place of samples, particularly if they are working models.

SPONTANEOUS

Pencil and paper. Whatever formal visual aids are used, one should always have a paper and pencil ready. This allows one to personalise the presentation, especially with well rehearsed 'ad libs'.

VALUE OF VISUAL AIDS

(a) They assist in explaining the product and its benefits. 'A picture tells a thousand words.'
(b) They enable you to plan the presentation by using the visuals in a pre-planned sequence.
(c) They help to get the prospect involved in the presentation.
(d) They help to ensure that all the relevant points are covered, by acting as a 'crib'.
(e) Spontaneous visuals will make the presentation more personal.

USING VISUAL AIDS

1 It is essential to keep control of the presentation and the visual aids. Do *not* allow the prospect to handle the visuals until you are ready.
2 Use visuals in sequence. Do not jump about from one to another and perhaps confuse the prospect.

3   Only use those visuals that are relevant to the presentation.
4   Articles from journals and customers' letters should only be used to prove a point, not to introduce one.
5   Remember you are selling *benefits* not products.

Appendix 7

THE PLANNED VISUAL PRESENTATION

Many salesmen believe that they can present their ideas and products to a prospect 'off the cuff', that is, with the minimum of planning or thought. In practice, so few men are so gifted that the concept is unacceptable. No military battle was ever won by sending out soldiers and hoping for the best; no politician was ever elected by making 'impromptu' speeches that were, in fact, impromptu; no business meeting ever reached a satisfactory conclusion without its content and strategy being carefully thought out by the participants; no football team ever won a match without planning the strategy for the game.

One of the major objections to a planned presentation is that it will sound unreal or 'canned' to the prospect. The answer to that is, of course, that it is up to the salesman to develop his presentation to reach the perfection an actor seeks when he performs a part. The great actor does not sound 'canned' when he plays Othello, because he has rehearsed the part over and over again.

In practice, it would be impossible to sell any product and not to develop some form of a planned presentation. After all, if you are selling the same type of product time and time again, you will certainly start to repeat some words or expressions. Don't let your presentation 'happen' like that. Make sure that every word or expression you use is helping to complete the sale. By planning your presentation and learning it word for word you can ensure that you don't confuse the prospect, or that irrelevancies won't encourage his indecision.

The main advantages of the planned presentation are as follows:

(a)   You will be able to concentrate on the delivery of the presentation. This will enable you to respond to the prospect more easily.
(b)   You will never have to search for words with which to persuade your prospect: these will come naturally in the most logical (and therefore successful) order.
(c)   When the prospect diverts the conversation (or there is an interruption), you will know precisely where you must restart your sales talk.
(d)   You will not easily be put off your style.
(e)   You will be able to build into your presentation the answers to the common objections. This prevents the prospect from bringing them up at a stage in the presentation that would damage your chances of securing the sale.
(f)   It prevents unnecessary talking on the part of the salesman. Most salesmen talk too much and take much too long to present their ideas and products.

Wherever possible, visualise your sales presentation so as to improve understanding and retention.

Some salesmen would say that when addressing a client personally they are employing the major perceptive senses of sight and sound – but are they? Although the sales interview is conducted within sight and sound of the prospect, very few salesmen employ any positive visual selling techniques. Instead, they rely on their voice to do the sales job and leave the prospect's visual receptiveness to concentrate on their appearance.

If one were selling tractors, the most efficient way to demonstrate would be to show them at work. Life insurance is not so tangible, but even so it can still be visualised to improve understanding and retention.

What is the object of using visuals in the sales process? Firstly, the salesman must strive to break down the complexities of his product into something his prospect can easily understand. If the manner in which your product works can, for example, be illustrated in a simple diagram, the prospect will more readily follow the salesman's train of thought. If he does that, he is more likely to buy.

Secondly, if the prospect can see the salesman's points simply illustrated on a sheet of paper, it will help him clarify his thinking. If, on the other hand, the prospect is asked to memorise the salient facts, he may not be prepared to make a decision there and then. The chances of closing a sale diminish, as every salesman knows, with the second and subsequent interview.

The professional salesman must constantly look for ways of illustrating his product. If he does this, it will improve his understanding of the product, make his presentation more acceptable to the prospect and increase his production.

There are two types of visual; one is permanent, the other is one prepared in front of the prospect.

PERMANENT VISUALS

Make full use of the sales literature provided by your company. Many companies are producing material that is extremely effective. Graphs or charts help explain visually the growth or sales of a product over a number of years. If you want to demonstrate an interesting build-up of a particular product, use a simple table which the prospect can easily understand.

Use an illustration form when selling a product. Don't expect the prospect to memorise all the facts and figures. Show him how his business can be improved and you will have an easier sale.

SPONTANEOUS VISUALS

Always carry a notebook with you. Use it (or the back of the illustration) to draw diagrams as you progress through the presentation. It has been said that a picture is worth a thousand words. It is also said that the prospect will understand more of what he both sees and hears than what he just hears.

When you have learned one presentation, start to develop others. Within a few months you will be able to use planned presentations to cover most of the situations that you will meet.

A planned presentation always produces better results. If you are currently successful but not using a plan, you will certainly improve your performance by adopting one.

Appendix 8

WHY IS A GOOD PRESENTATION IMPORTANT?

A presentation that is badly thought out and prepared, loosely worded, poorly delivered, and inadequately backed up will very soon lose the goodwill of the prospect. If the salesman loses his prospect's goodwill, how can he hope to win interest and desire for the product?

WHAT ARE THE MARKS OF A GOOD PRESENTATION?
An effective presentation is one which:
(a) *Interests* the buyer in your product.
(b) *Convinces* him that he needs your product.
(c) *Stimulates* his desire to possess your product.
(d) *Assures* him that your product is the one which will best satisfy his need.
(e) *Persuades* him to buy your product.

YOUR PRESENTATION SHOULD BE PLANNED
At all times your presentation must be a *pattern* of selling – never a patter! In planning your presentation ask yourself if it is:

(i)   consecutive,
(ii)   concise,
(iii) comprehensive,
(iv)   conclusive, and
(v)   clear.

WHY MUST A PRESENTATION BE PLANNED?
A planned presentation enables the salesman to:

(a) follow a logical sequence,
(b) cover *all* important sales points,
(c) avoid ambiguity,
(d) eliminate needless repetition,
(e) save time,
(f) give the impression of confident efficiency,
(g) control the interview,

(h) use sales aids to best advantage, and
(i) assess the moment to close.

Appendix 9

THE SALES SEQUENCE

Four tasks must be accomplished in sequence:

1 Gain *attention* with benefits.
2 Hold *interest* with good two-way communication.
3 Create *desire* by turning wants into needs.
4 Produce a specific response, ie *action*.

GAINING AND MAINTAINING ATTENTION
It is one thing to gain a person's attention. It is another to hold it. We must use devices to do this: colourful words, illustrations, names that ring bells, benefits.

HOLDING INTEREST
Who is the MAN? He is the person with the Money, the Authority and the Need. What does the MAN want? What interest excites and rewards him? We must discover, if we are to sell to him. Beware of projecting your own desires and preoccupations on to him. Empathy will help you avoid this trap.

CREATING DESIRE
The salesman must connect wants/needs. The MAN wants to know about the end result. 'Suppose I did buy your product?' must have an answer in concrete terms with vivid example. The MAN must be a central figure in this visualisation.

GETTING ACTION
Ideally the sale should be closed in such a way that the MAN believes he has made the decision entirely unaided. Looking beyond the decision to buy often achieves this. The MAN should feel he has bought, not that he has been sold to.

Appendix 10

AIDA – THE FORMAT FOR AN APPROACH CALL

In successful selling, planning and preparation are essential. To be a success the approach call must be carefully planned and then carried out in a controlled professional manner.
   Every approach call is different. It depends on the product, the benefits of that product and the prospect. Every prospect is different, so your approach must vary. Use the format in Fig. 28.2 to control the course of the Approach Call.

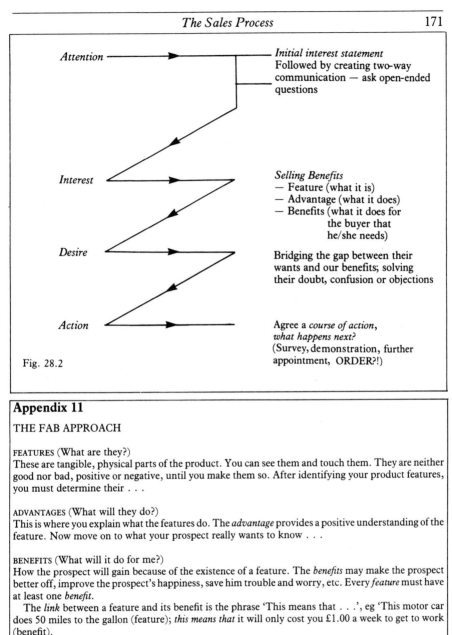

Fig. 28.2

Appendix 11

THE FAB APPROACH

FEATURES (What are they?)
These are tangible, physical parts of the product. You can see them and touch them. They are neither good nor bad, positive or negative, until you make them so. After identifying your product features, you must determine their . . .

ADVANTAGES (What will they do?)
This is where you explain what the features do. The *advantage* provides a positive understanding of the feature. Now move on to what your prospect really wants to know . . .

BENEFITS (What will it do for me?)
How the prospect will gain because of the existence of a feature. The *benefits* may make the prospect better off, improve the prospect's happiness, save him trouble and worry, etc. Every *feature* must have at least one *benefit*.

The *link* between a feature and its benefit is the phrase 'This means that . . .', eg 'This motor car does 50 miles to the gallon (feature); *this means that* it will only cost you £1.00 a week to get to work (benefit).

There must be a close match between the prospect's needs and the product benefits. Product benefits do not come singly. One leads to another.

Always sell the benefits of your product, and always explain them clearly and simply. Never *assume* that the prospect knows the benefit of a particular feature.

BENEFIT TEST
If the prospect can *logically* say 'So what?' after any given benefit statement, then you have *not* shown him the benefit.

BENEFIT PROOF
Basic rules:

1 Demonstrate the benefit.
2 Restate the benefit.
3 Expand the benefit.

Features have *advantages* giving *benefits*. Remember, sell the benefits that completely satisfy the prospect's needs.

Appendix 12

PLANNING AND MAKING AN APPROACH CALL

This is an exercise designed to give you practice in planning to control an approach call. Use the AIDA format already given you in Appendix 10.

The emphasis throughout the approach call is on two-way communication, open-ended questions – the answers to which will provide you with the information you need to build your sales case. Information that you can use to successfully control the approach call.

It is in the approach call that the very foundations of selling professionally come together. Remember you sell benefits, not products. You must answer the key question in selling – 'What's in it for him?'

1 Take the company you now work for and the products you now sell. Now, think of an actual 'prospect' company that you will be calling on in an attempt to make a sale. For the purpose of this exercise choose one that has *not* bought from your company before – one who is buying from a competitor perhaps.

Provide these details about such a company:

(a) What is the type of business? _____

(b) Why is it a good prospect? _____
_____

(c) What is the title of the man you want to see? _____

(d) For what purpose will they buy from you? _____

Now list below the *particular benefits* which your product has for this type of customer.

_____
_____
_____
_____

This will complete the basic 'pre-approach' stage. Now to work out your 'approach'.

Remember, the key question to be answered in making any sale is 'What's in it for him?' Bearing this in mind throughout, start to build up the plan for your approach call.

Begin by getting your whole 'approach' into perspective. You must build your case carefully and logically. Develop a pattern of discussion that draws the prospect to the 'action' position you want.

Before you can build up a case, you must have a good idea where you are going! Start by deciding what you want your prospect to do – or agree to – at the action stage. It could be to place an order, to agree to move on to a survey, to come to a demonstration at a customer's premises, or something else again.

2 Write down the *action* you could reasonably expect from your prospect at the end of your approach.

_____
_____
_____
_____
_____

The other vital point to aim for is agreement with your prospect over the *objectives* he would see as significant to him.

Remember, these are objectives he would be interested in achieving. Things like saving 10 per cent of the cost of a certain kind of process, or buying components with a shorter delivery time and guaranteed delivery date. You must clearly agree these objectives at the approach stage. They form the framework to which you attach the case you have made. Without this, you have no real power when it comes to closing the sale.

3   Write out the kind of objectives you want to lead the prospect to agreeing with you – the objectives on which you can make the sale.

_____

_____

_____

_____

Having clarified where you are going, you can now lay out the tactics you must use to get there.

All you have to sell are 'benefits'. You cannot afford to just fire them off as they occur to you. Firstly, you must put the prospect in a frame of mind to know that he wants the 'benefits' – then show him how you can give them to him.

You achieve this pattern by asking questions. Questions designed to tell you more about your prospect and questions designed to make him *think* about the 'benefits' you are offering him. These questions – and benefits – must be divided between the different stages of the 'approach':

Attention – Qualification
Interest   – Commitment
Desire   – Objectives
Action

4   *Attention.* Don't assume you will be given it. You have to make the prospect sit up and listen.

To do this you have to 'sell the interview' – and yourself – by choosing the most significant point which will make him think. You must put that point to him in a way that shows you think about *his* problems and understand them well.

Write out – word for word – the opening three or four sentences you would use to get his attention.

_____

_____

_____

_____

You now have the prospect's attention.

5   Bearing in mind your plan, and the benefits which you believe will be attractive to your prospect, what questions would you want to ask:

(a)   To move from attention to interest:

_____

_____

_____

(b)   To qualify the prospect – to check that he is a real MAN:

_____

_____

Note: Often the same question serves to both qualify the prospect and also to move him from attention to interest.

Lastly the *desire* to achieve something is a different frame of mind from being *interested* in what you have been saying.

6   What questions can you use to move your prospect to really understanding what it could mean for him if he goes ahead with what you suggest.

_____

_____

_____

_____

Those questions will tie in precisely with the objectives you want to agree with your prospect. In other words, you will have achieved both your aims:

(a) A firm basis on which to make the sale.
(b) The generation of the enthusiasm which will make your prospect go ahead with you to the *action* stage.

Appendix 13

THE SALES SURVEY

WHY A SALES SURVEY?
Sales surveys are expensive both in time and money. Before committing oneself to carrying out a survey, ask if it is really necessary. Is it essential, or could the order be obtained without it?

WHAT IS A SALES SURVEY?
A sales survey is a method of obtaining a quantity of information about a prospect, the company and the problems. This normally involves face-to-face interviews with several of the prospect's employees. Careful observation will also provide valuable information at this stage.

REASONS FOR A SALES SURVEY
1 To investigate the prospect's ability to purchase.
2 To identify the prospect's market for the product.
3 To provide sufficient, relevant information for a proposal.
4 To ascertain the 'feel' within the prospect company for your product.

CONDUCTING THE SURVEY
1 *Get top management association.* Helps to iron out the politics. As a number of personnel will be involved, it is essential to obtain the co-operation and permission of top management.
2 *Get all the relevant facts.* To make the survey as effective as possible, pre-plan the information to be gathered. Prepare the questions – in many cases a number of the questions will be similar from prospect to prospect. Pre-printed survey questionnaires can be very useful, as they will act as an aide-memoire to the questions to be asked. Make sure you see where your product fits 'into the line'.
3 *Is it practical and profitable?* Does he really need it and can he afford to buy it?
4 *Sell down the line.* See all those involved in the purchase and use of product, from the MAN to and including Fred (the operator).
5 *Take complete notes.* Either on a pre-printed form or on plain paper. However good your memory may be, you will not remember every detail of the survey. Don't be afraid to ask questions and record the answers.
6 *Control the survey.* You are a professional man selling time; this is *your* interview. Do not rush the survey and omit important facts, but do not take more time than necessary.
7 *Avoid the 'desk' survey.* Will it go through the door?
8 *What motivates the decision-maker.* Profit, greater efficiency, pride of ownership, keeping up with the Jones's.
9 *On completion.* Return to the MAN. Tell him what you are going to do, how long it will take, when you will return and, if possible, make an appointment there and then for your next visit.

Appendix 14

PROPOSALS

Most sales people hate preparing proposals and are unhappy about preparing a document which will have to work 'behind closed doors'. To compound this problem, marketing departments prefer not to be involved in 'one off' activities and therefore rarely contribute.

This doom and gloom is exacerbated because we know that the need to produce a proposal can often be highly suspect:

'Would you send me a proposal?' = Go away!

Our recent research on the effectiveness of a wide range of proposals identified the following reasons for failure:

1   Most proposals confirm nothing, stimulate confusion, inspire enquiries and therefore ensure delay.
2   Delay = failure. Your proposal may be the 'flavour of the month' now but beware of:
    (a)   Other schemes already in the pipeline.
    (b)   Management changes or reorganisations.
    (c)   Lost momentum and support.
    (d)   Sudden expenditure restrictions.
    'We've put it on a "back burner" for a while', ie it got cremated!
3   The quotation is really a proposal prepared when you don't have time to prepare a proposal.
4   No promotional content. Nearly all the proposals examined in our research contained nothing which could be confused with effective promotional activity.

However, we have to overcome these problems because the need to justify corporate decisions will increase. When we are sure that a proposal is needed; then it has to be a good one!

1   DO YOU REALLY NEED TO PREPARE A PROPOSAL?
    There are a number of important questions you need to answer satisfactorily before you commit the necessary effort to producing a professional proposal:

    (a)   Is preparing a proposal the 'soft option'? In some cases a proposal may have been prepared when a close could have been made.
    (b)   Do you suffer from misplaced professionalism? Junior sales people often tend to assume that always preparing a proposal is 'professional'. Older hands may have recognised the difference between being busy and being effective!
    (c)   Is the sale already lost? In crude terms the request for a proposal might be a prospect without the 'bottle' to say 'No' face to face.
    (d)   Is the contact too low? A proposal may have been requested because your contact is too lowly placed either to authorise or effectively 'sponsor' your product/service. In practice the proposal may still be the only way you get to the decision-maker, but this should be recognised and will affect both the content and the method of delivery.

2   A CHECKLIST BEFORE YOU START WRITING
    The meeting at which a proposal is requested must be used for you to decide the objectives, format and delivery method that will produce a result. The checklist in Table 28.A1 should form the core of the information you require and will tie in with the techniques described later.

TABLE 28.3   *Proposal request – suggested checklist*

Question/item	*Notes/implications*
Who is the proposal going to?	Why aren't they your contact?
What level are they in the company?	Have they the authority?
Will it be judged against competitors' proposals?	Stress/explain unique product strengths
Will your proposal be directly compared with those for other demands on the company purse?	Stress cost justification/savings
What is the normal approval procedure?	Good information and background
Is a formal meeting called to review the proposal(s)?	Can you actually present to that meeting?
What is the frequency of such meetings?	
Can your review meeting be booked now?	
What level of product/service knowledge will recipients have?	
How many copies are required?	Forget this and your proposal could be
When exactly is your proposal required?	photocopied on a 1932 Copier!

Note: If this all seems like an 'overkill', then just think how much time, work and risk is involved in proposal preparation.

3 WHAT IS THE REAL COMPETITION FOR YOUR PROPOSAL?

A common misconception is that the main objective of a proposal is to ensure that you get the business against the competition. This is obviously an important object but is frequently only 'Round One' in the fight to get your proposal approved.

ROUND ONE
Your proposal v Your competitors' proposals

ROUND TWO
Your proposal v Chairman's new car
v Two new lorries
v Staff Xmas party
v Paying the VAT bill

If your 'sponsor' in the company has been handled well, then 'Round One' may have been won before a proposal is even requested!

4 THE IMPLICATIONS OF KNOWING THE REAL COMPETITION

(a) Promote all the benefits even though some may also apply to your competitor's product/service.

(b) Keep it simple and include the obvious. The simple/obvious benefits should be prominently included for those without a detailed knowledge of the product.

(c) Satisfying the influencers. When the approval of a board of directors or finance committee is needed, then all the disciplines at that meeting should be satisfied or neutralised.

(d) Beware of the drones. The pen pushers will be looking for every spelling mistake, problem and ambiguity. This is the only task some administrators have to perform!

5 DEVELOPING THE REAL OBJECTIVES

The objectives below, recognised in the original research, should be used in the development of your 'standard' proposal structure.

(a) The proposal should be a promotional document. You need to ensure that the proposal is a 'free standing' selling tool for all the different levels of management involved in securing authorisation.

(i) The initial impression should be of an attractive document which will encourage the reader and ensure that your proposal is read in preference to others.

(ii) Simple yet effective reasons to purchase, capable of convincing even an accountant or purchasing director!

(iii) An impression of a professional document which itself would be 'worth the money'.

(b) Prevent delay. There are a number of objectives dedicated to preventing delay and the resultant risk of failure:

(i) The title page must employ techniques to catch the attention, supported by a document capable of being 'flash' read.

(ii) You have to ensure that even the most unenthusiastic reader will read your proposal. Keep it short and don't make it a chore to read.

(iii) You must answer queries, not start them, by completing each authoriser's job for him/her.

(iv) Use checklists and summaries, particularly when you have been requested to meet or exceed technical specifications.

(c) Make sure that the proposal has a close. The ordering procedure should be a part of the proposal. Requesting a letter of intent is a useful device. The proposal is your 'best shot'. If you leave the ordering until later then you reintroduce the opportunity for delay and failure.

6 SUGGESTED PROPOSAL FORMAT

The ideal proposal should be less than nine pages long. Pages 1 to 3 comprise the main 'promotional' pages, intended to summarise the proposal and to convince those authorisers who have no detailed knowledge of your product/service. Pages 4 to 9 expand and develop the benefits applicable to the particular functions of the major decision makers, eg technical director, finance director, purchasing manager.

Page 1 – Title page. This should prove that the proposal has been specially prepared and must summarise the main benefits in up to six simple statements.

Pages 2 and 3 – Benefit statements. The best reasons for the prospect buying, which reflect the customer requirements (and not what you want to say about your product/service). The benefits previously outlined on Page 1 should be repeated and amplified.

Pages 4 to 9 – 'Targeted' pages. A page for each of the managers/executives concerned with the purchase decision.

The page format we recommend is shown below.

> The benefits applicable to this authoriser (restated and expanded from pages 2–3 if necessary).
> --------------------------------
> The financial justification, simple cost and operating savings which would concern this authoriser.
> --------------------------------
> A question and answer section to cover his/her potential objections and queries.
> --------------------------------
> An endorsement from a similar application with perhaps an additional incentive to purchase.

This format will be adequate for most authorisers, but special attention should be paid to the finance people, who have been proved to be the most effective 'blockers'.

7 DELIVERING THE PROPOSAL
Wherever possible, deliver the proposal personally to assess the immediate impact and catch any problems or misconceptions 'at birth'.

8 EIGHT WHEEZES TO ENSURE YOUR PROPOSAL WINS
There are a number of proven techniques which will improve the effectiveness of your proposal.

(a) Always take credit for exceeding requirements and specifications and explain what this means in terms of reduced costs, longevity, etc.
(b) A relevant endorsement or case study is often more effective than special demonstrations or bench testing, etc.
(c) Do not hide the price, but keep it simple. Hidden extras and unspecified delivery/installation costs have been identified as a major cause of delay.
(d) Do not include unnecessary or 'offensive' payment terms, eg. 'subject to necessary credit checks', 'strictly 30 days net', etc.
(e) Include 'typical' cost justification or pay back figures when specifics are not available. They will normally be taken at face value.
(f) Offer supporting information if required rather than including possibly unnecessary information in your proposal.

(g) Try the 'induced panic principle' – tell them what one of their competitors is already doing with your product/service.
(h) Always include a number of payment options on the finance page. The management of even a large company could use a deferred payments or leasing option as a way of circumnavigating expenditure restrictions.

9 SUMMARY
If this summary had been at the beginning you would not have needed to read the previous eight pages!

(a) Before you write a proposal, is it really necessary? Or is it a sign that you have the wrong level of contact?
(b) Use the meeting at which the proposal is requested to identify what the proposal will need to do.
(c) The real competition is probably the other demands on a company's resources, not the competition!
(d) Promote the benefits, not the facilities, and really spell out the advantages for the non-technical authorisers.
(e) Keep it down to a maximum of nine pages or it won't be read; keep it 'attractive' or it still won't be read!
(f) The introduction should promote your product/service. 'Targeted' pages should satisfy the particular requirements of each type of authoriser.
(g) Deliver the proposal by hand, and if possible arrange a presentation of the proposal to the review meeting.
(h) Make sure you use the eight wheezes in the preceding section.

Appendix 15

SELLING TO COMMITTEES (DMUs)

1 Carry out a good reinvestigation:
   (a) Date of meeting.
   (b) Venue.
   (c) Names and position of members.
   (d) Decision-makers.
2 Pre-sell your contact.
3 Brief your contact – you may need his help.
4 Decide on objectives and treat as normal sale.
5 Get to the meeting place early.
6 Introduce yourself to the members as they go in.
7 Make seating plan and use names.
8 Prepare notes – remember that this is rather like public speaking.
9 Prepare and use handouts, and have sufficient – those who don't know, vote 'no'.
10 Use visuals.
11 Get everyone participating – use questions, positive suggestions, etc.
12 Avoid detailed discussion with single members.
13 Where there is no unanimous agreement, divide and obtain agreement section by section.
14 Remember, your manner, appearance, and method of speaking will have a tremendous effect on the group. There is no substitute for product knowledge. Telling isn't selling.

Appendix 16

SELLING THROUGH THIRD PARTIES

1 Don't accept this situation too readily.
2 Offer to accompany your contact to the meeting.
3 Ask questions in order to establish:

(a) Date of meeting.
(b) Personnel attending.
(c) Are they technical?
(d) Is it formal?

4 Offer to help with any report writing or specifications.
5 Brief your contact thoroughly with:

(a) Your objectives.
(b) Suitably marked literature.
(c) Visuals.

6 Get in touch with your contact just before the meeting to check final details.
7 Make sure your contact and the committee know where to find you during the meeting. Try to be available for consultation.
8 Remember, you are hoping to sell though absent; somebody has to do the job for you, so make sure your contact is himself 'sold'. If necessary, make yourself into a sales trainer.

Appendix 17

DEMONSTRATING THE PRODUCT

1 What are the objectives? Consider what are you setting out to prove.
2 Administration. This covers setting up the demonstration and ensuring that all goes well.
3 Check up! Don't rely on the original arrangements. Make sure by checking before the day.
4 Talk to others involved. This is particularly true of 'Fred'.
5 Check handouts and literature. Ask prospect *before* the demonstration.
6 Ideally, take the MAN and 'Fred' to the demonstration.
7 Tell – show – tell.
8 Show respect for the product. Don't knock it, either literally or metaphorically.
9 Encourage participation and ask questions. One question should be: 'Are you satisfied with what you have seen or is there anything else I can show you?'
10 Third-party reference. Should be to a firm in the same industry and of the same size. Customer must be able to identify with existing user.
11 Say thank you, especially to 'Fred'.
12 Take MAN (and 'Fred') back.
13 If a successful demonstration, *ask for the order*.

Appendix 18

OBJECTIONS AND HOW TO HANDLE THEM

How can objections, raised by prospective customers, be recognised and dealt with successfully.

(a) Accept them as a natural, inevitable interruption in the selling process.
(b) Regard them as an indication of interest.
(c) Welcome them as a means of discovering the prospect's attitude, needs and understanding of your presentation.

CAN OBJECTIONS BE USEFULLY CLASSIFIED?
(a) The real worries are *valid* objections, such as justifying cost or need, fear of making wrong choice, search for reassurance.
(b) *Invalid* objections include trifling excuses, blind prejudice, not wanting to surrender without a fight.
(c) *Hidden* objections need to be brought to light by careful questioning.

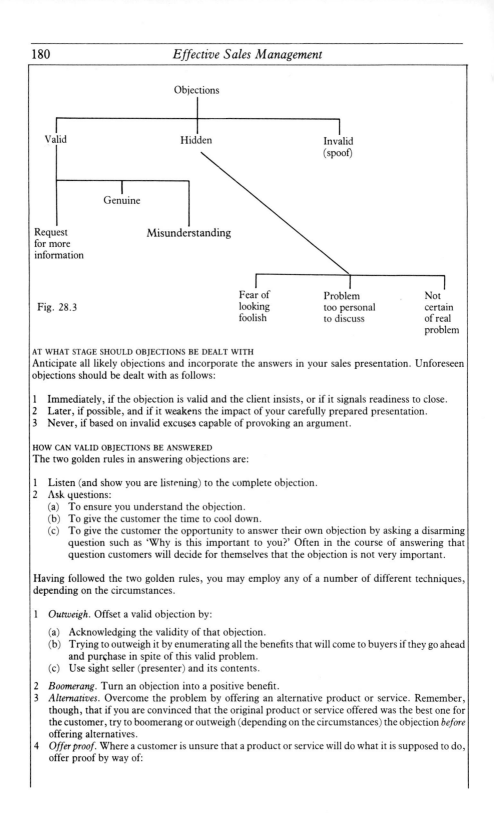

Fig. 28.3

AT WHAT STAGE SHOULD OBJECTIONS BE DEALT WITH
Anticipate all likely objections and incorporate the answers in your sales presentation. Unforeseen objections should be dealt with as follows:

1 Immediately, if the objection is valid and the client insists, or if it signals readiness to close.
2 Later, if possible, and if it weakens the impact of your carefully prepared presentation.
3 Never, if based on invalid excuses capable of provoking an argument.

HOW CAN VALID OBJECTIONS BE ANSWERED
The two golden rules in answering objections are:

1 Listen (and show you are listening) to the complete objection.
2 Ask questions:
   (a) To ensure you understand the objection.
   (b) To give the customer the time to cool down.
   (c) To give the customer the opportunity to answer their own objection by asking a disarming question such as 'Why is this important to you?' Often in the course of answering that question customers will decide for themselves that the objection is not very important.

Having followed the two golden rules, you may employ any of a number of different techniques, depending on the circumstances.

1 *Outweigh*. Offset a valid objection by:
   (a) Acknowledging the validity of that objection.
   (b) Trying to outweigh it by enumerating all the benefits that will come to buyers if they go ahead and purchase in spite of this valid problem.
   (c) Use sight seller (presenter) and its contents.

2 *Boomerang*. Turn an objection into a positive benefit.
3 *Alternatives*. Overcome the problem by offering an alternative product or service. Remember, though, that if you are convinced that the original product or service offered was the best one for the customer, try to boomerang or outweigh (depending on the circumstances) the objection *before* offering alternatives.
4 *Offer proof*. Where a customer is unsure that a product or service will do what it is supposed to do, offer proof by way of:

(a) A third-party referral.
(b) Newspaper/magazine articles.
(c) Examples.
(d) Demonstrations.

5 *Isolation*. Sometimes a customer continues to offer objection after objection, all of them of a relatively minor nature. Providing you are convinced that the product or service is right for them, and providing you do have a good answer for their latest objection, ask the following question: 'That's a valid point; providing I am able to solve that one for you, would you want to go ahead and purchase this item (service)'. If they say 'No', you haven't really found the real objection yet, so you can go ahead and probe for it. If they say 'Yes', answer the objection and ask a closing question.

REMEMBER
(a) Listen attentively.
(b) Ask questions to avoid misunderstanding.
(c) Answer questions to avoid misunderstanding.
(d) Answer convincingly.
(e) Never argue.
(f) Having dealt with an objection, always ask a closing question.

See also Appendix 19 – 'The Price Factor'.

Appendix 19

THE PRICE FACTOR

How important is the price objection – and how does the skilful salesman overcome it?

WHEN SHOULD THE PRICE BE REVEALED?
Understandably, every salesman fears the prospect who wants to have the answer to 'how much?' too soon. He realises the danger that a premature direct answer may disrupt the selling pattern or even kill it at the outset. He must consider ways of deferring the answer, without causing irritation, giving the impression of evading the issue, or of seeming to be nervously price-conscious.

HOW SHOULD THE PRICE BE REVEALED?
Just as the successful salesman does not try to sell his actual product but the benefits to be obtained from it, so he avoids selling on price but sells *value*. 'Price' then falls into its proper perspective.

Remember that price can be made to appear unimportant if the amount of money to be saved or made by using the product is fully stressed, eg in terms of increased productivity, saving in time, space, etc. But when you do mention the price, state it *confidently*, and remember that a very 'ordinary' price can sometimes be given a 'special appeal'.

WHY DO CUSTOMERS OFTEN OBJECT TO PRICES?
The salesman learns to regard the prospect's desire to 'haggle' over the price as a perfectly *natural* reaction – not a sinister spectre of sales resistance. Therefore, the price objection is a matter to be met with calm confidence and overcome by skilful conviction.

When a customer says 'It costs too much' he may mean that:

(i)   He has not got the money.
(ii)   He has not budgeted to pay as much.
(iii) He assumed it would cost less.
(iv)   He has in mind the lesser price of your competitor.
(v)   He is trying to bargain.
(vi)   He is using price as an excuse for some other reason.
(vii) You have not succeeded in convincing him.

In what different ways must these price objections be countered? Consider John Ruskin's views on price and quality:

There is hardly anything in the world that some man cannot make a little worse and sell a little cheaper and the people who consider price only are this man's lawful prey.

VALUE

It's unwise to pay too much, but it's unwise to pay to little. When you pay too much you lose a little money, that is all.

When you pay too little, you sometimes lose everything, because the thing you bought was incapable of doing the thing you bought it to do.

The common law of business balance prohibits paying a little and getting a lot. It can't be done. If you deal with the lowest bidder, it's well to add something for the risk you run.

And if you do that, you will have enough to pay for something better.

Appendix 20

THE SERVICE CALL

The service call is the call that you make on the prospect after you have converted him into a customer. To some salesmen this call is known as a 'courtesy' call, which is dangerous thinking indeed, as this implies that all you have to do is to wish your customer well, ask the inevitable question, 'Is there anything you want?', and, having received the inevitable answer, 'No, thank you', leave another card, another brochure and depart in a puff of goodwill.

Every call you ever make on either a prospect or a customer is made for one reason only – to get business for your company. In this respect the service call is no different.

Before making the call, ask yourself these questions:

1 Am I getting the maximum amount of business that I can from this customer?
2 Are my competitors doing business with this customer, and, if so, why?
3 Am I sure I am seeing the right man? Are there others I could be discussing business with to good advantage?
4 Have I asked about this customer's future plans, short, medium or long term (this is the one sure way to have your product specified).
5 Am I confident that, despite attack from my competitors, this customer will remain loyal to me?
6 Am I sure that this customer warrants the amount of attention and regular calling which I am giving him?
7 Have I really looked at the true potential on this account?

Remember, there are only a limited number of ways to increase your share of the market:

1 To develop (prospecting) brand new business.
2 To increase business with existing customers.

With (1) you will set out to obtain as much of your competitors' business as you can; with (2) your competitors will set out to obtain as much of your customer's business as they can. The best way to ensure that this does not happen *is to give your customer the good service to which he is entitled.*

YOU WON'T WIN EVERY TIME

Failure to obtain the decision you want, or failure to convince or persuade, must sharpen the edge of your determination. Just as it is important to analyse your reasons for success so you must examine critically your failures. What was the reason for failure? Can you learn something from this situation which will help you in the future.

Consider whether failure was due to the service, for the following reasons:

1 It was not suitable for his requirements.
2 Our prices really not competitive.
3 Time required to submit quotation too long.
4 Not the right type of specification.
5 Genuinely satisfied with existing service from our competitors.
6 The general state of the industry/market.

Perhaps failure was due to the prospect himself. Maybe he was:

1   Genuinely wanting to consider further.
2   Prejudiced, unreasonable.
3   Not in the right frame of mind to consider our proposals.
4   Lacking authority, afraid to commit himself, had insufficient money.
5   Never really in our market.

Perhaps the failure was the salesman's:

1   Did I fail to 'sell myself' in the first instance?
2   Lack of enthusiasm on my part.
3   Insufficient knowledge – unable to overcome the prospect's objections satisfactorily.
4   Failure to sell convincingly the benefits of our services and contracts.
5   Failure to capture his interest and maintain it. Poor two-way communication.
6   Poor finishing or 'closing'. Need for more determination to obtain his business.
7   Any special consideration you failed to realise at the time.

Whatever the reason, you must be resilient and determined to succeed next time. You must try again.

Appendix 21

CLOSING THE SALE

WHY ARE SALESMEN RELUCTANT TO ASK FOR THE ORDER?
Probably because the salesman is afraid that the prospect/customer will say 'No'. This would affect the salesman's ego, self-confidence and respect. In other words, it is the fear of rejection.
   The salesman should be trying to close right from the beginning of the interview or presentation.

WHAT IS CLOSING?
It is the logical and natural conclusion to a sales presentation. Closing is a means of obtaining a decision favourable to your company (this could, if the situation is appropriate, be no more than making an appointment for the follow-up call).
   It is a fact that most people are bad decision-makers and most people dislike spending money. Therefore, although your purchaser is in a decision-making situation, he probably dislikes making decisions and is careful about spending money. A skilled salesman can remove the uncertainty created by this situation. He can help the purchaser to make a decision.

WHEN TO CLOSE
Many sales presentations are faultless yet fail to secure orders. The salesman did not ask for the order. He never closed the sale.

1   Close the sale at the earliest possible moment.
2   Close when the buyer shows you he is ready to place the order.
3   Close when nothing else remains to be done.
4   Be ready to close from the first moment of the meeting.
5   Try to close all the time.

Always listen for closing signals.

HOW TO CLOSE
You are looking for a favourable decision: so make the decision easy, make it inevitable. Your manner should be confident, your words chosen with care. Once you have asked for the order, stop talking. The rest is up to him!

WAYS OF CLOSING
1   *Asking* (no recorded deaths of anyone who has done this!) Do not use this method on a poor decision-maker. He will roll into a ball.

(a) If 'Yes', thank him, take order, shut up and get out.

(b) If 'No', 'Not now', 'Not ever', ask the buyer why. The least he owes you is an explanation, and that helps to overcome the objection.

(c) Statistics prove that the average order is obtained after the third close.

2 *Indirect close.* For example 'Where would you like us to deliver the. . . ?' or 'Where shall we send the invoice?'

3 *Alternative choice.* For example, 'Standard model or the special?' or 'AC or DC?'

4 *Sale or return.* Let him try it, let him get his hands on it, let him see the advantages of ownership.

5 *The advantage list.* Compile a list of advantages on one side and disadvantages on another. Help him with the advantages. Do not help him with the disadvantages.

6 *Third party.* Tell him a story about a satisfied customer. 'Funny we should not be able to agree on this. Recently a similar situation happened to XYZ Company.' The example must be a company of similar size and category, which helps the prospect identify with the example.

7 *Fear close.* This is known in the insurance business as 'back up the hearse and let him smell the flowers'. All very well in insurance (and it works) but not for engineering. In desperation one can say 'If you do not buy now, the price will go up' or 'If you do not buy now, the model will change'.

8 *'Where did I go wrong?'* With a forlorn expression you pick up the briefcase and head for the door and then, hand on the handle, you turn towards the customer almost with tears in your eyes and say, 'Just for my own satisfaction can you please tell me where I went wrong?' Provided you are talking to a human being, he will ask you to return to the table and the discussion will continue.

Getting the order is the responsibility of the salesman. Your company relies on your skill and competence to 'clinch the deal'. The best way to close is to come straight out with it and in a pleasant, businesslike way just ask for the order.

The ideal situation is where the purchaser feels not that he has been sold to, but rather that you helped him to make a decision to buy.

Appendix 22

THE PROFESSIONAL SALESPERSON'S QUALITIES

What is a personal quality? It is a degree of excellence which can be seen in an individual.

The following is a list of some of the *personal* qualities which are highly desirable in the truly professional salesperson. These are probably not all the qualities but they are most of them and we can see such qualities in the successful people in any sales force.

EMPATHY
The ability to *understand* the other person's point of view; not sympathy.

INTEGRITY
Are you honest and truthful, about yourself, your company, your product? Remember there is a great deal of difference between telling lies and withholding the truth!

LOYALTY
Be loyal to your company, its products, its management, your colleagues and to your customers. Don't wash your dirty linen in someone else's backyard!

GENUINE ENTHUSIASM
Enthusiasm is a wonderful thing and is much admired by customers. But don't overdo it. Be sincere with your enthusiasm. Enthusiasm is infectious; so is the lack of it!

RESILIENCE
The old-fashioned word for resilience is *guts*. This, when applied to a salesperson, means that you have the ability to get up after being knocked down, not just once but many times.

SELF-MOTIVATION
People go to work for all sorts of reasons – money, job satisfaction, status, security and opportunity. Why do you work? Most people hope to achieve a balance between working efficiently for money while being good at their job, thus experiencing job satisfaction.

GOOD COMMUNICATION

The responsibility for good communication is with the communicator. If the prospect/customer doesn't understand you, don't assume he is either a fool or deaf – it may be you! Don't worry about a regional dialect or accent, it doesn't matter. It is only important to use the English language and to speak clearly. And remember that best way to learn something is to *shut up and listen*!

ACCEPTABLE TO PEOPLE

It is important to ensure that you are acceptable to your prospect/customer:

1 *Dress*. Never be excessively 'with it'; you may please some and offend others. Try a middle course – all things to all people.
2 *Habits*. For example, smoking. If it's obvious the customer doesn't, then don't smoke yourself. It will most certainly annoy. Another example, drink. If you do have a beer, a cheese and onion sandwich, or a curry, *have a mint handy*.
3 *Hygiene*. Personal hygiene is now something which people are more open about and consequently you want to make sure you don't become the subject of stories about toothpaste or soap. It pays to be a professional in all respects.

GOOD HEALTH

You may not be in tip-top shape right now and may suffer from a minor disability – but look after what you have. Don't over-eat, over-smoke, over-drink, under-exercise! Keep fit and alert, mentally and physically. It pays in the long run – for one thing you will be able to enjoy a long and happy retirement.

EFFECTIVE HARD WORK

Any fool can work hard; it takes considerable thought to work hard effectively. It has to be more professional to make four or five profitable calls than to make twelve calls for the sake of filling up your weekly call sheet.

BELIEF IN THE VALUE OF THE JOB

While many sales people are qualified (having served an apprenticeship of one sort or another), they have, by their own hand, opted to earn their living as a professional in selling. Are you proud of being a salesperson?

PART SIX

Motivating Your Sales Organisation

Success in selling could be said to be the result of the correct use of four factors:

1 Knowledge of company, products and customers.
2 Selling skills to establish customers' needs and help them solve them with product benefits.
3 Time planning and control.
4 Motivation.

Certainly more action has been centred in recent years on improving the first three factors but perhaps the most used yet least understood phrase in modern business is '*You* have got to be more motivated'. Yet, as we shall discover, many companies and managers have yet to pass the year 1900 in their understanding of what motivation is and how it works.

The 1900 attitude is represented by the believers of one or more of the following ideas:

(a) 'Money is the only motivation that works.'
(b) 'A good healthy dose of fear will always get all people to perform.'
(c) 'I can motivate my staff (whilst sitting in my office) without getting involved with them.'
(d) 'As all staff are basically the same, one idea will work for all of them.'
(e) 'So long as I set aside certain occasional portions of time for the motivation function, I can be my normal uninterested, uninvolved, whip-cracking self for the rest of the time.'
(f) 'As long as I keep telling others "You have got to be motivated", it does not matter how miserable I look.'

All these views are at least highly suspect, since practice has proved that:

1 Money is often more of a demotivator than a motivator.
2 While fear may get some people to act, it will cause just as many people to freeze.
3 The only way to know how to motivate someone is involvement.

4   People are not the same, we have just treated them that way.
5   Motivation, if it is to work, is a continual not spasmodic activity.
6   People respond more to how people act than to what they say.

What we want to do in these pages is to clarify what motivation is, how it has been used, and what modern thought suggests; and look at practical ways of improving results through motivational sales management. Let us, however, start with one basic premise. Anyone who wants to motivate others must first of all be highly motivated themselves and, indeed, need to want to be even more motivated.

29. *Motivation*

By definition and responsibility

The word motivation is derived from the word motive. A look at the dictionary will suggest two definitions of this word: the reason for something, and productive of motion. Therefore, a basic definition could be 'That (the reason) which impels a person to action'. Whilst this definition gives us a basis for understanding we will find it necessary to add to it as our discussion continues.

We also need to decide at the start why we want to motivate people, and the simple answer is because we want them to get results. Our basic motivation for wanting to motivate is, therefore, selfishness, and however much we wrap it up and pretend we are doing it through altruism and the benefit to the individual of being motivated, our basic reason is to get them to do what we cannot or do not want to do ourselves.

This is true whether we are talking about our work lives where no manager can personally provide all the results necessary to achieve his or the company's objective, or about our home life where we try to motivate others to mow the lawn or wash the car since we do not wish or do not have the time to do it ourselves. The reason for discussing this now is that it is vitally important, when considering something as potentially powerful as motivation, to accept that we, the motivators, have a responsibility for those we want to motivate: a responsibility to do that which is *also* in the interests of the individual we are motivating.

In practice

Let us review the methods of motivation practised by managers since the turn of the century. The year 1900 would be characterised by one word – 'fear'. Managers used fear in an obvious way. 'If you do not do what I tell you, I will dismiss you' and, of course, at that time it was a powerful motivator, since managers had the power to enforce the fear. A person could be easily dismissed and, when dismissed, starvation was a possibility for that individual and his family.

This form of motivation continued to operate until the middle 1940s when a new phrase started to be used in management language – 'the carrot and whip'. The idea was to offer some positive benefit as an inducement to move but, in case that did not work, to have the negative threat as a safeguard.

Of course, the only difference between the fear of the 1900s and the carrot and whip of the 1940s was the introduction of the positive carrot into the equation. Both parts still related to fear but now, in addition to fear of loss of job or starvation, fear of not getting something that was wanted had been introduced.

Reward theory

It is fair to say that many, if not the majority, of companies are still using carrot and whip as the primary motivator today, but since the turn of this decade our greater sophistication (or hypocrisy) has caused the name to be changed to 'the reward theory'. The fear has now been hidden and, instead, the concentration is on the reward or carrot, the suggestion being that if the individual needs the reward sufficiently he will perform as the motivator wants him to perform. See Fig. 29.1.

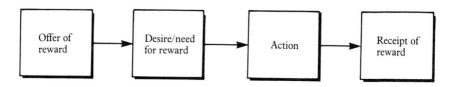

Fig. 29.1 *Basic reward theory*

While the reward theory as a theory seems practical, more and more managers have been finding that it either is not working as well now as it used to do or perhaps it is revealing inherent weaknesses. To discuss the reasons for these doubts, a number of different factors need to be considered.

First of all, there is the question of the nature of the reward. There are two values in a reward, extrinsic and intrinsic: extrinsic is what it costs to provide, ie its money value; intrinsic is what it is worth to the individual who is receiving it, ie its personal value. It will be obvious that the intrinsic or personal value of a reward is much more vital as a motivator than its extrinsic, money value. Yet many companies and managers have assumed the opposite – that the extrinsic value is all important. *Problem No. 1.*

Secondly, the fact that only the intrinsic value – the value of the reward to the individual – will motivate suggests that to motivate anyone the reward offered has to be designed specially for that individual. The problem here is that managers

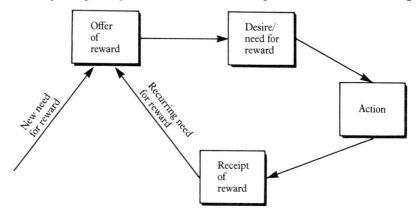

Fig. 29.2 *Reward theory*

have assumed that *a* reward will motivate *all* their staff. *Problem No. 2.*

Thirdly, by the very nature of the reward theory, motivation occurs in starts and stops, since as soon as the reward has been received there is no motivation to continue action until the next reward is offered. Therefore, reward theory has tended to follow the pattern of Fig. 29.2. Managers have had to search increasingly hard to find either new or recurring needs which they can offer to satisfy. *Problem No. 3.*

Fourthly, whereas the reward theory (the carrot) may well have been enlightened when it was first introduced, since at least it offered the opportunity of pleasure as well as pain (the whip), society has changed dramatically since then. The reward will motivate both because of the desire to have that reward and the fear of not having it, but society has acted to remove or diminish that fear. Let us take as an example one of the basic recurring needs, that of having a job and being paid regularly. In many countries there are now the following safeguards:

1 Laws to protect the individual from unfair dismissal. The fact that those laws were necessary because of bad and unfair management in the past is not in question. However, in practice their effect has been to extend the time it takes to remove someone from employment even when justified.
2 Society in many developed countries says that there shall be a level of income below which no one shall fall and, therefore, if individuals do fall below that level, Society will step in to give support. Again we are not arguing the ethical merits of this action but we are saying that the value of a reward which cannot be withheld is diminished. *Problem No. 4.*

Finally, two factors of human nature cause a further problem for the reward theory: (a) that which is given becomes a right, and (b) a person's level of expectation *begins* with what was received previously. In the case of the first factor, as soon as persons are given a reward, that becomes the norm for that task and they will expect to receive that as a minimum for future performance of that task. So as soon as someone is given an extra reward for certain parts of their performance, they will expect at least that in the future, and if that reward is not kept at least at that level, demotivation will occur.

As an example let us take the case of a company which has an excellent year and wants to thank its staff for its contribution to that success. The company gives the staff a bonus. The next year the company has another excellent year and gives the staff another bonus. The third year is a difficult one, so that the company cannot afford the cost of the bonus. A few members of staff may decide to work harder the following year, but the majority will say 'What have you done with *my* bonus', because that bonus has become theirs by right in their own mind.

When we come to the second factor – the rising level of expectation – the problem is made worse, since not only do people expect to have the reward repeated, they also expect the reward to increase or at least to be different. For instance, a company decides to offer an incentive to its sales force and offers, say, a weekend trip to a local resort in return for a particular level of performance. It may well generate interest among the sales force but what to do next time? It is no good offering the same prize, because it will at best get a lesser response and at worse no response. The company will have to offer more, and this is the first step into a spiral where the costs of the reward increases and quite often the performance progressively decreases. Some companies that started off with low-cost weekends in local resorts are now giving three weeks in far-away places and getting a *lower* response than for the original weekend.

In spite of all these factors, the majority of companies are still using reward theory as their basic motivator (and in many cases their *only* motivator) to achieve increased performance. They are finding their costs increasing alarmingly and productivity decreasing at the same rate. More and more companies are starting to say there has to be a better way – a different way to increase staff motivation.

30. *Theories of Motivation*

Maslow – the father of modern motivation

To cure ourselves of the reward theory syndrome we have first of all to stop thinking about motivating people *en masse* and start thinking about motivating the individual. The first rule of motivating others is that to motivate someone you have to make them see the benefit to them of your idea. It follows therefore, that in order to make them see the benefit, that benefit has to relate to that individual's needs and wants. To motivate someone therefore, we first have to establish what that person's needs and wants are.

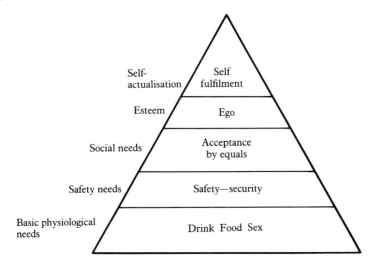

Fig. 30.1 *Maslow's Pyramid*

The late Professor Abraham Maslow has become known as the father of modern motivational thought, since he set out the five-stage priority of human needs in what has become known as Maslow's Pyramid (Figure 30.1). Professor Maslow's theory can be extended as in Figure 30.2.

The basis of the theory is that the bottom level is prime in that a person who is starving because of lack of food or dehydrating because of lack of water will be unconcerned about anything else until those needs are satisfied. However, they are no more important than any other level, since each of us will be motivated only by the *lowest unfulfilled need*. For example, when someone has just had a large meal, the offer of food will not motivate, since that person will have moved on to the second level, the need to be safe and feel secure. This second level applies

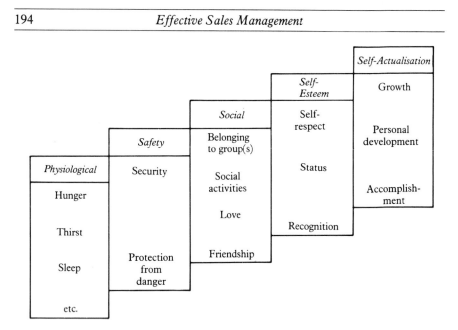

Fig. 30.2 *Maslow extended*

whether we are thinking of safety from physical attack or security from losing our job.

If we feel safe and secure then another level of needs affect us, the social needs. We need love, friendship and to belong and be accepted as a member of a group.

The next level of need, self-esteem, is the need for self-respect and to be respected by others. This need, said Maslow, can be classified into two sets: 'Firstly, the desire for strength, for achievement, for adequacy, for confidence in the face of the world, and for independence and freedom. Secondly, the desire for reputation or prestige (defined as respect or esteem from other people), recognition, importance, attention or appreciation'.

If all the needs for esteem are satisfied, the individual is then motivated by the highest need, self-actualisation, which is the desire to make full use of one's own abilities and talents. In other words, if all the lower needs are satisfied (and this only occurs for a small proportion of us), then the artist must paint, the guru must commune with his god and the 'born' salesman must sell.

A mistake is often made in assuming that a person will automatically remain in one level of need for long periods. This may not be so. Wherever you are in the pyramid now, you can in a relatively short time move into another level: for example, if you were denied food and drink or warmth, it would only be a matter of hours before nothing else would matter until those needs were satisfied.

That then is Maslow's Pyramid, but what does it mean to us as sales managers and how can it help us to motivate our staff? Surely what Maslow does is:

1 Confirm that we cannot motivate from behind our closed office door, since the only way we can motivate is to establish what are our staff's current needs – not yesterday's or yesteryear's but today's needs.

2 The only way to do that is by two-way face to face communication.
3 What Maslow gives us is a series of pigeonholes, of signposts to help us to place those current needs into recognisable slots.

Fig. 30.3 is a checklist to help you to (a) see if you know what are the current needs of your staff and (b) complete the profile where there are blanks.

IDENTIFYING INDIVIDUAL NEEDS

Salesman	Basic need	Safety need	Social need	Esteem need	Self-actualisation need
Name:	1	1	1	1	1
	2	2	2	2	2
	3	3	3	3	3
Name:	1	1	1	1	1
	2	2	2	2	2
	3	3	3	3	3
Name:	1	1	1	1	1
	2	2	2	2	2
	3	3	3	3	3
Name:	1	1	1	1	1
	2	2	2	2	2
	3	3	3	3	3
Name:	1	1	1	1	1
	2	2	2	2	2
	3	3	3	3	3

Fig. 30.3

Of course what Maslow does not tell us is how to satisfy those needs. You do not have to be a genius to know that if someone is starving, you can offer them food, but then very few of our staff suffer from that most basic of the physiological needs anyway. It becomes much more difficult when we are considering safety, social or esteem needs. For the answers to this problem we have to look further forward to people like Herzberg and McGregor.

Herzberg – action caused by desire

Professor Frederick Herzberg has promoted a theory of motivation which goes a long way forward from the original theory of 'carrot and whip' or, indeed, its extension, 'the reward theory', which we have already stated is still used by many managers and companies to try to exhort greater efforts from their staff. It stems from two statements:

1 What makes people happy and motivated at work is what they do.
2 What makes people unhappy and demotivated at work is the situation in which they do it.

Managers are going to have to become familiar with three new letters that are going to become increasingly important in the management of people in the future. The three letters are QWL – standing for 'Quality of Work Life' – and managers who want to motivate their staff are going to have to improve their QWL.

This starts by defining people as they *are*, not as we *want* them to be. Many workers who we have assumed to have the characteristics which we wanted them to have are now saying: 'We are not like that. Treat us the way we are, not the way you believe us to be'. So the big revolution managers are going to have to face is that of accepting the needs of the people, not their own projected needs.

Herzberg, working from the basis set by Maslow, has suggested that these needs fall into two categories. The first set of needs defined by Herzberg are called *hygiene needs*, and deal with a person's relation with the environment. They consist of how people are treated at work:

1   Do you pay them well?
2   Good working conditions?
3   Human relations – the nature and quality of their supervision.
4   Technical supervision.
5   The nature of the company's policy and administration.

They are called hygiene factors, because, if they are right, they prevent people from being dissatisfied in their working environment. They keep people from being unhappy, which is their function, but they do not motivate.

One form of hygiene that has long been practised is to deny people fair treatment at the beginning. For example, 'I am not going to pay you as much as the going rate, but prove you can do the job, and I will make it up to you later'. The trouble is that you can never make it up. That lack of fair treatment at the beginning will never be forgotten, and normally leads to a revenge psychology on the part of the employee. In other words, he or she will get back at you later because they cannot forget the remembered pain. The principle here is very simple: treat people fairly, because it is in your own and their best interests.

The other set of needs of people is caused by the fact that they are human beings and, therefore, not only do they not want to be hurt – so treat them well (hygiene) – but they want to *do* something. They want to grow and show what they can do. They want to be able to say at the end of the work experience not that they vegetated but that they are more than they were (know more, can do more and, therefore, *are* more), and the only way to measure this is by what they have done in that experience. They are, therefore, asking these questions:

1   Do I achieve? Am I contributing?
2   Am I given increased responsibility?
3   Am I advancing and growing?
4   Is what I do meaningful and significant?
5   Is my ability recognised?

These are the *motivators*. These are the variables that managers can use to motivate people, because people who want to do something, want to do it – that's motivation.

Referring back to carrot and whip, Herzberg suggests that anyone can be made to do anything, so long as they are threatened or bribed enough, but do they *want* to do something? The answer is no. In other words, people can be got to move by what he calls 'KITA' – Kick in the Arse – and if more movement is needed, more KITA is needed. KITA can either be positive – offering people a reward, bonus or an incentive – or negative – threatening them. By the use of KITA, then, people can be got to move, but unless they want to do a good job because they *want* to do a good job, they are not motivated.

One of the other problems about applying KITA is that it normally causes a short-term improvement in productivity, at the cost of a long-term decrease in the average day's work, because of that 'reward once given becomes a right' effect.

Therefore, if we want to talk about motivated performance, we have got to talk about the motivators, which are:

1 Achievement.
2 Recognition for achievement.
3 Meaningful and interesting work.
4 Increased responsibility.
5 Growth and advancement at work.

In other words – the quality of the human experience at work.

A point that Herzberg insists is vital is that the motivators are not more important than the hygiene factors. Each of them has to be given equal importance, because *each* of them is vital if motivation is going to be strong.

One of the most important variables in creating motivation is training, because motivation is a function of ability and the opportunity to use that ability. So the more ability you can give people by training them, the more they will want to do. To explain this equation of

$$Motivation = ability + opportunity$$

Herzberg posed the question: 'What would determine my motivation to play the piano?' The first and obvious determining factor is 'Can I play the piano?', since no amount of leaping about and pressing hot buttons will cause me to play if I cannot play. The second and equally important factor is 'Is there a piano to play?', since I may be a master pianist but with no piano there will be no music.

One problem that has been very evident in industry is the lack of the second factor in the equation – that of opportunity – and Herzberg has, therefore, promoted the job enrichment movement. So what should a job contain? The following factors are necessary:

1 A range of responsibilities and activities to keep a person interested.
2 Areas of growth, since all jobs should be a learning experience.
3 Direct feedback, since how a person is doing should not be dependent upon someone else telling them – they should be able to see for themselves.
4 The responsibility for checking one's own quality, because that responsibility cannot be delegated to a control system.
5 Direct communication between that person and the people they need to communicate with, not via supervisors or managers.

Herzberg suggests that the situation will improve and productivity will improve when management is prepared to say: 'It is our fault. We didn't know how to manage people well, we just knew how to hurt them well. We didn't respect them enough or challenge them enough or give them enough satisfaction'.

The reader will recall that we began Chapter 28 by defining motivation as 'That which impels a person to action'. Perhaps now is the time, in view of the impact of Maslow and Herzberg, to amend that definition to 'That which impels a person to action because that person *can* act, has the *opportunity* to act and therefore *wants* to act.'

Before we can turn Maslow and Herzberg into specific action areas for the manager we have to examine one more factor and one more person's work. We must consider McGregor and his examination of the attitude of the manager and the response of staff to that attitude.

McGregor – the theory of X and Y

Douglas McGregor suggested the management's attitude towards staff had a very significant effect on staff motivation or lack of it. Many managers believe in Theory X, which is the assumption that:

1 People are inherently lazy.
2 They will not work unless you force them to by using carrot or whip.
3 They are not interested in and do not want to take any responsibility.

McGregor suggested that if this is true, it is because, since the beginning of the Industrial Revolution, managers have expected their staff to react in this way, and if you treat a man like a beast of burden, then he is likely to act like a beast of burden. It is significant, though, that many of those same people who react without interest at work go home and work extremely hard at a hobby or take the responsibility of contributing to or helping to run volunteer organisations.

McGregor suggested that if managers accepted and adopted Theory Y, then employees would work harder and more willingly if:

1 Employees and management shared common goals.
2 Employees were given some responsibility in determining how productivity could be increased.
3 They were given a chance to develop their abilities.

In other words, McGregor suggests that if you expect people to be lazy, they will be lazy, but if you expect that people will want to contribute, they will want to contribute.

We can now go on to look at practical methods of motivation.

31. *The Hygiene Factors*

Herzberg suggested that while the hygiene factors did not in themselves motivate, they were as vital as the motivators, since if they were wrong, they would cause dissatisfaction and could cause people to leave.

The hygiene factors are:

1 Company policy and administration.
2 Working conditions.
3 Salary.
4 Technical supervision.
5 Interpersonal relations.

Let us look at these in more detail and show perhaps why they tend to at least demotivate more than motivate, and what the manager should do to minimise their negative effect on the sales force.

Company policy and administration

Almost inevitably sales personnel see this as restrictive and unhelpful in doing their job, and even improvements will only cause a temporary attitude change. Additionally, the majority of managers only have the power at best to affect this area marginally. All the manager can really do is try wherever and whenever possible to contribute to positive changes.

Let us, for example, look at reporting procedures as a part of administration. In Part 5 we discussed the design and installation of a good sales control system. Any good system should require the minimum amount of work from the sales force to give the maximum amount of practical information to management. It is fair to say, however, that in the majority of cases the reporting systems that we have reviewed in recent years have reversed this rule, and what is worse, the results have only been used as a cudgel to beat the salesperson with rather than as a positive management tool. So in this area sales managers should carefully review the existing reporting system on the basis of:

1 What information do I really need in order to manage properly?
2 Am I going to be able to use the information? Otherwise, why ask for it?
3 How can I reduce the amount of writing the salesperson has to do in favour of ticks and numbers?

If this results in a new, simpler, more practical reporting system, the result will be an improvement in sales-force attitude and, therefore, in the quality of reporting.

199

However, the manager who expects that this will forever stop the moans about the reporting system and ensure that all reports will be submitted on time is guilty of self-delusion. What it will do is reduce the area of contention and dissatisfaction, which is what the manager is trying to do in the hygiene factors.

Working conditions

Again the manager must attempt wherever possible to improve conditions, but the best he/she can hope to do is get a temporary improvement. Take one of the most contentious things to a sales force – the cars they drive. Having to spend many hours behind the wheel makes the car an important part of a salesperson's working conditions. However, how long will a new car motivate an individual? With most people only until one of the following things happens:

1 The first time the car breaks down.
2 They get the first knock while parking or parked.
3 They realise that everyone else has exactly the same car.

The period of motivation is at best likely to be a matter of months, followed by a period of disinterest, followed by increasing levels of demotivation until the next car arrives.

We have ignored the fact that many longer service salesmen become totally bored with driving anyway and, therefore, the fact of driving at all is a negative aspect of their job. So all the manager can do is to provide the best car that the company can afford. It is likely, however, that dissatisfaction will be decreased by allowing the salesperson more choice in the model and colour of that vehicle.

Salary

The method and size of remuneration has in many companies been the primary motivator, yet even the value of this factor has come more into question in recent years. The issue is clouded by the fact that, if asked what motivates them, most groups of sales people would respond with the word 'Money'. Yet more and more managers are finding that the significance of money as a motivator has at least been overrated.

The motivational theorists would suggest that money only motivates in one of three ways:

(a) When it is below subsistence level.
(b) When it means a drop in the standard of living.
(c) When it is seen to be unfair (someone is getting paid more for doing the same or an inferior job).

It is significant that all of these are negative motivators, ie someone will do something about it because they are unhappy because of (a), (b) or (c).

That the theorists' view is simplistic is open to discussion. All of us know some sales people who really are money-motivated, but even for them one questions whether it is the money itself that motivates rather than the money being a symbol to satisfy one or other of Maslow's needs.

The prime problem here surely is the earlier discussed factor of the individuality of motivation. The fact is that what motivates one person will demotivate another, so how can managers define a method of remuneration which will motivate all. The simple answer is that they cannot. It could work perhaps if a manager created an individual package for each individual in the team, but then sooner or later the 'unfairness' factor would arise, even if such a scheme was possible to administer.

Another factor about money is that in adverse trading conditions managers often have little that they can do to affect the income of their sales personnel. Salary has in many countries recently become subject to the *annual* review, and with many countries fighting the effects of inflation small percentage increases have become the norm.

Even commission earnings are becoming pegged and, of course, short supplies of the product or service adversely affect this method of payment. When it is possible to increase income, what is the effect?

Let us say we offer our sales staff an increase of 20 per cent. Some of them may be comfortable on their existing income and, therefore, unaffected more than marginally; some of them would think this increase is merely their right because of their last year's efforts; and certainly some of them would be motivated because this increase is an indication of their worth to the company – in other words a form of recognition. But how long would it last? How long would it continue to affect them positively?

At best in most people only until:

1 their expenditure rose to the level of the new income.
2 they realise how much tax is going to take out of the increase, or until
3 they get used to this level of income,

and this ignores those companies who stupidly act unfairly and give some people higher rises than either the norm or the individuals deserve. So even where the raise does positively have an effect initially, the effect does not last long.

Let us review the current methods of paying sales people.

Commission only

In practical terms this offers companies a highly cost-effective way of remunerating sales staff, since they only have to pay on results. It is usual, therefore, for the company to be able to employ a larger number of sales staff than would otherwise be possible. Another advantage is that this method, because it offers unlimited income to the highly successful, does attract some highly capable sales personnel.

The disadvantages of this system are that:

1 In order to give sufficient income, the commission has to be set at a high level, which may prove to have an adverse effect on unit cost and/or profit.
2 This sort of payment method also attracts candidates who cannot get into selling where the company is paying a salary, and therefore people tend to

come, fail and go very quickly. Turnover of staff can become unacceptably high.

3   It is extremely difficult to motivate 'commission only' staff to do anything that interferes with selling, since they have the constant pressure of making a living. Service tends, therefore, to be a problem.
4   The pressure already mentioned tends to affect different people in different ways, and even some very good sales people find it difficult or impossible to work under these conditions.
5   Although the sky is the limit in income terms, most companies using this scheme find that sales people reach a level of income where the extra reward is not worth the extra effort.

Small basic salary, high commission potential

Again this has the advantage of limiting the company's fixed costs and additionally should increase the quality of the candidates applying for jobs. However, this method still suffers from most of the disadvantages of the commission only system.

High basic salary, low commission or bonus

Here the company should attract a high quality of candidate, and certainly the system allows the company to be selective about the choice of that candidate. The disadvantages are:

1   The company *has* to be far more selective, since the basic cost factor is much higher and the reader may recall that in Part 3 we said that 'the best that any interviewer can hope to do is gradually cut down the number of times he is wrong'.
2   It is also unlikely that the small amount of commission or bonus available is sufficient to have any effect on the salesperson one way or another.

High basic, high commission

This system can only be operated in the very small sector of selling where the product or service is highly profitable, but does have advantages in that it can attract and keep both the high quality candidates who need the security of a high basic and those who enjoy the challenge of high commission potential.

Straight salary

From the comments on the methods listed above both the advantages and disadvantages of this system will be fairly clear. However, more and more companies are deciding that the advantages outweigh the disadvantages and are opting for this method of remuneration.

The remuneration method that an organisation chooses is much more likely to be based on its financial status, type of product or service and industry than on its

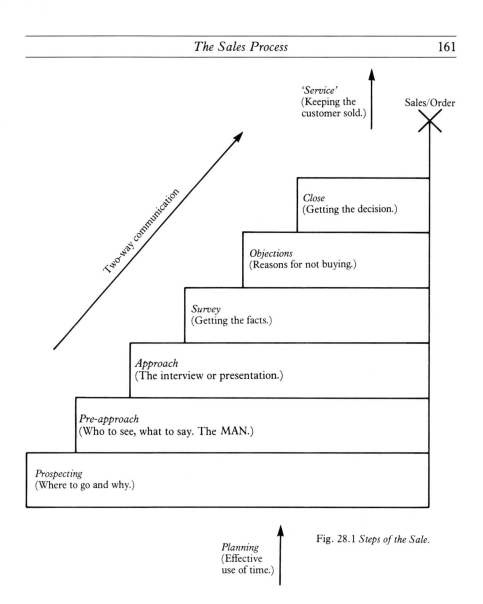

Fig. 28.1 *Steps of the Sale.*

Professional selling

The funny thing about selling is that everyone thinks they can do it. To even hint at selling immediately draws forth stories of how expert the teller is at getting rid of houses, cars, bicycles, boats etc. However, could that person do the same thing day after day, week after week, month after month and year after year? Probably not.

But the *professional* salesperson has to and should enjoy doing so, while making an increasingly good living. As with any other profession (and done properly it is a profession), there are qualifications to be earned, hard work to be endured and, in the early stages, probably a degree of financial sacrifice. So how is selling different belief in the motivation of one method or another. It is significant that the companies we have been dealing with in recent years all have similar problems of motivation, whichever of these methods they are using, which tends to support the following suggestion.

Choose the method that is right for your company's financial status, industry or type of product or service, but do not expect that that method will motivate for very long, if at all. If the right method has been chosen it will attract and help to keep the right candidates for your company. They will then be available to be motivated.

Please do not think from what we have said that money is unimportant because it is vital to pay as well as possible. It is just that companies have assumed that it motivates rather than realise that its real function is to minimise demotivation.

Technical supervision and interpersonal relations

Since this whole book is about improving the quality of supervision it is not our intention to discuss this area at great length here. Let us just repeat that the more that we as managers do to improve our treatment of people at work, the less dissatisfied they will be and the more chance we will have to use the motivators to increase their desire to work.

32. *The Motivators*

The primary areas we have to work on to motivate people were listed by Herzberg as:

(a) Achievement.
(b) Recognition for achievement.
(c) Meaningful and interesting work.
(d) Increased responsibility.
(e) Growth and advancement at work.

In Fig. 32.1 we list some of the primary action areas under each of those headings. Some of these action areas are dealt with in depth in other parts of this book, but some require further amplification here. It will be noticeable that the different headings in Fig. 32.1 interlink, since positive action under one heading will cause positive effects under other headings; where this link is highly relevant we have shown it thus $\longleftrightarrow$.

Achievement

Fair and positive targets

It may seem strange to some managers to hear about targeting in a chapter about motivation, since in many companies the targeting system is an entirely demotivational event. Part of this is due to the way the targets are set, by whom they are set and how they are communicated.

In many companies the targets are originally set at boardroom level, sometimes by scientific methods (or as scientific as targeting can get) but equally often by the 'wet thumb in the air method' of last year plus a percentage.

Once it has been decided that this is the sales target for next year, it is left to the sales director to implement. The first thing he/she does before dividing it among the divisional sales managers is add on the 'fudge factor'. This fudge factor is the amount he/she increases the target by to allow for shortfalls from any one division. The first thing the DSM does is to add on his/her fudge factor and so on down the line through the various levels of manager until it reaches the salesperson who has actually got to achieve the target.

In many cases this final figure can be umpteen per cent more than originally intended because of all the fudge factors. Is it any wonder that the salesperson rejects the targets as unreachable?

Often this target will have been handed to the sales staff in sealed envelopes at the end of a sales meeting, presumably on the assumption that they will not go outside, tear open the envelopes and compare the unpalatable results. As a result

Achievement	Recognition	Work itself	Responsibility	Advancement and growth
1 Fair and positive targets	1 Verbal praise Person to person Sales meetings	1 Improve job content	1 Increase authority	1 Training in current job
2 Other meaningful work objectives	2 Written praise Memo Letter Sales bulletins League tables	2 Ensure variety	2 Deputising for Manager	2 Development training for next job
3 Encourage individuals to set personal goals and objectives	3	3 Special projects Field training assignments Manning show/exhibition stands Marketing assignments Special selling assignments	3 Manning show/exhibition stands	3 Counselling
4 Inject fair competition		4 Double calling	4 Involvement in sales meetings	4 Career structure or path
5 Incentive schemes		5 'Blitz' selling	5 Acting as representative of sales dept on internal committees	5 Promotion
6 Award schemes	6 Field accompaniment	6 Delegation		
7 Effective performance appraisal	7 Family recognition	7 Invite involvement in decision-making process		
8 Accurate job descriptions	8 Reward	8 Job rotation	8 Acting as representative of company on external bodies	
9 Performance standards				

Fig. 32.1 *The Motivators*

of the above and other management malpractices in this area the difference between target and actual has become so gross that the two have little relation to each other.

The first principle of good targeting is that the target should be CBA+, ie it should be:

(a) Conceivable.
(b) Believable.
(c) Achievable plus
(d) Aim high.

In other words, the individuals have to be able to *conceive* that they can reach the target. More than that they have to *believe* that they can reach it and it has to be realistically *achievable*. Also it should be *aim high* in concept to make it worth achieving.

The second principle is that the target has to take account of the individual and his/her current state of ability, the area and its potential, the products and their acceptability, and the current state of political and economic activity and their effects on demand.

Many companies have decided that there has to be a better way of target setting than that outlined above and, taking note of the two above-mentioned principles, have asked themselves the question: 'Who is the person who can most accurately assess what can be achieved in a sales territory?' Providing that person is experienced, it has to be the person who is working the territory, ie the salesperson. These companies have, therefore, reversed the targeting procedure and started it not at board level but at salesperson level. On receiving this suggestion, many sales managers' first reaction is to suggest that the sales people will set the target artificially low. Of course, any manager who just says to the sales force 'Set your target for the next period' and then accepts that figure without comment is not managing: he/she is abdicating. However, in the countless cases where this method is now used the too-low target is very much the rarity; in fact usually the salesperson is too optimistic rather than vice versa.

What should happen is this. The salesperson is asked to set the target but also to state how that target is going to be achieved, e.g. what proportion will come from existing customers in specific terms, what proportion will come from new customers – who from and how much etc. The salesperson and immediate manager then sit down and negotiate, and this will, as already stated, normally be a process of lowering the figure to the realistic rather than raising it to the acceptable. Having gone through this process with each salesperson, the manager then has the team target, which is negotiated upwards with the next in line and so on up to board level, where it becomes both the target and the forecast.

On first adopting this idea, few companies stick to it completely. The senior sales manager usually becomes the fulcrum, with a target still coming down from the board and now a target coming up from the sales teams. However, there is generally little variation between the two figures – quite often the figure coming upwards has been higher and even when the figure coming down is higher, the sales manager has the information to be able to say: 'This is the best I can see us doing in this period unless you can help with increased promotion or other aids'.

In the majority of cases, before long, the process has become a totally upwards one, resulting in greatly increased accuracy between target and actual, and vastly greater commitment from the sales force, since its members have been instrumental in setting the targets rather than being in receipt of 'tablets of stone' from above.

One problem is what to do about new products which are going to be launched, since the sales people, when setting their targets, will not be aware of them. Firstly, the fact that they are not aware of them is due to secrecy, and we would debate the desirability of that secrecy. However, if there has to be secrecy, then the manager has to set a secondary target for new products which will then be transferred to the sales force's targeting system in the second year.

With this method of targeting, the opportunity for motivation through achievement is very high. Not only can the salesperson achieve success in reaching the target, but also he/she has the satisfaction of having set the target correctly in the first place.

Other meaningful work objectives

While the target is perhaps the most obvious achievement area, the manager should not discount the value of setting and having the individual set other worthwhile work objectives. These objectives can be both individual and team objectives, since both give the opportunity to achieve success. Listed below is a set of meaningful work objectives for the individual.

1   Increase the number of calls over last month by one-fifth.
2   Increase the ratio of sales to calls by 10 per cent.
3   Increase the average value of each sale by 15 per cent.
4   Get better balance of sales among products offered.
5   Lower ratio of expenses to sales by 5 per cent.
6   Exceed quota in more months this year than last.
7   Make two more service calls per week.
8   Co-operate better with credit department on late payments.
9   Achieve an order for a new product with one old customer every week.
10 Allocate 10 per cent more time this week to the highest-margin product.
11 Make more extensive use of sales information from the head office.
12 Make more presentations to buyer groups.
13 Call on one new account, at least by 'phone, every day for a week.
14 Work out how to reduce travel miles per call.
15 Conduct one more dealer or distributor meeting per month than currently.
16 Create a market information update for the company.
17 Conduct a survey of your top ten customers.
18 Build a profile of ten prime prospects who should buy in the next six months.

Personal goals and objectives

Since most people's work and personal life cannot be separated, it is fair to suggest that the more an individual is goal-orientated, whichever part of their life these goals relate to, the more it will affect the other part of their life. It makes sense, therefore, to encourage the individual to have personal non-work goals, whether they be goals to have something or do something, since the more goal-orientated the individual is in private life, the more he can be encouraged to be goal orientated in his work life.

Fair competition

One point we have not as yet discussed is the fact that it would appear that sales people tend as a breed to have a high 'will to win' element in their make-up. This should be encouraged by injecting a competitive element into activity as often as possible. This competition must be fair and each party must have the opportunity to win but, those provisos apart, most sales people enjoy competing.

The competition does not have to be formalised in the incentive or award schemes discussed later. It can be as simple as announcing at the end of a sales meeting, 'I have noticed that the most sales we have ever achieved in a month of Product 'X' was A and the most sales any individual has achieved is B. Let us try this month to beat those records'.

Incentive schemes

In our earlier discussions in Chapter 29 about the difficulties of using the reward theory, we briefly mentioned some of the problems attached to incentive schemes, particularly the difficulties encountered by these companies who have been using such schemes as their prime or only motivator. However, as part of a total motivation package, as outlined in Fig. 32.1, a well run incentive scheme can certainly help, since it gives yet another opportunity to achieve.

We list below a set of suggestions of do's and don'ts to help you make your incentive scheme work.

1   Don't run too many schemes because:
    (a) The effect will lessen as schemes become more the norm.
    (b) It can upset both your profitability and distribution patterns – one company we know got to the stage where 64 per cent of its total sales were occurring in the nine weeks of the year in which it ran incentive schemes.

2   Short schemes work better than long ones. It is very difficult to maintain interest in a scheme that lasts months or a full year.
3   Make sure you can afford it. The strategy that usually operates is to pay a bonus in either travel, merchandise awards or cash for sales you would not have made if you had not run the scheme. Make an optimistic forecast of your sales without a scheme, work out how much you can pay for sales beyond that figure and plan your prizes accordingly. Ten per cent of the additional sales volume should be considered to be the upper limit on expenditure, but it does, of course, depend on your margin.
4   Short-term incentive schemes can be highly effective in directing the efforts of the sales force in specific areas. For example, we mentioned in Chapter 31 the difficulty of getting sales people on commission only or low salary and

high commission to perform necessary non-selling functions. Incentives can help in this area.

5   Try to ensure that everyone has a chance to win either by setting 'beat your previous best' criteria or by offering rewards for different types of success.

6   Change the style or type of incentive scheme regularly, preferably each time you run one, and introduce different elements.

7   Set clear objectives and make them specific. If you do not know in advance what you want to achieve, how can you measure the results?

8   Bring the sales people into the setting up of the scheme. They are the ones you are trying to motivate, so get them to work designing the scheme and choosing the prizes.

9   Promote the scheme extensively. This will mean kick-off meetings and regular bulletins.

10 Having a theme will help in the promotion.

11 Keep it simple. The more complicated you make it, the more difficult it becomes to administer and the more chances you have to spoil the motivational effect.

12 Do not be afraid to get help. There are now many professional organisations who can help you in arranging contest details and finding the right prizes, but keep control – it is your scheme.

13 Make sure the awards are worthwhile. Prizes that do not work properly, or travel in third-class hotels, will be a remembered demotivator. Better something small with quality than something large without.

14 Keep the score properly and analyse it afterwards. Did this scheme really work for me, the company and for the sales people?

Award schemes

Another form of incentive is award schemes, such as salesman of the month. Many managers ignore this, usually because the idea does not and did not motivate them when they were selling, but they should remember that they are trying to motivate others not themselves. If their sales people like the idea, then it is worth trying, since it is yet another opportunity to achieve.

A number of companies have found graded award schemes highly successful. They have the benefit of everyone being able to win, since they are awards for reaching various levels of performance. Again, some of these levels can be used to highlight the necessity of competence in things not necessarily to do with the sales target, such as cost ratios or profit ratios.

Performance appraisal

In many ways good performance appraisals offer satisfaction in all the motivator areas, since they are an opportunity to set achievement goals, to recognise good performance in the past and so on.

Contrary to most people's belief, performance appraisal was introduced and designed to be a motivational experience for both the parties. Unfortunately what it has become in many companies is exactly the opposite – a totally demotivational experience!

The reasons for this are many and varied but among the main ones are:

1   The fact that it has become the *annual* event.
2   Often the appraiser is:

   (a)   Ill-prepared.
   (b)   Ill-trained in this important activity.
   (c)   In consequence, demotivated before it starts.

3   Often the subordinate is:

   (a)   Ill-prepared, usually because he/she has not been invited to prepare.
   (b)   Demotivated before the event starts because of previous bad experiences.
   (c)   Unhappy that 'God-like' judgements are going to be passed on his/her previous period's work.

4   Often the appraisal is:

   (a)   Held in the wrong environment.
   (b)   Takes place in the wrong atmosphere.

The primary purpose of an appraisal is to help the subordinate. The reasons for appraisal are the following:

(i)   To provide knowledge of individual performance.
(ii)   To plan for future promotions and successions.
(iii) To assess training and development needs.
(iv)   To provide information for salary planning and special awards.
(v)   To contribute to corporate career planning.

The three main principles for appraisal (and counselling) interviews
1   Everything written should be shown and shared, since secrecy breeds suspicion, and suspicion destroys a counselling relationship. Two specific aspects often withheld are those relating to (a) poor performance, and (b) potential promotion. In the first the secrecy reflects the manager's own anxiety – telling someone he is doing badly is not easy. The second, promotion, is difficult, as telling the subordinate of potential promotion is very likely to be interpreted as definite, with keen disappointment if it does not happen. If there is something a manager feels he cannot communicate to a subordinate, then that is probably a good enough reason to exclude it from the appraisal report.
2   The appraisal report should be finalised in the presence of the subordinate.
3   The subordinate should contribute a major part to the appraisal. Self-appraisal is particularly effective in two areas.

   First, in the area of weak performance most individuals will be surprisingly open and honest about themselves, if the appraisal/counselling is a supportive relationship. Analyse rather than criticise!

   Secondly, in the area of career progression, managers tend to see a subordinate's future in terms of the other people in the department and how, particularly, the manager's own progression developed. If the manager gives the subordinate the chance to talk, however, he may reveal totally different aspirations.

Emotion in appraisal

There is always an element of emotion in appraisal interviewing. Both manager and subordinate each have positive and negative feelings, and appreciating what they are can help understanding. Taking the manager first, let us consider his feelings:

(a) He wants to be helpful and understanding but may be inclined to offer advice too closely related to his own experience. He needs to remember the subordinate is an individual in his own right.
(b) He wants to be kind and tolerant and liked by his staff. However, he must be prepared to point out the realities of any situation.
(c) On the other hand, he may be fearful of the interview itself and whether he may make a mess of it. This feeling will diminish with practice.
(d) He may fear the interview becoming emotional and perhaps creating hostility in the subordinate. He may be overcome by developing relations where expression of feelings is normal.
(e) He may envy the subordinate's youth, health, qualifications or career opportunities. He must control these feelings.

Let us now look at the subordinate's feelings:

(a) He wants to be liked by the boss, but must not allow this feeling to make him dependent and subservient.
(b) He wants to be helped to improve.
(c) But the most likely feeling is fear of criticism of work or behaviour. Until this fear is allayed by the manager, the interview will achieve nothing. *Only the manager* can allay this fear by establishing a counselling relation, which shows he is fair and can be trusted.

Process of appraisal

So how should a performance appraisal be run to ensure that it is a practical and motivational experience? The first question is how often should appraisals take place? Annual appraisals are too far apart. At best the appraisal should be quarterly, at worst twice a year.

Advise staff well in advance. Get the subordinate to complete a copy of the appraisal form on himself or herself and include the question 'How well was I managed this year?'

The appraiser's preparations should include:
(a) Reviewing the period's results.
(b) Studying the last appraisal result.
(c) Checking the appraisee's personal file and job description.
(d) Talking to any other managers concerned.
(e) Completing outline copy of appraisal.

The appraisal interview should take the following lines:

(a) As both appraiser and appraisee have completed the form, the interview is not the appraiser telling the appraisee what the company (or appraiser) thinks of him/her but a discussion about the points of agreement and a negotiation about the points of variance.
(b) The appraiser should try to keep the appraisee talking and concentrate on listening.
(c) When the evidence has been brought to light, they can then go on to diagnose the problem areas. It is vital that the diagnosis concentrates on things which can be improved, not on basic character traits.
(d) When the problem areas have been dealt with, an agreed appraisal can be written and signed by both parties.
(e) It is now possible to move on to the most vital stage, which is to *agree* a plan of action to overcome the problems. This plan should be time-targeted. In the event of agreement not being possible the appraisee should have the right to a further interview, with the appraiser's superior.

If the interview is to be effective it must not be confused with a salary review. That is quite a separate interview.

After the interview the appraiser should complete any other paperwork straight away. The action plan should be progressed and monitored on a regular basis.

Accurate job description (JD)

One vital aspect of motivation is for people to know, without comment from others, how they are doing. A good accurate JD can give this immediate knowledge, since it lays out plainly and specifically what that person should be doing. The format for and method of building a JD is laid down in Chapter 15.

Performance standards (PS)

As an extension to good job descriptions, more and more companies are using PS as a method of giving immediate feedback. There can also be opportunities to achieve, since a PS is a statement of the conditions which will exist when a part of a job function is being performed properly. It should be noted that a PS is not a hoped-for goal, it is something that the individual will be able to attain within a recognisable and measurable period. This means that the individual will constantly be able to see new achievement areas by updating that standard, which should be set by the individual in co-operation with his/her immediate manager.

A performance standard may be defined as a statement of the *conditions* which will exist when a duty or responsibility has been (or is being) satisfactorily performed. It is quantitatively expressed, and devoid of vague, ambiguous language – eg 'efficient', 'prompt'. It is attainable because it is feasible, committed to by the performer, and accepted by the performer's supervisor. Unless all these specifications are met, there is not a performance standard.

Performance can be measured against past performance, against what *others* are doing, and those things that the company's objectives make mandatory. Performance standards, in performer–supervisor relations, are a tool for:

1 Releasing the performer's *initiative* while strengthening the supervisor's *control*.
2 Obtaining the performer's *commitment* to personal responsibility and the supervisor's *acceptance* of that commitment.
3 *Self-analysis* for the performer against performance yardsticks agreed to by supervisor.
4 Management at all levels to *assess* performance of others.
5 All levels of organisation to reach continuous agreement on company-wide objectives and methods.
6 Identifying problems (a) when performance deviates from standards, and (b) when changes in standards are indicated.

Writing performance standards is illustrated in Fig. 32.2.

'I do these things' (job description)	'For these purposes' (individual and company objectives)		'as evidenced by these conditions' (performance standard)	
ACTIVITIES Format – 'I + transitive verb + object'	PURPOSES Format – 'In order that/to……..		STANDARDS Format – Performance is satisfactory when . . .	
Examples				
1 I submit proposals for marketing programmes	1a	In order to get them approved promptly and efficiently	1a	When X% of them are approved after not more than Y revisions within not more than Z days after initial submission
	1b			
	1c			
2 I handle customer complaints	2a	In order to achieve customer satisfaction at the lowest cost in time, money and effort	2a	When not more than X% of complains per year are dealt with by higher authority and not more than Y% result in additional costs
	2b			
	2c			
3 I review cost reports	3a	In order to see the variances are either eliminated or explained promptly by my superior	3a	When my superior does not bring to my attention more than X times a year that he was not given accurate, meaningful, or timely information on variances
	3b			
	3c			
4	4a		4a	

Note: When you have more than three purposes to an activity, break down that activity. When the same purpose reappears in three or more activities, combine activities. Standards should cover all the purposes listed for each activity.

Fig. 32.2

Summary

Under this heading of Achievement we have set out numerous ways in which staff can be given the opportunity to achieve. The reason why this is one of, if not the most important of, the motivators is that motivation occurs not just in the striving but in actually getting there.

Imagine if you were standing on top of Mount Everest, just about to plant your country's flag on the peak. You would already have enjoyed the challenge of conquering each problem as it occurred, but imagine the elation of actually having reached the top!

A word of warning, though, the manager must be constantly ready to help the individual recognise and accept new challenges to achieve, or the individual may cease to strive. Similarly, the manager must not forget to recognise the success that has already been achieved, since, for most of us, half the enjoyment of achieving is being recognised as an achiever.

Recognition for achievement

Most managers spend much more time finding fault than offering praise, yet praise is a far more important and successful promoter to doing better in the future. As described in the 'praise sandwich' principle discussed in Chapter 24, if you want people to want to do better, tell them first all the good things they have already done. So this section is about the opportunities and methods to praise people when they have performed well.

Verbal praise

The words 'Congratulations, you have done well' are some of the most attractive words to hear in the language, not just because they offer a boost to the ego but also because they show that the praiser has taken the trouble and interest to seek you out. So, in using those or similar words, the manager not only motivates but also gains the respect of the individual. Take the opportunity whenever it arises, therefore, of telling people how well they have done. It is worth remembering that even though a task may not have been totally successfully achieved, there will always be something that merits a positive comment.

The old principle of 'praise in public, discipline in private' is still valid. So whenever possible issue that praise in public.

This means that sales meetings (see Chapter 37) are a vital opportunity to praise individuals in front of their peers and also to praise collectively. They are not the opportunity to 'tell-off' the individual.

A 'good news' session should, therefore, be included in every sales meeting, so that the manager can not only praise but can also train by asking those who have succeeded how they achieved it, in order that others might learn. As discussed under the 'Increased responsibility' heading (p. 219), sales meetings have other values in the motivation process.

Written praise

Managers should also take the opportunity either to confirm the verbal praise or to praise more formally in writing by memo and letter. Verbal praise is one thing, but to see that praise in writing enhances its importance. The salesperson who receives a letter in the morning congratulating him for success is more likely both to want to succeed and have the confidence to succeed during that and following days. It also enhances the importance of that letter if it is copied to a manager's superior and that fact is noted on the letter.

Occasionally a non-motivation-inclined senior manager will ask why you wasted his time by sending him a copy. Just say politely and gently, 'Well actually I was not trying to motivate you . . .'

Another opportunity for written praise is to use regular bulletins or newsletters to the sales force. The principle here is the same as that employed in local newspapers – the more names you mention, the more copies you sell!

One method which can add to the interest of the bulletin or, in fact, be issued separately, is to use league tables. Some managers shy away from these because the same name always appears at the top of the list, and therefore, the others become demotivated. We would suggest that this is because the league table concept is not being used properly:

(a) The topic of the league table should be changed regularly to highlight a different area. This has the added advantage of reminding people of other areas of importance besides the target.
(b) It should on different occasions be measured in different ways, eg rather than always measuring in terms of numbers, look at percentage of target or greatest improvement over last month.
(c) Do not always publish the total list. Sometimes only publish the top three or the top half of the list.

If you keep changing the league tables, people will continue to be interested, and it gives you the opportunity to praise different people. It also has the hidden advantage that those who like to see themselves at the top and often do because they are high producers will, when finding themselves lower down the order in a different list, strive that much harder to attain the top ratings in that area also.

Incentive/award schemes and performance appraisals

All these apply in this section, since not only do they offer the opportunity but also have the recognition factors built in. The incentive/award schemes have their rewards and titles built in, and performance appraisal has its basic opportunity to praise for past performance.

Field accompaniment

A very real opportunity to praise exists here, but even more important is the fact that field accompaniment is itself a very real recognition of the importance and value of the individual. One of the reasons often stated for experienced salespersons 'going off the boil' is that no one ever takes the trouble or shows sufficient interest to go out with them. This will be discussed more fully in Chapter 33.

Family recognition

For many people their family is the most important thing in their lives, yet many companies fail to capitalise on this as a motivator. In fact, some companies ignore this through a feeling within management that for anything to be more important than the job is almost unbelievable, if not a sin!

More companies are now realising how important family motivation can be, and are trying to encourage family participation. The letter of praise, for example, is a good way for salespersons to show their families how they are doing.

Among the other ideas under this heading are:

1 Birthday cards to members of the family.
2 Incentive prizes directed to the family.
3 Inviting wives/husbands to attend the sales meetings on occasion, particularly if that meeting can be combined with a social event in the evening.
4 When the sales staff are going to have to spend a period of more intense effort or longer hours than normal, a note to their family acknowledging this.

Reward

We have already pointed out the problems attached to reward in Chapter 29, but it must not be overlooked that reward, whether it be financial or non-financial, is in itself a form of recognition. As important as the reward itself, however, is the method chosen to announce or present that reward. A prize presented to an individual at a full sales meeting is likely to have double or triple the effect of something sent through the post.

Meaningful and interesting work

We are fortunate that the majority of jobs in selling are much more likely to be both meaningful and interesting than those in many other types of work. Even so, a lot can still be done to improve this element – to add to the interest, to widen the range of activities.

It is worth noting that the cross-over effect between work itself and responsibility is almost universal. Anything we do to add to the job interest is likely to increase the responsibility, and anything we do to increase the responsibility is likely to make the job more interesting.

Improve job content

A review of the job description often points to areas where activities which should be performed by the salesperson are being performed by others. It is also common to find that managers have kept to themselves what are really portions of the salesperson's activity, either because they (the sales managers) enjoy doing these things or because they do not trust the salesperson to do them properly. If it is because of the former, there is no excuse; if it is because of the latter, there is still no excuse, since they should train the salesperson to ensure that he/she can perform those tasks.

Over and above the review of the job description the manager should continue to search for activities that will make that particular job in selling more interesting.

Ensure variety

This needs almost no clarification, since the more variety there is in the task a person performs, the easier it is to retain interest in that performance and its quality.

Special projects

As soon as the person can perform a task well, the manager should start to consider what special short-term or one-off tasks that person can undertake. These tasks both stretch and develop that person, and give him fresh interest in his routine activities when he returns to them after a break. As examples of such special projects, one should consider the following:

Field-training assignments
Most people actively enjoy helping others, and in so doing learn themselves. Field-training others, therefore, can be very motivational. It also helps the manager, since few have sufficient time to spend on the vital activity of field training. A word of warning, though – beware of the 'learning from Nellie' approach, discussed in Part 4. Before allowing anyone to field-train others, make sure that person uses the standard, successful selling techniques and has been taught how to field-train properly.

Manning and managing show/exhibition stands
Here is another opportunity for introducing variety into the salesperson's life, since exhibitions are a different environment from normal selling assignments and to an extent require different selling techniques. Before carrying out this type of assignment, the salesperson should, of course, be made aware of that different environment and taught these different techniques. The management responsibility should be shared out, and not always given to the same person.

Marketing assignments
The sales staff are one of the single best sources of marketing information available, yet most companies fail to make use of this source, which is daily updated in the marketplace. One way to capitalise on this asset and to bridge the gap that often exists between marketing and sales departments is to give selected sales people short-term marketing projects to fulfil, eg marketing surveys and new product test launches.

Special selling assignments
Often companies need short-term special activities performed. Examples include reducing an over-stocked item or clearing end-of-life stocks. Most companies tend to spread these activities throughout the sales force, where often they are seen as negative interruptions to other activity.

Depending on the size of the assignment, it may well be best to treat this as a one-person project on the basis of the ability to perform. In that way a recognition of ability and an opportunity for the salesperson to do something different from the norm are combined.

Double calling

One thing that companies often fail to recognise or discuss is the loneliness of the selling job. You could, of course, say that sales people are with people all the time, but most sales people actually spend less than 1½ hours per day with buyers and these buyers are on the other side of the fence. Is it any wonder then that many sales people are inclined to do too many comfort calls on those people with whom they are friendly or where they can be sure of a welcome and a cup of coffee?

One way to help overcome this loneliness is to suggest that sales staff spend a day or two working in pairs occasionally. This is particularly appropriate where each has strengths that the other can learn. For example, putting together the salesperson who is good at selling benefits with another who is good at closing can help each of them. Another way to help overcome this problem is to have the occasional 'blitz sell'.

Blitz selling

In this case a larger group, perhaps the whole team, is brought together to work for a week separately but close enough to meet each other in the morning before work, at lunchtime and at the end of the afternoon. A vacant territory or the launch of a new product is often a good opportunity for this activity.

The elements of immediate competition, of close communication and growth of team spirit are all important assets of this activity. Equally, since each person has a relatively small area to work, they will be more likely to call on places which would otherwise be missed, which leads to business expansion. Another advantage is that the manager has three opportunities a day of holding short sales meetings and the opportunity of accompanying every one of the sales people during that period.

While not every type of selling lends itself to this activity, the advantages of a well-run blitz can be high. Two notes of warning, however:
(a) It *has* to be well run, which means ensuring that the territory divisions work and that all other logistics are carefully prepared.
(b) Because of the excitement that can be and is generated in this type of event, the manager has to ensure both that people are restrained from either exerting too much pressure or over-selling, and that the person who follows up the blitz has to be highly capable.

Delegation

That delegating properly is an art is often misunderstood. We believe that it is also quite difficult to get it right, which is why we deal with it in some depth in Chapter 9.

Many people who delegate do so simply to reduce their own workload. While this is important enough, equally important is the opportunity it gives to the person who receives that delegated task to have a more interesting, more responsible job to do.

Invite participation in decision-making

Often we hear managers say 'We wish our people were more interested in what goes on in the rest of the department and the rest of the company'. We would suggest that this lack of interest usually stems from the fact that 'our people' only understand what they themselves do.

To overcome this problem, first of all explain more about what goes on and then ask for their opinion and suggestions. Everyone has a contribution to make in both his own and other spheres, but if not asked, no one is likely to offer. If we start by allowing and inviting people to participate more, make more of the decisions that affect their own activity, then see what other contribution they can offer, we may well be in for a pleasant surprise.

Job rotation

One reason why people do not perform certain parts of their job well is because they fail to see the importance of those tasks, and the effect that their poor performance has on other people's jobs. One example is the salesperson who is a poor or slow reporter, who does not realise the trouble he/she is giving to the order or sales administration clerks. However, you rarely find a former clerk reporting poorly, since he knows the detrimental effect it has.

A number of companies are, therefore, introducing the policy of allowing people where possible to experience at first hand the linking of jobs to their own. This experience is kept short (often a week), but as well as being instructive, it often forges bonds of great value between people of different departments. Sometimes technical expertise makes it impossible for that experience to be totally first hand, but even watching someone else perform his job can be highly valuable.

Another aspect is for people to exchange jobs for short periods. In spite of resistance to the idea, more and more sales managers are swapping salesmen from different territories for, say, a month, with very encouraging results.

The resistance often comes from genuine concern about such things as the importance of the customer–salesperson relations that have been built over a period and the extra costs. However, swapping the salesperson who has a rural territory for a month with another who has an urban territory can have very positive results for both the people and the territories concerned.

Increased responsibility

While responsibility may not cause the same degree of high level motivation as say recognition or achievement, its effects are likely to be enjoyed over a far longer period.

Increased authority

More and more companies are now talking about the need for the salesperson to be the manager of his/her territory. Unfortunately, though, in a lot of these companies they are only paying lip-service to the idea. If they really want the sales person to manage, then they have got to give that person the authority so to do. Let us examine one or two areas of that authority.

1 The power to negotiate

In many companies different strata have different negotiating powers, eg the salesperson can go to 5 per cent, the area manager to 10 per cent, and so on up to the managing director, who can give the product or service away! This is wrong. The salesperson should have the total power to negotiate the level of discount on his/her own territory.

Some managers, when this idea is put to them, immediately say 'But they will give it away'. Of course they will, if they have not been taught how to negotiate, if they have not been shown how much extra you have to sell in order to overcome the effects of discounting.

The rule again, therefore, is train first, then give the opportunity and the power to act.

2 The power to settle complaints

In any business things sometimes go wrong, and when that happens, the quicker the problem is solved, the shorter is the memory of the person who has had to complain. Often, though, so many different people come into the settling of a complaint that it takes a long time to settle it. Equally, by going through such a number of people, the opportunity for further problems is increased.

Give the salesperson the authority to settle complaints and the procedure is considerably shortened. In addition, you are complementing and adding to the relationships between buyer and seller, because the buyer sees the salesperson as a problem-solver. It may be necessary to put an upper cost limit on this power, but this should be avoided if possible.

These are just two areas in which the salesperson's authority can be increased but there are many others, eg the self-setting of targets (p. 204).

Deputising for the manager

Many managers tend to delegate upwards when they are going to be away from the sales team on holiday, etc. Why not start delegating down, so that people in the team who are looking to be promoted can have the opportunity of practice and the enjoyment of responsibility?

Special projects

These have been dealt with earlier (see p. 217).

Greater say in sales meetings

Sales meetings have already been mentioned under Recognition (p. 216) and will be dealt with more fully in Part 7, but in the context of giving more responsibility, one aspect of them is relevant here. No one ever said that the manager has to do *all* the presenting at sales meetings, and, in fact, we are by no means certain that the manager has to run every meeting of the sales team.

The more say an individual has in the running of a meeting the more he will enjoy it, and the more he will retain the information and act afterwards, so that the manager should whenever possible delegate parts or even whole meetings to others who are qualified to do so. We can even make a strong case for allowing the unqualified to contribute to meetings in the following way: someone who has a particular weakness will work very much harder to improve if asked to make a presentation at the next sales meeting on that subject.

Of course, the sales manager may well have to help in preparing the presentation and will certainly have to ensure that before the meeting the presentation is first made to him/her. This is to guarantee that the information given to the meeting is correct and to ensure that the individual is lifted rather than diminished by the experience.

Acting as representative of sales department on internal committees and acting as representative of company on external bodies

As business becomes ever more complex and as more companies realise that they have, in order to succeed, to become one organisation rather than numerous departments, it is inevitable that more committees are formed both internally and externally. Some managers are now finding themselves spending almost more time sitting on committees than they are managing. Spread this responsibility around among the members of the sales force, since it not only adds to their responsibility and interest but also capitalises on their experience and ability.

Growth and advancement at work

Under this heading we are looking for ways in which we can help those who want to advance and grow to do so. One temptation is to think only in terms of promotion. With many sales forces either not getting larger or even growing smaller, this is dangerous since there are in many companies less opportunities to promote now than perhaps there used to be. This heading, therefore, is concerned not just with promotion but also with helping people to advance and grow within the job they are currently performing.

Training in current job

Hertzberg said that motivation is a function of ability and a function of the opportunity to use that ability, and that training was therefore one of the most important variables that a manager has to motivate staff. It is certainly true that the more salespersons are able to sell, the more they enjoy selling and, therefore, the more motivated they are. So one of the most vital aspects of any manager's job is to train the staff, not just initially but also continuously, so that they can advance and grow in the job they are performing (see page 107).

Development training for the next job

Someone once said that if you want to be promoted yourself, develop two people to do your job as well or better than you can. Some managers are afraid to do this because of the spectre of redundancy, but those that discount this spectre find their own jobs more fulfilling and the staff they are developing more motivated and, therefore, productive.

It is vital though, if you are training someone for the next job, that you allow them the opportunity to practise those skills or they will become frustrated and may eventually leave. The old saying 'use it, or lose it' is also true.

Counselling

Development counselling, of which formal appraisal is a part, is about helping people to prepare for and see the opportunities in the future. The counselling interview is also a practical approach to dealing with staff problems.

Deciding to hold a counsel interview

Where a situation is wrong, and is obviously going to get worse, take the positive decision to hold a counsel interview. It is the only way. Face the problem – do not simply hope it will go away. Prepare for the interview by brushing up on the interviewee's background.

Give the interviewee a general idea of what the interview will be about when arranging the time and place to have it. When that time comes, make certain that the meeting will not be disturbed in any way.

Getting the facts

Ask questions to get the other person talking. It may be that the answers to some of the questions are already known. That does not matter. What is being looked for is a key, something to unlock and let out the real cause of the worsening problem. Get the person to unburden him/herself.

Agreeing cause of problem

Once the interviewee has admitted there is a problem, and given the details, the counsellor can start to rebuild the situation. Only after such a frank discussion can the real causes of the problem be agreed. This agreement is essential to a cure. Without it there is a strong likelihood that it is effects, not causes, that are being dealt with.

Allowing interviewees to speak for themselves

In any situation like this it is much better for the interviewees to solve their own problem. So let them talk and provide their own suggestions for what should be done. That way they will have a far higher level of commitment to taking action.

Deciding the course of action
The counsellor has to listen to the interviewee's suggestions for putting the situation right. Between them they can then agree what should happen. This is a vital stage. Always establish a programme for the course of action to be taken.

End with positive agreement
The counsellor and interviewee have thoroughly aired the problem – and agreed what to do. At the end the interviewee will feel much better. This is partly due to having had the opportunity to talk, and partly to being able to see an end to the trouble. Make sure that any counsel interview ends up with positive agreement – a commitment from both sides to solving the problem.

As managers, we are responsible, primarily, for those under us. We should know them well and keep an eye open for a problem area. As soon as we recognise the symptoms of an approaching problem, we should decide to hold a counselling interview.

Career structure and path

Development counselling is of little value if there is no opportunity for the individual to develop and grow. A clearly defined career structure and path (while it is in reality a hygiene factor) is, therefore, vital, since it is no good looking at a map if there is nowhere to go.

Promotion

Where the person is qualified and the opportunity arises, we can obviously promote him or her. However, care should be taken in the way this is done, since two emotions follow each other very rapidly when someone is promoted – elation at this recognition of ability which has been struggled for and achieved, and fear whether one can cope. Promoting someone, therefore, has to be carefully handled and will certainly require able counselling to ensure that the person swims rather than sinks.

Senior managers often quote the 'Peter Principle' which states, 'In a hierarchy every employee tends to rise to his level of incompetence', when discussing someone they have promoted who has failed. Perhaps what they should quote more often is the other 'Strafford/Grant Principle', which asks 'Who failed him?' So often the failure is the fault of the superior rather than the person promoted.

Summary

In this chapter we have looked at numerous different motivational ideas. In fact, as each of these ideas can lead to many different specific action points, there are probably hundreds, if not thousands, of different ways the manager can motivate as a result of this chapter.

We would recommend that the manager reviews Fig. 32.1 constantly, to see what can be done to help the motivation of staff and specifically whenever he/she has a member of staff who needs motivating.

It is worth reminding oneself of the definition of motivation: that which impels a person to action because that person *can* act, has the *opportunity* to act and, therefore, wants to act. It is also worth remembering the fact that motivation is an individual process which needs to be continuously monitored in order to obtain the best results that people are able to give us.

33. Coping with Troughs and Levels

Troughs

With the techniques already discussed, motivating can be relatively straight-forward. Perhaps a more difficult problem is to try to stop certain people from becoming demotivated.

There are certain inherent factors in selling which are inclined to contribute to demotivation. Negative hygiene factors and loneliness have already been discussed in previous chapters. In addition, selling can be extremely discouraging. The best planned sales presentation still sometimes results in a 'No', because failure is inherent in the job of selling. Of course, success is there to compensate for failure, but inevitably sales people usually get more 'Nos' than 'Yeses'.

It is easy when the series of 'Nos' become too long for doubt in one's own ability to chip away confidence. When this happens, some sales people have the ability to work on through or even increase activity to reach the successes; others enter a trough.

The 'trough' is a state of mind in which a salesperson loses drive and self-confidence and starts to believe 'Nos' are personal, not simply refusals to buy the product. As a result, their sales presentations become less effective, which in turn leads to even lower sales. The spiral down can in some cases become so steep that the salesperson sees no alternative but to leave the company or even leave selling.

Troughs can appear at any stage in a salesperson's career, but are normally more destructive to the inexperienced, since the more experienced are likely to have fought through troughs previously.

Fighting the trough

A good sales manager can help to overcome this problem in the following ways.

Recognising it early
Most things are easier to deal with if they are caught early enough. Two things aid the manager here.

Firstly, a good daily reporting system gives early warning of a downturn in performance (see Chapter 26). If the manager acts early enough, the trough will not develop.

Secondly, constant contact between manager and salesperson will give clues to a pending trough situation before it is reflected in results. This contact is even more vital for companies where the sales process is so protected that reports can only reflect activity rather than results.

In this latter situation it is vital that the manager conducts a specific weekly telephone discussion with each salesperson to allow them to boast about the good things that have happened and discuss problems. As a spin-off, the manager can pass good ideas from one person to another.

Make sure the salesperson keeps score

Knowing the normal ratios of call to success can help the salesperson put the failures into proportion. If it normally takes Salesperson A five calls to hit a sale and he/she has just had their eighth 'no', then they have to be rapidly approaching two successes. In addition, knowing the existing ratio makes it easier for the manager to suggest striving to improve that ratio.

Field training

When the manager sees signs of a developing trough, he/she should immediately react by field training. This field training should concentrate on rebuilding the person's confidence and on making selling 'fun'.

Take the pressure off

Often the salesperson in a trough can be trying *too hard* to climb out of it. Trying too hard can be as non-effective as not trying hard enough and, therefore, if this is the problem, the manager should for a short period act to reduce the pressure. 'Let's go out for today not to get sales but just to create some leads for later follow-up' can often result in a bumper sales day because the pressure has been removed.

Give a helping hand

Sometimes a trough in the inexperienced salesperson is either caused by or made worse by a specific area of skills need. Train to overcome the need.

Try to give the salesperson a success by either providing a qualified lead or by creating a sales situation in which that person can win.

Job rotation

This may well be the right time to arrange a short-term swap on to another territory, as discussed in Chapter 32. The salesperson will enjoy a change of scene and change of faces, and may well spot selling opportunities missed by the regular salesperson, which will boost his/her ego.

Double calling

This may also help (see p. 218).

Levels

A 'level' is a period during which the salesperson is satisfied with the current level of achievement and is happy to cruise at this pace. Unlike the salesperson in a trough, who would do anything not to be there, the levelled salesperson is quite content at this pace. He/she feels that additional sales are not worth the additional effort and, therefore, contests and awards have little or no effect.

The long-service salesperson is the most likely candidate in this context. A person who has worked hard in the past to develop the territory, he has not the same financial needs any more (mortgage paid off, children at work) and is now working just hard enough to not become subject to management static! This level of activity may still keep him/her at a relatively high level of results but it is well below that individual's capacity.

Equally, younger sales people can become content with current performance and exhibit the same symptoms.

Management action to motivate

While the answers are likely to be found in Chapter 32, 'The Motivators', we would specifically recommend the following.

For the levelled younger salesperson
If more than 10 per cent of the young sales people in the team are levelled, it would suggest shortage of one or more of the following:

(a) Challenge.
(b) Competition.
(c) Incentive – financial or more likely non-financial.
(d) Field training.
(e) Immediate feedback from a good reporting system.
(f) Clear and realistic objectives.
(g) Clarified promotion opportunities.

For the levelled longer-service salesperson
This is a more difficult problem since it is likely that this salesperson had already had most of the motivational concepts tried on him by previous managers. These salesmen have 'seen it all before'.

Another problem in dealing with these cases is that sometimes managers, particularly younger ones, have their own attitude problem to contend with. This can be caused either because the manager cannot understand why anyone should want to remain a salesperson all his life or by fear of the salesperson's greater experience.

As regards the manager's inability to understand, it should be recognised that not everyone wants promotion. It makes just as good sense to be a career salesperson as it does to be a career family doctor.

As for the fear element in the manager, that has to be recognised as a lack of self-confidence, and it needs to be remembered that just because others have failed to get the best out of this person, the current manager has not necessarily to fail also.

Certainly companies should recognise that this career salesperson may be levelled but may still be one of their most vital assets.

One of the major reasons that experienced sales people become levelled is that managers have stopped giving them the necessary attention. 'Salesperson X does not need field training because he is successful' is an all too often expressed view of managers, just as 'I need to spend my time with the inexperienced or problem cases' is so often said. Yet these views are both disastrous and do not make economic sense.

Firstly, everyone needs the attention that good field training can give and, secondly, a 1 per cent improvement from a good salesperson will probably produce more results than a 10 to 15 per cent improvement from a weak or inexperienced salesperson. So rule one of handling the levelled experienced person is to give them equal field training attention as you give the rest of the team.

The answer, however, has to lie within Fig. 32.1, The Motivators. Everyone has a 'Hot Button' somewhere; it is just a question of finding it!

There follows a list of suggestions for motivating levelled sales people. While most of the ideas will work in any organisation, you will obviously need to discount the inappropriate.

Also, obviously, you will not want to use all of them at once or even necessarily regularly. Find the one or ones that work for the individual you are concerned about, then implement them.

Motivators for levelled salespeople

1. Make the job more interesting

(a) More often than not the levelled salesperson is a long-serving, experienced member of the sales force so use that experience by making the person a specialist in a product, or a market sector with the title and responsibilities that are appropriate.
(b) Use the person as a trouble-shooter for difficult accounts, special situations or indeed salespeople who are in a trough.
(c) Involve the salesperson in recruitment activity.
(d) Give the person training responsibilities for new staff but first of all train the trainer.
(e) Use the person as a pioneer for new products or as part of a pioneer sales force.
(f) Have the person act as the company expert on certain types of customer, on important competitors or a product group or line whose advice and information can be requested by any person in the company.
(g) Get the person to carry out special marketing or research assignments.
(h) Get the person to plan and run a sales meeting or make a special presentation at one.
(i) Increase the person's personal authority in conducting his/her job, such as negotiating power.
(j) If you have an annual national sales meeting or conference make him/her the co-ordinator.
(k) Recognise the person's experience and ability by involving them in higher level decision making.
(l) Ask for the person's help in producing the company news letter or sales force bulletin.

2 *Make more recognition opportunities*

(a) Invite the person to participate in or run exhibitions/trade shows.
(b) Create a management advisory group and invite him/her to be part of it.
(c) Interview him/her and print success stories in the newsletter/bulletin.
(d) Invite him/her to speak at the next annual conference.
(e) Use family recognition by sending birthday cards to his/her family or gifts to their partners in recognition of special activities.
(f) If you have operating units abroad consider sending him/her on a visit to them.
(g) Get the managing director to invite him/her to lunch or another social occasion.
(h) Create a club for senior long-serving company staff and invite him/her to be a member.
(i) Offer special status by paying for the individual's memberships in professional or trade assocations.
       In short, make this person feel important.

3 *Provide opportunities for self-growth*

(a) Suggest specialist courses of study for membership of a professional body such as the Institute of Marketing.
(b) Invite the person to attend externally run high-level seminars and training courses.
(c) Counsel the person on the opportunities available within your company.

4 *Increase hygiene*

(a) More liberal expense account.
(b) Create a share-purchase plan.
(c) Reduce unnecessary administration.

34. *Who Motivates the Motivator?*

One question often asked by managers is 'Who motivates me?' The answer in a forward-thinking company is obviously 'the manager's manager', but, in practical terms, it is fair to say that the higher a person goes the less other people think they need motivating.

Of course, this is not true. All of us need motivating by something or someone, but in most respects the manager is going to have to rely on self-motivation to do the job.

Self-motivation is obviously equally important and helpful to the salesperson. Some people would suggest that you either are or are not self-motivated. They hold the view that if you are, think yourself lucky; if you are not, accept it.

We believe that anyone can become self-motivated, provided they develop sufficiently important goals in life – goals that will provide overpowering reasons to act. The problem is that most people do not have even short-term objectives, let alone long-term ones. So if we want to become self-motivated, what have we got to do?

Checklist for self-motivation

Stage 1   Take thinking and planning time and really honestly ask ourselves some questions:

    (a)   What are we really looking for in our business and social life?
    (b)   What do we really enjoy about life?
    (c)   What are the really important things in life to us?

Each time we decide on an answer, the vital thing we have to do is *write it down and keep it in a folder that we can refer back to.*

Stage 2   Having decided what are our major goals in life, we must also ask ourselves:

    (a)   Why are these things so important? Only by so doing can we find out about ourselves, and we shall also help to answer question (b).
    (b)   How do we achieve each of our major goals?

Each time we decide on an answer to why these things are important, the vital thing we have to do is *write it down and keep it in a folder that we can refer back to.*

Stage 3   However, because our major goals are normally long-term, before we can answer the question 'How?' we have to break each of our major goals down into a number of 'step goals' and relate each step goal to the maximum time we will allow for its achievement. Then we can see a pathway to achieving our major goal relative to the time taken. The reason for this is the maxim 'That which you can conceive and believe, you can achieve!'

Our major goals may well be of such an 'aim-high' order, that taken as a whole, they are difficult to believe and, therefore, seem impossible to achieve. So, to achieve our major goal we have to be able to move towards it by going past a number of smaller, highly believable and highly achievable milestones.

In this way we can not only monitor and measure our progress but, more important than this, the sense of satisfaction we gain in achieving our step goals will act as self-motivation to help us carry on to achieve the next step goal, because success breeds success.

As we decide on our step goals the vital thing we have to do is *write it down and keep it in a folder that we can refer back to.*

Stage 4   The next stage after deciding on our step goals is to ask ourselves how we are going to achieve each of these Step Goals. Look at this question in terms of the methods, tools, techniques which we have to employ to achieve our aims. They normally can be defined in terms of learning and practice.

As we answer this question we again *write it down* . . .

Stage 5   Now we have to decide when we can honestly expect to achieve the first step in our pathway. How long will it take to get to the next milestone? etc.

This stage is important because without a time factor our plans become vague and descend to the 'this year, next year, sometime never' variety.

Once we have decided, we must *write it down* . . .

Stage 6   The final stage of our self-motivation plan is to ask two more questions:

(a)   Who can assist us to reach our major goals by helping us achieve our step goals?
(b)   Where can we get help when we need it?

What have we done by following this process?

1   We have given ourselves an action plan for our future life, because, without planning, success is only achieved by chance and is normally not really appreciated because we are not aiming for it.

Also when we 'trip' over success, we have missed one of the major motivational factors that will accelerate us to our next goal – *motivation through achievement of objectives*.

2 We have decided what we want out of life, which will help us put into the right perspective the negative events that sometimes happen

3 We have given ourselves a set of aim-high but believable and achievable objectives.

4 Most important of all, we have given ourselves a great many 'Hot Buttons'. These are mental buttons which, when pressed, will give us an overriding, overwhelming reason to get into *action*.

Remember the following:

(a) Don't be afraid when setting major goals to aim really high. The main difference between the man who climbs Mount Everest and the man who goes rock climbing is that the first aims *higher*.

(b) Don't be afraid to adjust your action plan upwards, but always avoid adjusting your major goal downwards. It may take you longer to achieve one or more step goals than you had planned, but if you keep your eyes on the summit, ie the major goal, you will be drawn towards it. If you find you are reaching your step goals too quickly, you have not aimed high enough. Reset your goals higher.

(c) As soon as you have decided on your action plan, start to act *immediately*! Delay can be fatal.

You may be asking yourself, 'Why all this business of writing it down?' There are three reasons:

1 The act of writing it down helps to clarify the mind and confirm the action.

2 It is too important to leave to memory.

3 When things go wrong in life, reviewing the folder both reminds us what is really important to us and helps to reduce what may seem overwhelming to its proper perspective.

PART SEVEN

Communications

Human beings have inhabited this planet for about 10 million years, give or take about 5 million years, depending upon the particular authority to which you subscribe. The nature and scale of time makes this quite a reasonable estimate, a discrepancy of plus or minus 5 million years representing a mere moment on the true time-scale.

These millions of years of experience and progress, enhanced by the incredible human computer located between our ears, should have made us good communicators. We have had a few million years to practise and improve. It must be one of the few areas in which mankind has made relatively little progress – in fact, it may have been retrogressive.

We live in an age of so called high technology and we can blame this for our communication problems. At least we can hide behind the high technology screen.

This is ludicrous. It is doubtful if this atomic age is any more technological than the era of the invention of the wheel, or the industrial revolution, relatively speaking.

One thing for sure, it is different. Previously it was 'what man can do' that governed our existence. For thousands of years the great philosophers and teachers tried to show their fellow human beings how life on this planet could be improved. For most of that time man's control of the environment has been limited by what he could observe others actually doing: that is, simple physical, mechanical observation and then copying, hopefully with some improvement. Written and verbal communication have improved over the last few hundred years, with a consequent improvement on the evolutionary development processes.

As we approached the turn of the century, however, there was a drastic change. We were no longer governed by what we could do or demonstrate. No longer was it necessary to do small-scale experiments, building small laboratory prototypes and then scaling them up for the real thing. The microscopic approach that had governed development for thousands of years was changing.

The era of Thompson, Rutherford, Bohr and Einstein introduced a significant change. They did not even know what an atom was, yet they were contemplating taking it to pieces. The atom was still the smallest fundamental particle; no one had ever seen one, yet they were calculating energy releases from theoretical atomic thought experiments. The idea that the atom was the ultimate smallest

233

particle of matter – the idea that was given to us by Democritus and the Greek philosophers over 2,000 years ago – had been exploded. Taken apart by the power of human thought. They had named the particles that made up the atom before they had 'observed and identified' them.

The microscopic world had arrived. Will the micro world of the atom be the key to man's prosperity or his destruction?

Within the micro world of the atomic age have come the great developments of the computer, space travel and robotics, and doubtless there are many more fields of development still to come. Yet the change is fundamental. If man thinks of taking an atom to pieces, he does it. If man thinks of living at the bottom of the ocean, he does it. If man thinks of a voyage to the moon, he does it. We are no longer limited by what we can do, demonstrate, copy and improve. It is now more a question of *what man can think?*

Hence change and development in this era is phenomenally fast compared with previous times. All that we mere mortals can do is try to live with the rapid change.

There is an old saying: 'What the mind of man can conceive and believe, He Can Achieve!' This perhaps is the single most important factor that we as managers must communicate to our sales people.

35. *Communicating with your Sales Force*

Your sales force is out on a limb

Frequent, constant, simple, effective, persuasive positive communication from you to your sales force is vital for their survival in the icy climate of the commercial jungle. It is, indeed, an unusual environment. Stimulating, exciting, challenging, rewarding, providing opportunity for growth and development, it still demotivates and destroys more people than it builds and develops.

Unfortunately it carries a lot of passengers who are not performing adequately – those who 'like driving around and meeting people'. They told us that at the interview, remember? Perhaps they would have fulfilled their role better as taxi drivers or bus drivers and could have driven around and met people all day. Alas, that is precisely what some of them are doing and they are not earning their keep!

The solution then is simple, isn't it? All we have to do is recruit the right material in the first instance, then train them thoroughly, wind them up and let them go. Add a few magical management ingredients occasionally, such as motivational shots in the arm, topped up with improved human relations, a dash of job enrichment and job enlargement; then mix in promises of instant promotion carrots, shaken with transactional analysis, body language and all of the other 'flavours of the month' that have made headlines in sales management magazines and text books over the last 25 years. Now you will have created a Molotov cocktail that will clear that icy jungle out there of all known forms of life – including that rare species, the customer.

Sales management is without question one of the hot seats of management. You are literally only as good as yesterday's results. You cannot hide behind your peer group of managers in other departments, such as production, inspection, accounts etc. Your figures and the analysis of those figures are laid out, bare, for all to see. Your figures are the result of the activities of your sales force; if the figures are not ahead of target then you have failed. QED.

What a tangled web we weave and we were not practising to deceive anyone.

Perhaps we could iterate that saying quoted earlier . . . 'What the mind of man can conceive and believe, He Can Achieve!' It really is back to the mind . . . it's all in the mind.

We live today in a Golden Age, an incredible age that man has worked for, dreamed of, for thousands of years; yet now it is here, we somehow take it for granted. It still is an age of wealth and opportunity in spite of the world recession hiccup of the 1980s. We enjoy a very high standard of living, that is a fact, despite the plight of our unemployed millions.

Whatever the definition of management to which you subscribe, it really is a matter of getting your work done by getting other people to do theirs. The central theme of good management must, therefore, be good communication. Whatever the enterprise and whatever the task, whether it is installing new equipment, treating customers fairly, laying off personnel, increasing sales, etc., management decision and management action are necessary. The whole enterprise can only decide, behave and act as its managers do. The enterprise by itself has no real purpose.

Good, simple, effective and persuasive communication is the key to good management, consistent with the requirement of economic responsibility, ie supplying goods and services at the right price, the right quality, the right time, to the right market place and with the best service available.

Good, simple, effective and persuasive communicating is all that we have to do to occupy the hot seat of modern management – successfully? Not quite: there are a few other basic requirements, as we have tried to show in the other chapters, but whatever the topic or function, communication is vital to the good manager. If the sales results are down, then our sales force are not thinking right, and that may mean that we are not communicating the right, simple, effective, persuasive and positive message.

The right message may range from basic human relations, on the one hand, to raw inspirational motivation, on the other, but whatever the requirement it is your responsibility. Somewhere along the line you have failed to convince them of the basic truth that what the mind of man can conceive and believe Man Can Achieve!

Repetitious? Yes, but repetition is an important part of communication.

There is really nothing capricious in the nature of good sales management. You would not conceive and believe an idea that was totally impossible. If, therefore, you tried to 'sell' your team on an impossible scheme, you would almost certainly fail to get their commitment. Failure to achieve the task would be inevitable, for two main reasons:

(a) Their own basic innate intelligence.
(b) Your own words and body language, which would reveal your lack of belief in and commitment to the task.

Our skill in communication affects the way that people think. The way that people think determines their actions. If, therefore, we are not getting the desired results, it is probably because we are not producing the right actions in others, and this may be a direct result of bad communication.

Notice particularly that we are talking about simple, effective, persuasive and positive communication. This is not meant to imply the need for *more* communication. Far from it, there is good evidence to suggest that we have become entangled in these 'flavour of the month' management topics and we are in danger of communicating too much. This is especially true with the computer churning out masses of paper. The happiest people in this situation are the staff of the computer department, justifying their takeover of the whole enterprise through indispensability, and the paper manufacturers celebrating escalating profits year over year. The average salesperson neither needs to know nor wants to know every trivial piece of information. Frankly, it is more likely to demotivate than motivate, and there are too many agencies in the icy jungle doing that already.

A particularly useful acronym, which should hang on every office wall, over your bed (and they should not be the same room), in the front of your presentation kit, etc. is

K I S S

KEEP IT SIMPLE STUPID

or

KEEP IT SWEET AND SIMPLE

The key word is SIMPLE. It is the easiest thing in the world to get too complicated too quickly, and when you do, how much communication is taking place? Very little!

One of the problems is that we sometimes think that we are doing a fantastic job with big words, high technology and fast talking. In truth, all that we may be achieving is an ego massage, and that is of little value because the opinion of the receiver is likely to be rapidly formed and detrimental to the communicator.

The real need in today's management is for improved communication, more effective communication; in fact quite simply better communication. That may mean less communication.

We also need excitement and enthusiasm in our voice when we communicate. Written communication also demands excitement and enthusiasm in the words and style that we use. How many people do you know that meet these requirements?

The next time someone is talking to you in that pathetic low-key manner adopted by many people, ask them if they feel fairly happy and positive. If the reply is yes, then enquire 'Why don't you tell your face?'

We must certainly communicate to our sales force in a confident and enthusiastic manner most of the time. We owe them that much of our effort and energy. If you are in any doubt about what there is to be happy about, just try this short checklist:

(a) You are alive?
(b) You are well?
(c) You have a good job?
(d) You work for a good company?
(e) You market good products or services?
(f) You have a good team?
(g) You have worthwhile family and friends?
(h) You have stimulating, challenging and rewarding problems to solve?

If you are still in doubt, then remember that we live in a Golden Age, a stimulating exciting age, the age of atomic energy, computers, robots, the age that man only previously dreamed of in science fiction, with space travel now a reality and the ancient alchemists' dream of 'turning base metals into gold' a possibility (although not yet commercially economic). Life to you should be a stimulating, exciting adventure, it should never be a bore. There now, that really turns you on, doesn't it!

If any doubt still remains, if perhaps you think that you have too many problems, we have an answer for that too. Thank God for your problems. Pray that He will send you some more. Remember that the only people without problems are dead. (Current research suggest that these people, at least, have no mortal problems.)

Still some slight degree of doubt? Well it's probably your own fault anyway because you don't communicate in a simple, effective, persuasive and positive manner, with excitement and enthusiasm. You have probably created your own negative environment and got the situation you deserve.

Make your people think that you are genuinely glad to have the opportunity of working with and talking to them. It really does matter, you know. The last and greatest most unexplored area of the universe is the human mind. People *react* according to the way in which you act towards them.

People behave according to the way that they think, and you can influence that. It is, on the one hand, an awesome responsibility, but, on the other hand, a stimulating, exciting and rewarding field of activity.

Make your sales people feel that you care about and share their activities by demonstrating that you have empathy, total empathy with their situation, and you demonstrate that by communication. Perhaps the simplest, most effective activity within which to demonstrate such motivation and empathy is field training.

The snag with textbooks is that they always have an all embracing simple answer that is difficult to apply in practice. It would be perfectly reasonable to pose the question: 'If it's so easy, why isn't everyone an instant and continuous success?'

The reason is simple. It is back to the power of the human mind, setting meaningful objectives and tapping human motivation. That is why managers must continuously demonstrate simple, effective, persuasive, positive actions with enthusiasm. Like laughter, enthusiasm is contagious. Some of it will rub off. Some people require more exposure but we must never stop trying. It is a prime requirement of modern management.

Simple, effective, persuasive and positive communication is still difficult to achieve in a business, political or even social sense. Development in simple communication between humans has not kept pace with developments in commerce, engineering, science and technology. The high technology era has made simple communication more difficult. The increasing use of jargon sometimes makes understanding impossible for the uninitiated; the simple law of always using polysyllabic words when monosyllabic words would describe the situation more effectively, and frequently more colourfully, has increased the problem.

Shakespeare did not say 'Males of advancing years characteristically exhibit a significant and inexorable deterioration of the recollective faculty'. He said 'Old men forget' (*Henry V*). Three simple words instead of fifteen more complex words. Which message communicates better?

Or perhaps, 'The design and integration of the individual and machine requirements in this system environment impose severe visual acuity problems', may cause you to think for a few moments to decide that the writer is telling you in plain (but not simple effective English) that 'the pilot will find it difficult to see his instruments'.

Consider this brief extract from a recent advertisement: 'The ability to interface effectively with sales and production management at early stages ensuring on-going purchasing ability'. Take another one: 'After a period of induction training concentrated on user and key account selling, you will assume complete responsibility for the export sales management function, which you will set up against marketing guidelines and report direct to the Managing Director. You will recognise the company commitment to a philosophy of profitable sales attainment consistent with company marketing policy and production capacity'.

What does it all mean and how did we get into this situation? Examination of the second extract suggests:

(a) You will receive induction training – that's good.
(b) You will have complete responsibility but report to the Managing Director. A doubt may occur to you at this point, because you are setting this up within existing marketing guidelines. There may be no room for innovation here; the managing director may stifle any creative thinking.
(c) 'You will recognise the company commitment to a philosophy of profitable sales attainment . . .' Would you want to work for a company that did not want to make a profit.
(d) '. . . consistent with company marketing policy and production capacity'. Does that mean if you sell too many, they will sack you?

Jargon seems to be floating all around us, in the atmosphere. You may think that you are reading this, but nothing could be so simple in the 1980s: you are 'interfacing' with the book. Simple language is out of vogue; we must now play a translation game.

We need 'hands-on' experience of everything working in 'fast moving environments'. We must be totally profit-orientated, self-motivated, dynamic, determined, aggressive, disciplined and dedicated. It doesn't seem to have occurred to the writers that if you possessed all these qualities, you would probably be grossly overqualified for the post advertised, or the most obnoxious egomaniac. How your colleagues would enjoy working with you!

Words like factory, site or working conditions are too crude. Use 'environment', it has a more up-market appeal, or occasionally 'facility', just to ring the changes.

'Function' is another good word to add dignity and status. Frequently it can be omitted from the sentence without any loss of meaning, eg 'experience in accounting function', or, 'the person will be required to develop and implement an effective training function'. The latter means simply 'the person must develop effective training'.

'Experience' is out – you must now have been 'exposed to' various situations. How foolish! An idiot could be exposed for many years to a process or method of operation and learn nothing from his exposure.

Companies are no longer large or small. No one wants to be considered small and how large is large? 'Major' is preferred. 'We are a major manufacturer of . . .' Major has the added advantage of 'importance' being implicit in the word. 'Substantial' is another useful alternative. Furthermore, 'major' or 'substantial' appeal to the enquiring mind. Do they mean 'quite large' or 'larger than small' or 'not quite large enough to be called large' or exactly what? One thing for sure, they are important.

'Limited' is the in word to replace 'small', implying 'select' or specialised. 'This particular model is being demonstrated to a limited number of distributors . . .', or 'The company has a limited number of vacancies for . . .'

We owe it to our companies, our sales force and, indeed, ourselves to protect and simplify our communication. We have all heard some of the examples of gobbledegook used on official government pamphlets, usually explaining something or stating a required action on the part of the reader. That there is ambiguity is obvious, but unfortunately a total lack of understanding is often produced.

Melville said: 'A man of true science uses few hard words and those only when none other will do, whereas the smatterer in science thinks that by mouthing hard words people will think that he understands hard things'. Surely Churchill, one of our greatest orators and master of the simple language proved the point with 'Never in the field of human conflict has so much been owed by so many to so few!' The speech that stirred a nation to action contains eighteen words, four words of two syllables and fourteen single syllable words.

Perhaps this little story of the Hungarian refugee, stated to be a true story, strikes at the heart of the problem.

The Plumber versus Bureaucracy

In the 1970s a plumber discovered that he could clean drains with hydrochloric acid. He was a Hungarian, living in Brooklyn and struggling with the English language – American style. He was so pleased with his discovery that he wrote to the Government in Washington to tell them.

The reply came back: 'The efficacy of hydrochloric acid in this application is indisputable but the toxic residues produced create severe environmental disposal and pollution situations and the electro-chemical attack is incompatible with metallic permanence'.

Overjoyed, he wrote to thank the department for approving his idea and the reply this time was: "There is no doubt about the effectiveness of hydrochloric acid, but the responsibility for the production and disposal of toxic residues is wholly yours and you must be accountable for the excessive corrosion of any metallic components in the vicinity'.

Again joy, and he and his friends wrote to thank the helpful department and they all signed the letter. One week later the third reply came back: 'Tony, don't use hydrochloric acid, it eats hell out of pipes!'

Yes our salesmen are out on a limb. The real problem however, is that some sales managers are busy sawing through the branch to isolate them completely. Since the inevitable fall may mean annihilation and the success of the sales manager depends upon the success of the sales force (individually and as a team), then the only sensible conclusion would be that some managers are hell bent on self-destruction.

Remember, when communicating:

(a) We should not be attempting an ego massage – even a mild one.
(b) KISS, Avoid jargon. It really does pay to KEEP IT SIMPLE SALES-MANAGER.

36. *The Nature of Communication*

The business world has posed many paradoxes. One of the classic paradoxes is that of progress in all fields while real communication has stood still. We said earlier that when the situation demonstrates poor communication, then we can dismiss it on the grounds of high technology. Technology with its endless jargon and ever longer words creates barriers to simple, effective, persuasive communication.

Productivity has been increased in many areas. It had to be improved or companies would have been liquidated. The survivors in the steel industry and car industry are a leaner but healthier lot. Yet with all this progress and productivity there is a weak link in the chain of development. All the increases in productivity have been as a result of technology – bigger, better, faster, machines, greater theoretical and practical understanding leading to improved processes.

The one factor that has not improved is human beings. We are being paid more and more for physically doing less and less. The old cliché 'a fair day's work for a fair day's pay' still holds, but the emphasis has shifted. The norm for the fair day's work is moving inexorably down while the norm for the fair day's pay spirals upwards.

In selling we have no machines to make life easier or improve productivity. But we see our colleagues in production, inspection and accounts working fewer hours in jobs that are being made appreciably easier by machines, and getting paid more for doing less.

This is a bitter pill to swallow. Selling is down to you and me and maintaining a well motivated sales force, and the single most important tool at our disposal is *communication*.

In these situations the demands on us to communicate better are even greater – and we do not. With experience, understanding and technology we should communicate better, but, if anything, communication has taken a backward step. True, we have improved telecommunications – more links, telex machines, satellites, lasers, computers. The technology of bigger, more and faster has grown at a phenomenal pace, but better communication? No!

Now that we have all these sophisticated techniques, the pressure is on – we *must* use them. The real problem is we did not communicate well before they arrived. In truth we are poor communicators. We do communicate too much at times.

Hertzberg asked a classic question: 'Do you think that if you tell your wife (or husband) everything, that she (he) will forgive you?' Of course not. Similarly we can flood our sales force with useless information that certainly does not motivate.

If we tried to build a simple model of communication, our rationale would probably follow these lines:

241

If	wishes to communicate	person
person	————————————————————→	
A	with	B

Person A has to take the following steps:

1 *Thought*. Everything starts with a thought process, ie thinking the message through carefully.
2 *Encoding*. Putting the 'message' into the right code.
3 *Deciding method*. Write, talk, telephone, signal, etc.
4 *Transmitting*.

What happens at the other end of this simple communications process is the following:

1 Receipt of message.
2 Decoding.
3 Thinking about the message.
4 Action – physical or mental, or both.

This model may be oversimplified but it is adequate for our purposes.

If communication is as simple as that, how can it go so terribly wrong? How is it that husbands cannot communicate effectively with wives and vice versa, children cannot communicate effectively with parents and vice versa, unions cannot communicate effectively with management and vice versa, managers cannot communicate effectively with subordinates and vice versa, nations cannot communicate effectively with nations, etc. How does such a simple process get so horribly snarled up?

To know that the problem exists is good. To be able to define that problem and discuss it is even better. But to take positive action to rectify the problem is the best thing of all. Part of the problem lies with the human beings themselves and the other part with the words they use.

Some of the factors combining to cause a breakdown in this simple process are the following:

(a) The message must be carefully thought out, but thinking is hard work, so that the trouble starts with the very first step.
(b) We must have something useful to say.
(c) Person B must have an interest in the message.
(d) The situation must be free from distractions and interruptions.
(e) The code should be carefully selected – Person B may not speak our language.
(f) Prejudices, likes, emotions, reactions all get in the way of simple effective communications. Murphy's Law of Random Perversity says: 'If things can go wrong or be misunderstood, they will, and that which goes wrong will be that which will cause us the biggest problem'. Emotions and prejudices probably account for more miscommunication than all the other factors combined.

One really efficient way to screw up the communication machinery is to pass the message via a third person 'C'.

The words themselves must take part of the blame. Our language does contain anomalies and ambiguities. For example, try this on your sales force at the next meeting. Condition the group by telling them that this is an experiment and you simply want their first (not their second) image of understanding. You don't want them to think about it, you want an instantaneous reaction, a gut feeling. Then print in large capitals for all to see the four letter word LEAD on the flip chart or blackboard. Their reactions will be diverse and interesting: follow the leader, to lead, dog lead, electrical lead, lead in a pencil, the metal lead and so on. Surprisingly few think of a 'sales lead' as their first reaction. One would reasonably expect sales people to, but they do not.

This leads us to a vitally important deduction:

WORDS DON'T HAVE MEANINGS . . . PEOPLE DO!

No matter how the *Oxford Dictionary* defines the words, the only things that matter are:

(i)   What did the communicator really mean?
(ii) What did the receiver understand him to mean?
and
(iii) The message has been passed if (i) and (ii) are identical.

Long explanations often fail to remove the ambiguity of words: for example, 'bath for sale for baby with enamelled bottom' or 'coop for sale for twelve chickens with wheels'. Our model should take care of this, of course, at the very first stage, 'thinking the message through carefully'. Any ambiguity should be identified and removed. Is it always done that carefully?

Long sentences, written or spoken, are generally bad, because they introduce ambiguity. There are exceptions, of course: to a novelist a long sentence is often the most effective way of creating an effect or atmosphere. For business or technical communication the general rule is that shorter sentences make easier reading and better understanding.

One subordinate clause is enough, so try to use only one 'which' or 'this' or 'that' in a sentence. Take the following sentence, for example: 'The strength required in a complex metal forging with reentrant angles must be measured by different methods, depending upon the direction and type of stress and the temperature experienced in practice, and this can become the most important factor'. What does 'this' refer to? Is it the complex design, the type of stress, the temperature or all of them? It is not clear.

One thing that annoys a reader or audience is having to perform unnecessary mental gymnastics to understand badly constructed sentences. Sometimes the ambiguity is such that it is not possible to understand the real meaning of the sentence. This, of course, highlights the need for good questioning – but in the written text the author is not there to answer questions.

Wordiness usually results in confusion. This may arise from circumlocution or tautology. Avoid the following:

1   'In the field of' when 'for' is better.
2   'Due to the fact that' when 'because' or 'as' is better.
3   'At this present moment in time' when 'now' is better.
4   'As well as' when 'and' is better.
5   'In the case of' when 'with' is better.
6   'In actual fact' when 'in fact' is better.
7   'In this respect' when 'therefore' is better.
8   'In so far as . . . is concerned' when 'concerning' is better.

Avoid the unnecessary repetition of 'adequate enough', 'classified into groups', 'connect together', 'descend down', 'divide off', 'final completion', 'necessary prerequisite', 'new innovation', 'first commence', 'inside of' and 'review again'. It is true that impact can be obtained by some repetition, but it should be treated with care.

We are all guilty of breaking the rules in 'some cases', which is itself a case of circumlocution. The word 'case' normally means a box or container but we misuse it in various ways. For example: 'in the case of oil flowing through a pipe', it would have to be a very large diameter pipe to enable a 'case of oil' to flow through it.

The order of words in a sentence can produce ambiguity, and careful construction (syntax) is essential for good communication. Although it may lead to humorous situations, as, for example, with the 'bath for sale for baby with enamelled bottom', it is best avoided. Watch out for the 'hanging participle', ie verbs ending in 'ing', as in 'Being toxic, the chemist was unable to process the material satisfactorily'. Is the chemist toxic? Another example is 'Searching for an appropriate theory to explain the Phenomenon, many became available'. Leave it to Many, therefore, he'll do it. Take a third: 'To perform satisfactorily, the operator must adjust the pressure according to the ambient temperature'. Do we mean for the operator to perform satisfactorily or the equipment?

Perhaps one more example should suffice to ensure that we are never again guilty of creating ambiguity. The story concerns a poor chap rushed to hospital with badly scalded feet. The doctor asked him how he managed to get so severely scalded. The man explained that he was preparing a can of beans for lunch and the instructions on the label clearly stated 'Stand in boiling water for ten minutes'.

There are other problems with communication. One of these is programmed into us by the nature of our upbringing at home and teaching at school. It is demanded of us that we are quick to respond to any question. The next time that you are addressing your sales force direct a simple question at one of them – for example, 'three times five?' There will be a slight pause, then most times you will get the correct answer. How do you know the answer is fifteen? You probably never proved it. If there are more than just a few seconds delay, someone else in the group will be tempted to answer. Check with them, and you will find that they all wanted to answer it. They resisted the temptation because you directed the question at one person and they have matured since their classroom days – but the tendency to want to be first with the answer remains.

You know that the answer is fifteen because you were brainwashed when learning your multiplication tables. You were also brainwashed into the 'must be first with the answer' requirement, or standing in the corner wearing the dunce's hat was your penalty. Don't be alarmed, there is nothing wrong with brainwashing, providing it is being done for good reasons. We are brainwashed continuously. Every event or experience feeds another programme or modification into our computer.

Unfortunately, this tends to produce very rapid responses when faced with any question or problem. Sometimes our response is unnecessarily rapid; we may jump to conclusions without analysing all of the evidence or facts. We make too

Fig. 36.1 *Motorway*

many assumptions and you know the problem with the word assume – ass . . . u . . . me, it makes an *ass* of *u* and *me*. Naturally you must make some assumptions or you would never cross the road, but we tend to make too many because of an innate desire to be first with the answer.

There are other problems too. Look at Fig. 36.1 at a distance of metre or so. It is a poor picture. It lacks detail, clarity and is merely shades of white, grey and black. In spite of its lack of clarity, we have a clear understanding of that picture in a fraction of a second. We see it as a typical roadway scene, nothing odd; the road appears to narrow as it recedes into the distance, but we know that is not so, it is simple perspective. However, there is an unrelated piece of information: superimposed across the road are two white areas. Most people will conclude that the upper white area is longer and wider than the lower white area. That is a false conclusion. They are identical. It is very easy to cause this marvellous computer of ours to malfunction and jump to the wrong conclusions concerning our understanding of a simple event or piece of information being presented to it.

There are two very important conclusions to be drawn about this simple event:

1   We easily jump to the wrong conclusions about quite simple information or events.
2   We see the road 'getting narrower as it goes into the distance'. What distance?

There is no depth, no three-dimensionality in the picture, yet we 'see' an impression of depth. The picture cannot possibly have 'depth'; it is on a flat piece of paper and has only width and height. The impression of depth is entirely ours. We put it there. We are distorting a picture that is flat, and producing a 3D effect because we want to see it that way. We see things the way we want to see them, hear things the way we want to hear them and understand things the way we want to understand them.

We may try to dismiss this fact as trivial. That is another of our problems. Our computer rationalises everything. We may say that this is a simple pictorial illusion, and we have seen such illusions many times.

The truth is, yes we have seen many illusions in the past that fooled us and we will see many more in the future that will fool us. We live in a world of pictures. Those pictures are created by events we see, sometimes by descriptions in words we read or hear. We think in pictures, so our eyes can fool us, our ears can fool us and our brain can fool us. Even in a simple piece of communication we can get 'the wrong picture'.

We live in a world of illusions, created either by poor communication on the part of the sender or receiver, or, unrelated information presented at the same time causing confusion. Consider Fig. 36.2. Most people see some degree of curvature in the picture, two roller surfaces touching. Curvature implies depth and 3D effects. Remember there is no depth in that picture – we put it there. Furthermore, there is not a curved line on the diagram. The shapes are all simple rectangles.

Once again our perception and understanding are influenced by our experiences, and we see things the way we want to see them – even if it is wrong. It is a classic situation of 'Don't confuse me with the facts, my mind is made up'. We all know how infuriating that attitude can be when displayed by someone else. Yet

Fig 36.2 *Chessboard*

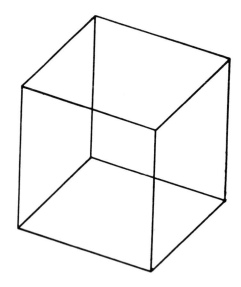

Fig 36.3 *Cube*

we are all guilty.

Perception and comprehension are very personal responses and not always related to intelligence in a direct or simple manner. Consider Fig. 36.3. Pictures are seldom more simple than that. Our perception is a collection of lines in a regular pattern leading to your comprehension of a cube. We immediately give it a depth, a 3D interpretation. Remember the depth is supplied by us, not the picture. There is something else, however: our perception and interpretation of that simple picture changes as we look at it. Sometimes we appear to be looking up at it and other times down upon it. Sometimes what appears to be the front face flips and becomes the back face. What a crazy world!

This simple picture illustrates one of the most important conclusions in communication: The way in which we see and understand something now may be different from our understanding of the identical situation or event sometime later – a few seconds later, a few days later or years later. If our own understanding of a simple event can differ, it is not surprising that other people sometimes 'see' things differently from ourselves.

Miscommunication is a very likely event.

Perhaps it is time for a 'recap' (which, as Penelope Keith says 'always sounds slightly vulgar').

Rules of good communication

1 *Listen.* Most people talk too much. Our objective should be to get others talking, and when they do, *listen*. Listening is hard work – it requires effort to concentrate, analyse what is being said and relate it to the situation.
2 *Ask questions.* (a) to check for understanding and (b) to get others talking. Ask

open questions. Open questions start with who, what, where, when, how, why and which.

3 *Talk with people.* Avoid talking down to them or blinding them with science, which creates barriers to good communication. Too much jargon or too much of our opinion produces emotional responses that are generally unfavourable. That is why asking questions is so important; it helps to break down the barriers.

4 *Look for signals.* Be alert for their responses. What they say, the way they say it, the body language can give vital clues to their understanding or interest. If they do not understand or lack interest, how much communication is really taking place? Very little. We are just talking to ourselves.

5 *Promote two-way communication.* This is essential. One-way communication is bad. Items 1–4 help to promote good two-way communication.

37. Sales Meetings

There are many reasons for holding meetings, no matter what title we give: sales meetings, management meetings, committee meetings, the number of possible titles is enormous. Many of the objectives that we hope to achieve from meetings overlap and the number of objectives are therefore reduced by a rationalisation process. This at least helps to simplify the agenda.

Unfortunately in sales we are obsessed with numbers. Everything must be instantly quantified: how many hours spent on research, on preparation, on planning (route or call), on product knowledge, on knowledge of the whole business, on sales skills and techniques; how many telephone calls for exploration, for appointments, how many appointments obtained; and so the list goes on.

Then we look at ratios: phone calls/appointments, appointments/presentations, presentations/quotations, quotations/sales, etc. The possible combination of each of these can keep us and our computers very 'usefully employed' for hours; and we have not even started on the percentage increases over last quarter, last six months, last year, and projected increases next quarter, next six months, and so on.

Detailed analyses of these figures demand a simple efficient reporting system, a desk computer and a sensible management approach to the figures, and even more meetings to discuss them. The whole thing becomes a vicious circle: more detailed reporting ⟶ more analysis ⟶ more meeting/discussion time ⟶ less time selling ⟶ higher objectives on sales ⟶ greater demands on sales force ⟶ higher percentage increases ⟶ more sales ⟶ more reporting . . .

What a treadmill!

That inexorable process may turn us on as managers – that is why we went into management, remember? – but how many of our sales force are turned on by the treadmill? If the answer is 'all (or most) of our sales force are motivated by this process', then one of the three main possibilities exist:

(i)   We are geniuses at motivation (and there aren't too many about).
(ii) We are incredibly lucky to have a group of real entrepreneurial sales people.
(iii) We are deluding ourselves.

Objectives are important. Quantifiable objectives are also important, so we have to play the numbers game whether we like it or not. There are, however, two objectives of meetings that transcend the quantifiable:

1 To achieve simple, effective, persuasive and positive communication. No apologies for reiteration. It is after all the vital requirement of management and, therefore, worthy of repetition.

2 Make everyone glad that they attended our meeting today. How often have we attended meetings and, when the meeting ended, walked out thinking 'What a waste of time! I missed a day's (or two) sales production to attend that!' or 'What was all of that about? I feel more like going home than facing prospects', etc.

  If meetings should achieve anything at all, it should be motivation of the sales force, and unless we achieve the two objectives stated above, our chances of achieving the third objective are very small. The next important objective, therefore, becomes:

3 To achieve motivation of others towards the desirable goal.

There are, of course, many other objectives of meetings. They too are important but our chances of achieving them are determined by the degree to which we achieve the three objectives stated above. Other objectives may be:

(a) To inform.
(b) To educate.
(c) To inspire.
(d) To plan.
(e) To discuss and analyse past performance and decide a suitable plan of action.
(f) To increase turnover (with suitable action plan).
(g) To alter sales mix (with suitable action plan).
(h) To discuss and analyse cost ratio and plan accordingly.
(i) To discuss and plan new product launch.
(j) To discuss and plan promotion of various products.
(k) Development of new accounts (with suitable action plan).
(l) Development of existing accounts (with suitable action plan).
(m) To discuss any policy, territory or company changes, with specific plans for implementation.
(n) Any management activity that requires reporting to the sales force and plans for any changes that may arise.
(o) Any change of operations required because of poor performance in certain areas or with specific products, with corrective plans agreed.

Many of the topics can be classified into relatively few management areas, and this helps to streamline the agenda, particularly with the all embracing 'any other business' as the last item. But frequently there are too many topics on the agenda to be adequately covered in the time allocated for the meeting. This immediately produces the 'quart in the pint pot syndrome' and leads to annoyance and frustration.

  The agenda requires careful thought. Some managers use a standard agenda for each meeting, and although this is not the best method, it can work if proper thought and planning are put into it.

  Perhaps a few check questions should be honestly answered before we rush headlong into the next meeting.

(i)   Specifically what topics do we want on the agenda?

(ii)   Are they sufficiently important to warrant a meeting?

(iii)   Is there a real need for this meeting, is it simply to satisfy our manager's ego, or is it simply 'time we got the lads together again'?

(iv)   How many hours of preparation time will we personally commit to ensure that this meeting is a success.

There may well be many other questions that will occur to us from time to time when arranging certain specialist meetings; we should add them to our checklist, pin them on the wall and use them. The four proposed above will suffice to answer a vital question of distinction:

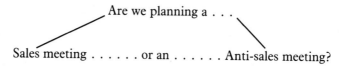

Are we planning a . . .

Sales meeting . . . . . . or an . . . . . . Anti-sales meeting?

We must answer this question honestly, because most meetings fall into the second category. Since it makes no sense to hold anti-sales meetings, what can we do about it?

Perhaps we could add the following suggestions to our checklist:

1   Choose a suitable venue and date as far in advance as possible, and advise everyone accordingly.

2   Be fair in your choice of location: try to make it convenient or central for all. This is not always possible, so a change of venue 'to be seen to be fair' is advisable.

3   Try to arrange the venue out of the office if the budget permits. The telephone and those urgent 'must see Fred' requests can ruin a meeting.

4   Inspect the venue yourself if you have not been there.

5   Give careful thought to the agenda. It must be in line with the objectives that you set. Have a theme for the meeting, and display it as a main heading on the wall, on the flip chart and on the copies of the agenda. Refer to it frequently throughout the meeting, as it should relate to one of the main objectives of the meeting.

6   Circulate everyone with a detailed working agenda at least one week and preferably two weeks (or more) before the meeting. A working agenda is not simply a list of topics: it states why the topic is there, who are expected to make major contributions and gives them a time allocation to state their case. This way everyone has plenty of time to prepare their contribution.

When we write to them with the agenda venue and date, what vital thing should we try to achieve? SELL IT! Yes, *sell* the idea of the *meeting*. Talk up the value of meetings. Point out how beneficial the individual contributions will be. Talk about positive constructive discussion. We must tell those who are coming that we are looking forward to getting their ideas and commitment.

It may take a little time, particularly if previous meetings have always produced the response 'I travelled 100 miles to attend that?' It does work.

We are sales managers, aren't we? Well then, we should be able to *sell* this *service* to them.

7   Encourage the delegates to prepare visuals to support or illustrate any contribution that they make. Simple overhead projector transparencies or flip chart sheets are usually adequate.

8   Arrange the agenda sequence carefully. A meeting *must* finish on a high note.

9   Be ruthless on time allocation. Urgent items are frequently not very important and must be guillotined.

10 'Any other business' – eliminate it from your agenda. If it is not possible, then put it first, with a severe time restriction. Most times 'any other business' is an excuse for bad planning. Nothing should be on that agenda that you have not had a chance to consider beforehand. Anyway, most AOB sessions become negative, griping sessions, and that is something we do not want at a sales meeting. That should be reserved for management or anti-sales meetings.

11 Insist upon positive constructive participation, and encourage it throughout the meeting by prompting with questions. This way we can encourage the shy or reticent.

12 Put coffee, lunch and tea breaks on the agenda, and discourage alcohol at lunchtime. We should not try to win the popularity poll by bribery with alcohol.

13 Put in a film for change of face and pace if possible.

14 Allocate 50 per cent of your agenda time to *training*. This should be mainly sales-orientated training rather than product training, which should be done at other times.

Again we could go on adding to the list but we have enough points here to drastically improve most sales meetings.

Let us examine a few of the implications.

(a)   No AOB. This is not an attempt to stifle discussion or sweep problems under the carpet. Quite the contrary. If one of the sales force wants a particular item discussed, then he should notify us a few days before the meeting. We can then discuss and make appropriate suggestions, perhaps solving the problem. If the problem is not solved to his (her) complete satisfaction, then we request a brief report, stating the problem, summarising the discussion and suggesting possible solutions. One to two pages only is required and this can then be circulated to all the delegates well before the meeting. Guess what will happen? Most of the 'problems' are not worth the effort of a one-page report for the meeting to discuss. The raiser of the problem probably wanted attention to satisfy his ego. We can provide far better ways of satisfying egos.

(b)   If we allocate 50 per cent of our time to training, we will need to axe some other items – or greatly increase the duration of our meetings. One item that we may choose to omit is 'Discussion and analysis of last session's results'. Sacrilege? Not at all! There are three important aspects here:

    (i)   Are all of your teams or people performing well and above target? If yes, then it should be the theme of your meetings and shouted from the rooftops.

(ii) If the answer is no, do the under-achievers know who they are and by how much they are below target? If they do not, then we should not be in management.

(iii) If they do know who they are and by how much they are below target, do we seriously believe that we are capable of discussing that at a public meeting without it becoming a humiliating, embarrassing crucifixion?

Do we seriously think that having crucified them, and reduced them to the depths of despair that we can raise them to the heights of inspirational motivational excellence to break the company sales records in the next session? If we can achieve that, then discard this book, write and tell the world how you do it, you will have an instant bestseller.

Caution! This is not an attempt to get us to abdicate our responsibilities, avoid unpleasantness and let them struggle on in mediocrity. On the contrary, they know who they are, they do need help and guidance from us. They need our regular help by telephone, letter or day-to-day face-to-face contact. They need our help in the most important area of all – field training. They do not need us to take them apart publicly. They do need our help in a special meeting at which the problem is discussed fully, analysed and the positive motivational recommend-ations and conclusions are agreed by both sides; then they can report the recommendations and conclusions in a highly motivational way to the main sales meeting.

Some people, but very few, thrive on being crucified. It somehow seems to lift them to above-average performance for a session or two before they slide slowly down the results table, awaiting another masochistic attack that gets the excitement and adrenalin flowing again. Be careful, we need to know our people well to play this game.

We may doubt the wisdom of this approach, in which case consider this: last session's results are now history, but can we change history? Categorically no! So the only thing worth discussing is how to achieve a better future – that is more positive.

Furthermore, there is nothing really new in management, Hegel told us in 1800: 'What experience and history teach is this – that people and governments never have learned anything from history, or acted on principles deduced from it'. At about the same time Samuel Taylor Coleridge said: 'If men could learn from history, what lessons it might teach us! But passion and party blind our eyes and the light which experience gives is a lantern on the stern, which shines only on the waves behind us'. These are clearly overstatements but there is an important principle: don't dwell too long on the analysis of your past results; it is far better to concentrate your efforts and energies on planning a great future. The one way is very risky and probably demotivational, the other is positive, constructive, inspirational and motivational.

How much time are we prepared to put into the planning and preparation of our meeting? There is one law of nature that we cannot violate. We get out of life in exact proportion to the effort that we put into life. This is certainly true of meetings. We cannot go along with the attitude 'Time we had another meeting, I hope it goes all right'.

We must really *want to* hold a successful meeting. That is the basis of good motivation. If we really *want to*, then we will commit the necessary effort and energy to plan and prepare it.

Furthermore, in terms of communication, which is really the purpose of meetings, remember that we are managers. We cannot have 'the power and the glory'. Sales people need the glory; they thrive on it, so let them have it. No one really questions our power or authority. Let them run part of the meeting. Let them get on their feet and talk. We can afford to let them do this for most of the training section.

Psychologists tell us that all people, including managers, have certain basic requirements. One of those requirements is emblazoned across our chest in very large capital letters:

MAKE ME FEEL IMPORTANT

Some people have a more highly developed ego than others but we all have it to some degree. One way of satisfying this requirement is to allow salespersons to conduct part of the meeting. This may range from a formal teaching/lecturing session, through role play, to giving inspirational talks.

Let them do it. It is one way of getting the adrenalin flowing and ensuring that *they* enjoy attending our meetings. This is another aspect of delegation but like all delegation it requires careful planning between the manager and the person concerned, then frequent checking before the day of the meeting to ensure that their thoughts are in line with our requirements. It may well take more of our time than doing the entire job ourselves, but the mileage that we derive from it later is worthwhile.

This approach ensures that the members of our sales force are being well trained in public speaking and are, therefore, better equipped to handle group presentations. They feel more a part of the whole process, and this provides an excellent base for motivation.

Sporting stories provide good motivational impact and, indeed, there is a close analogy between success in sport and success in sales. Many characteristics – drive, effort, overcoming obstacles, keeping going, going the extra mile and developing the will to win – are common to both. Get them all participating in this way. It really does make better use of their energy than a griping session.

Here are a few ideas for topics that would make good training sessions or talks at your future meetings. They form a good change of pace when used judiciously with formal training and role play sessions on 'opening the interview', over-coming objections, closing, planning etc, that must always be an ongoing requirement of meetings.

Suggested topics for presentations

1 How to hit and exceed targets.
2 How to break records again and again.
3 How to get more out of your territory.
4 How to plan effectively.
5 How to sell better.

6 How to qualify prospects from suspects.
7 Records and reports without tears.
8 Maximise your business – develop sales across the range.
9 How to be a professional.
10 The importance of human relations in selling.
11 The importance of good communication in selling.
12 How to improve human relations and communications.
13 Overcoming objections.
14 Handling specific objections.
15 How to solve problems.
16 Brainstorming sessions as a business aid.
17 The importance of image.
18 How to really sell the company.
19 Logic and system in sales.
20 The essential steps in a good sales presentation.
21 Opening interviews.
22 Breaking through the preoccupation barrier.
23 The importance of various personality traits in sales people.
24 The importance of belief and sincerity.
25 The importance of benefits.
26 How to convert technicalities into benefits.
27 How to use third party referrals effectively.
28 Marketing and the salesperson.
29 Overcoming the price objection.
30 How to sell quality.
31 How to sell service.
32 Developing quality and service in your presentation.
33 How to improve your closing skills.
34 How to improve your demonstrations.
35 Streamlining the paperwork problem.
36 How to improve your handling of customer problems and complaints.
37 How to improve advertising layout and designs.
38 Quotations versus proposals.
39 Quotations that sell.
40 Why we should use the phone more.
41 Telesales techniques.
42 How to prospect effectively.
43 Cold calls should be *gold calls.*
44 How to use your time more effectively.
45 How is your self-image.
46 Positive mental attitude.
47 My best sales.
48 How to handle tricky situations.
49 How to score over the competition.
50 The magic ingredients for success in selling.
51 How to write good reports.
52 How to accentuate the positive and eliminate the negative.
53 How to develop enthusiasm.

54 Self-development.
55 Reopening lapsed accounts.
56 How to become salesman(woman) of the year.
57 Have different people devise quizzes on topics of selling theory, practice and product with ideal answers.
58 Hand out inspirational stories from newspapers, magazines and books and have people make personal presentations from them.
59 Call upon people to talk for a short time on different topics of the products or business, explaining them in a lively but complete way.
60 How to set objectives.

Do not be afraid to repeat training sessions. Ignore the cries of 'We've done it before' or 'We've seen this film before'. Repetition is an essential part of learning.
    At the end of the day, analyse the proceedings honestly:

1 Have you achieved your objectives?
2 Was it worthwhile from your and their point of view?
3 Are they better trained and motivated?
4 Did you really finish on a high note?

This is by no means an exhaustive treatise on communications in meetings. If it has made you think of one change that you can implement for the better in your meetings, then this text has been worthwhile. Let us remember, they should be *sales meetings* not anti-sales meetings.

38. *The Printed or Written Word*

Sales bulletins and newsletters

Many of the guidelines that we have established so far apply to sales bulletins and newsletters. Remember the acronym KISS (Keep It Simple Salesmanager) and the 'Make Me Feel Important' requirement. A bulletin should always be packed with good, positive motivational news and stories – never negative and demotivational.

The weekly or monthly bulletin need not be an expensive item in the sales budget, and the motivation it engenders should produce a good return on the investment. If you are in any doubt about this, change it.

Have the art department design a good front cover, not necessarily elaborate or multi-coloured but appealing and eyecatching. Choose a good positive name for the bulletin. The design and title have to last for a few years.

A simple and effective title such as *Spoilight*, and the front cover consisting of a theatre spotlight in the top corner shining a beam into the centre of the page, which then represents a stage, would do fine. The names of those people who have performed well during that week or month appear in the centre spotlight.

The following pages contain short success stories of the high achievers and, at the back, league tables of individuals and teams appear. No comment is made on under-achievers. That is not the purpose of this bulletin.

We must acknowledge the importance of the bulletin to the sales force and therefore to our own and the company's success. We must ensure that:

(a) Only motivational, enthusiastic material gets into the bulletin.
(b) Recognition of a good job and lavish praise for teams and individuals is the order of the day.
(c) We see it as a means of developing people as individuals and fostering team spirit.
(d) It provides a feeling of participation and belonging.

If we think that sales people don't bother to read sales bulletins, we are probably right. If we include references to them somewhere in the bulletin, and photographs, league tables and good action-packed success stories with training in mind – then they will read them. If sales people don't read bulletins it is our fault.

If we have a large sales force, or some are producing well below target, then don't publish the full individual performance table. Have a sensible 'cut off': perhaps the top half or top two-thirds would supply the necessary motivation.

Include references to salesmen's wives, particularly the 'housewives' of the group. These are the forgotten army who get little acknowledgement for their efforts, patience, support and motivation. We should also remember, if they dislike our company, product or being deprived of their husbands, they can demotivate the salesman far more effectively than we can ever motivate him. Presumably the reverse is also true, ie husbands demotivating saleswomen, but it is perhaps not so common an occurrence because of the smaller numbers.

Use plenty of headings, sub-headings and space in the layout to add to the motivational impact.

Company business news, most times, is not motivational and should be omitted. If the company has just acquired another company and it may mean more sales for everyone, then it is worthy of mention. But general policy changes, procedure changes, another item required on a report form, salesmen not phoning the office at the required time, etc., are not for the sales bulletins or the sales newsletter. These are anti-sales items.

Make it motivational, make it live, KISS and ensure that it is posted off on the same day each week. Always speak highly of the bulletin yourself, refer to it frequently and always ask, whenever speaking to a salesperson, 'Any items for the bulletin this week'. Encourage them to write brief but punchy items. It will pay off, and it is another vital link in the whole communication chain.

Correspondence

Companies do sometimes change products, designs, procedures, forms etc. Sometimes this is good; frequently, however, it is bad news for the sales force.

Well, not really bad news, but simply that any extra task, whatever its nature is seen as a threat unless there is instant, obvious financial gain. Well, we were salesmen once, weren't we! We had to operate in the commercial jungle. Remember how we felt when things changed 'unnecessarily'?

We must sometimes communicate 'non-productive' news, or issue edicts or reprimands. Never put them in the bulletin or newsletter. First, we should ask two questions:

(a) Is it an important change or requirement?
(b) Does it need to be on record in the file and hence necessitate a formal memo?

If the answer to both of these is yes, then try one other check. Would it be better to tell him or her, preferably face to face but telephone will do, before he or she receives the memo?

Usually the answer is yes. Remember we are discussing these topics under the main heading of communication and, in particular, better communication. No matter how clever we are with words, Murphy's Law still applies – 'If things can be misunderstood, they will be misunderstood – and 'things' always look worse in writing. There is something very superior, very absolute about written communication when issuing orders, edicts, changes, etc.

So, tell them first.

The golden rules still apply – KISS, use short words, use short sentences. One of the problems is that we write to salesmen infrequently, so when we do, we feel a little apprehensive and it comes as a complete shock to them.

We don't always need to have the letters typed: handwritten with a carbon copy for file is often better than total formality with copies to the main board. If it is a letter of praise, always send copies to appropriate directors.

We should strive to be ourselves when we write, avoiding stuffy phrases and formality:

It has been brought to my notice . . .

I would like to draw your attention to . . .

I feel that I must make it absolutely and categorically clear that . . .

In accordance with your request I have given very careful thought to and analysed your suggestions. At this present moment in time I find it difficult to accede to your point of view; however in the normal course of events in the very near future in actual fact I sincerely hope that I may be able to reconsider the situation and answer in the affirmative.

Just look at that. Before we scoff, however, are there any phrases there that we use occasionally? First, there is very little 'sincere' about it although the word 'sincerely' is used towards the end. 'In accordance with your request' is superfluous. 'At this present moment in time' means 'now', and so on. All we are really saying is 'not now but perhaps later'.

We should not try to impress; we don't have to score points in this way from our sales people.

Send them a handwritten note when:
(i)   They have had a good day.
(ii)   When you need them to 'phone you urgently, either for business reasons or to apply some corrective measure. If they will need any paperwork or information to hand, tell them in the note to have it ready.
(iii) When they are negotiating a large order, congratulate, express your confidence and request they contact you on the appropriate day with the good news.
(iv)   If they have written a good report or letter, tell them.
(v)   If they have done anything well, a few words are well worthwhile and appreciated.
(vi)   Write separate thank-you letters to their wives.

Remember, much of this is part of the 'make me feel important' ego psychology. It shows you care. It helps foster good team spirit and above all it *motivates* to even greater action.

The good-news aspects will also appear in the bulletins, but no one will ever complain of that repetition. For a really outstanding performance, send his wife a bunch of flowers. She has earned it, too.

Once again, all communication should be simple, effective, persuasive and positive communication and there is an ulterior motive: to motivate them to even greater action. Whatever form of communication we are using, we should have that objective clear in our mind.

39. *The Infernal Telephone and Other Machines*

Expensive though it is, the telephone is useful, and we do not make enough effective use of it.

It is rapidly approaching £30,000 ($42,000) per annum to put a salesperson on the road and a face to face call costs in excess of £30 ($42) average for industrial selling – whether anything is sold or not. The telephone call costs about 30p (42c). With care it can be really cost-effective. So why don't more salesmen use the telephone to make appointments or to replace some face-to-face calls? Part of the answer is the old 'fear of rejection'. We can get a lot more rejections per day by telephoning than we can face to face. So our ego is preserved in face-to-face situations: less calls, less risk of rejections. Our computer rationalises that subconsciously, and we make less telephone calls by subconscious decision.

Since we don't use the telephone enough now, presumably we shall use it even less as we talk more and more to computers at the 'other end of the line'. The cold blunt instrument will become the cold blunt computer, and Orwell's Big Brother comes a step nearer.

Until now industry has geared itself to the robot revolution to replace people and relieve them of dangerous, laborious or boringly repetitive work – freeing people to do the more intellectual and stimulating tasks that a robot cannot perform. How does this affect sales and marketing. Perhaps we should tread warily.

The Robot Institute of America defines a robot as a 'reprogrammable and multifunctional manipulator designed to move material, parts, tools or specialised devices through variable programmed motions for the performance of a variety of tasks'. That sounds dangerously close to the definition of a salesperson and, remember, when we have them programmed to that extent there won't be too many managers needed.

Too futuristic? Be careful, we used to think that Flash Gordon and space travel was pure science fiction. 'They' once said: 'It is impossible ever to get a heavier than air machine to fly in a controlled manner'. 'They' once said: 'It is impossible to send recognisable sound with the complexity of the human voice by wire; only morse code is possible'.

'They' were wrong, but before we scoff, let us remember who they were; they were scientists and boffins of the day. They were intelligent people.

We can build robots as tough as tanks or capable of handling eggs without cracking them. We can get them to mine coal or stir a cup of coffee, they can dig soil on other planets or examine and repair the feet of submerged oil rigs. They can be operated at one quarter the cost of blue-collar workers. They never complain, never ask for raises, are seldom 'off sick', always start on time, take no coffee breaks and need no holidays. If that tempts you, tell the story of the fully robotic, totally automated, transatlantic Jumbo flight with no crew on board, just airborne, and the voice synthesiser is announcing to the passengers: 'This is a wonderful piece of high technology. It is much safer than conventional man-controlled flights and nothing can possibly go wrong . . . go wrong . . . go wrong. . . .' Well, be careful, experience has shown that robots really are more reliable than humans.

The 'steel collar' revolution is upon us. Blue-collar and white-collar workers beware! We can already 'talk' to computers and get logical responses. It will not be too long before there is a real dictaphone that types the letters. There are some applications already where computers are accepting voice instructions and others which read print and translate it to a 'reading voice'. The machine can even get the emphasis on the right syllable and put in pauses for effect.

Where does this incredible technology take us? A prospect, a robot of course, wants a particular machine to perform certain well defined tasks. It dials a central information bank, states what it requires of the machine, and within seconds has a visual display and print out of all of the suitable manufacturers, today's prices and delivery, all details of installation or commissioning. Your move! You argue on price, it negotiates an availability, delivery to particular sites and eventually you have a mutually agreed deal. Time elapsed – seconds. It can't happen?

Perhaps this really tells us to do our own job better now or the steel-collar replacements may be closer than we think.

More efficient, effective, persuasive communication is needed. People still like to deal with people, so let us make sure they want to deal with us.

We should be in daily telephone contact with our sales force if we can't meet them. It doesn't matter whether that is 9–5.30 or evening contact. If evening contact annoys us because it clashes with the requirements of good-time management with which they indoctrinated us on the last management course we attended, then have another tranquilliser or sip of wine and phone them anyway.

Obviously they should phone us at a predetermined time, but we shouldn't get too excited if they don't. Have another sip of wine; they may have got entangled in some revelry at an opening celebration of a newly repaired section of the M6 or M1 or somewhere.

We need to know what they have done, whether it went according to their plan, whether any further action is required and particularly if we need to involve anyone else. Remember, make them feel important, and make them think that we care. We then need to discuss tomorrow and the rest of the week with them, ie communicate and motivate.

We should also be giving them information on changes or advise on technical matters that may affect them. Above all, we should congratulate them on a job well done, give ample praise and recognition, trying to finish on a high note so that he/she will be well motivated for the right action tomorrow.

Suppose there is no good news; it was another disaster day and it's all negative problems. Oh, it's him again is it? Well, when did you last field-train him? Was it a really effective field-training day? Was a detailed field-training report completed? What does it tell you? 'The fault, dear Brutus, may not be in our sales force but in ourselves' that things are not going well.

We had better find something to get enthusiastic and motivated about, even if it is only that tomorrow presents us with another golden opportunity to do a fantastic job, and it looks like a golden opportunity for the best day's field training we ever performed.

At least the telephone provides us with instant communication, and therein lies a problem. It is still only as effective as the thought and planning that has gone into it. We should have a checklist in front of us before the call, with the highlights that must be discussed. To have to recall because something was forgotten can be very demotivational, and if it is our fault, then we are not communicating properly.

One aspect of training that should be on the meeting agenda frequently is telephone techniques. Organise role-play situations and discuss them in detail until everyone is proficient at simple, effective persuasive communication. When they are proficient, then have 'live' telephone conversations with real prospects, for appointments, demonstrations, follow up and actual sales calls.

This is particularly good training for proper use of the voice for telephone, face to face, public speaking, demonstrations and interviewing. We are lazy with respect to speaking properly. We don't think and plan, we don't move our lips fully, we don't script our 'speeches' with sufficient care. If we would just remember the seven golden rules for speaking in any situation, we would improve quickly and dramatically. Here they are:

1 Think and plan carefully what message you wish to impart.
2 Vary the *volume* of your voice.
3 Vary the *speed* of your speech, ie talk rapidly in some parts, slowly in others; this is nothing to do with the duration of the speech.
4 Use deliberate *pauses* for effect.
5 *Emphasise* key words and phrases.

NB. Nos 2, 3, 4 and 5 are *easy* – we used these with great effect when we were children. We could sell anyone on our ideas then. What went wrong was that we substituted the serious, dead-pan, stiff upper lip approach.

6 *Modulate* your voice, ie vary tone or pitch. This is more difficult, but if we follow rules 2–5, modulation tends to follow naturally.
7 Keep a *smile* in your voice. It costs you nothing and it really does help to lubricate that communication machinery.

The experts tell us they can tell when the person at the other end of the line is smiling. One thing for sure, if we smile we feel better, if we feel better we communicate better, if we communicate better, we sell more.

At least these seven simple rules will put some enthusiasm into the situation. If rule 7 only produced one extra sale per year, it would be worth getting enthusiastic and smiling about, wouldn't it?

40. *The Sales Conference*

Whatever the frequency, this should be communication *par excellence*. Hawaii Hilton or Heathrow Hotel, this is going to take a lot of planning time.

Every meeting, from monthly sales meeting to annual convention, requires careful planning. We said earlier that the success of any meeting depends upon the effort, energy and time that we put into planning it. We ought to plan all meetings with equal care, but, somehow, the annual convention gets more attention, probably because the main board will be there.

Question. If the annual convention is that important, shouldn't the wives or husbands be there? If the answer is no, then does the company want to be seen as a marriage-wrecker?

The planning of all meetings should start with clearly defined objectives. Think them through carefully.

If increasing sales is a prime objective, then cost-effectiveness is presumably a part of it. We must be careful immediately. There is nothing to suggest that the annual convention is any more successful in obtaining cost-effective sales than the normal monthly meeting. Why should it be? Have we suddenly discovered some startling principle that will revolutionise selling that we are keeping secret until the convention?

If the budget is unlimited and the annual convention is famed for its lavish living and entertainment, then we may get some mileage from announcing next year's venue and the individual and team targets that must be achieved to ensure that this sales force can win its way there. The annual convention is seen by most people as the company's way of saying thank you for a job well done in the past. It is not seen as 'payment up front' for the fantastic job that they are about to do during the forthcoming twelve months.

The inevitable upwards spiral problem can cause us a few headaches. However lavish last year's event was, this will have to be better or it is seen as a penalty. Comments like 'I suppose next year it's Scunthorpe' hardly reflect a high level of motivation.

These philosophical reflections aside, the annual convention really does put us in the spotlight. We really do have a chance to prove that we are the very epitome of organisation and planning.

The first thing that we have to do then is delegate. Immediately appoint a convention coordinator and an acting convention coordinator. They will probably need to be head-office-based so that they have instant access to typing and to us for instant decisions. Don't laugh, there is real mileage in this. For example, the Southern Area Manager may be our chosen man. He will get a tremendous kick from this because he will now have the longest title in the company: Southern Area Sales Manager and Senior Hawaiian Convention

Coordinator. This is real motivation at work. Our only problem is no one ever wants the distinction two years running.

If you are planning a convention for the first time, watch your budget carefully, in particular the hidden costs. Remember that we are going to lose a number of days of sales production. This will be more than the actual duration of the convention, for there is the euphoria that precedes and follows such an event. There is also the cost of secretaries, managers and executives that assist or participate in any way.

Then the real planning starts and we need a checklist that must be rigorously followed until our return from the convention. Perhaps the following guidelines may help:

1 Decide on the realistic objectives and get executive management approval and backing. Don't promise a substantial increase in sales as a result of the conference. If we do, we may never be allowed another, someone will ask if the sales increase can be obtained in another (cheaper) way.
2 Decide venue and dates. We may have to check it out ourselves, if not ask someone we can really rely upon. Remember size of room, seating, lighting for video filming and blackout for film, seating and comfort, ventilation and smoke control, outside distractions and noise. The venue should never overlook a swimming pool or busy street. Don't forget power points location, separate projection room, lectern, top table, screens fixed and tilting for overhead projector, foyer or space outside for refreshments. Ease of location with respect to airport, car parks, lifting in any equipment you are taking. Agree carefully what equipment you wish the hotel to provide and its quality. The number of times so-called international conference hotels have inadequate equipment is quite alarming. Remember the old rule, 'Don't *expect . . . inspect*'. 'It will be all right on the night' is not really good enough, and you can't pass the buck.
3 Decide upon a firm agenda with accurate time limitations. No one can have the luxury of overrunning at an important convention, not even the company chairman.
4 Allow your co-ordinator to start co-ordinating with all delegates and participants.

What 'props' will you need? Are any teams putting on a 'show'? Are costumes required, and should you hire there or take them with you? All travel arrangements will need to be stated several times. If visas are required, the co-ordinator should get them – that means he needs everyone's current passport. That is good, hold on to them or someone will forget on the day. Any vaccinations required? Keep reminding them in the bulletins, or someone will forget.

Start 'talking up' the whole convention in the bulletin. Get everyone excited, let them have some brochures of the hotel and surrounding district, state temperatures for that period and suggest clothes to take. Mention these aspects at least every month.

5 Ensure that every participant knows exactly what part he is playing and exactly what time allocation he has. Ensure everyone knows that if they are

speaking, then a guillotine will operate, even on the managing director – it is not his convention nor the chief accountant's.

6   Do you want a photographer for the meeting or for the dinner or social activities? If you book through the hotel or conference centre, then check a sample of his work on arrival, and if it is not good enough, change him.

7   Do you want a cabaret? If you use one of the regular acts employed by the hotel, then check it out if possible.

8   Ask every major speaker if they need slides, transparencies, etc., and ensure that they are being properly prepared and on time.

9   Ensure that the meals give adequate variety of menu.

10   Do you want a cocktail party on arrival, or bouquets of flowers for wives at the airport or at the hotel?

11   Arrange meetings for all major speakers to discuss timing, rehearsing, any scene-shifting or special apparatus or requirements.

12   You will need careful planning for the opening and closing 'ceremonies'. It need not be quite on the scale of the Olympics, but it does need to have impact. Have a brainstorming session for ideas.

13   Ensure that every day is loaded with positive motivational ideas and plenty of praise and acknowledgement for good performance.

14   Ensure that each session has a chairman who is well briefed beforehand and can therefore stimulate discussion on the main points.

15   Everyone must participate. They have to feel that the conference was worthwhile.

16   If partners are attending, arrange coach trips or films for them during business sessions. Usually they will only want to attend prize-giving ceremonies.

17   Before you organise the next one, ensure that you set particular performance requirements for a salesperson to 'win' the whole package for two. Have other target levels to win 75 per cent, 50 per cent, etc., of the total cost and thus offer them the opportunity to attend by paying the balance.

Conventions are inordinately expensive and they consume enormous amounts of our time in planning and organising. We should ensure that we are totally committed to our personal investment in time and effort before we rush into conventions. Remember there must be a follow through action plan arising from discussions, and we will have to monitor that, too, on return.

With proper planning and preparation, with total dedication and determination to make them succeed, conventions are worth it. With the right performance targets built in as a prerequisite for attendance, they can also be highly motivational and almost financially successful. We must get the targets right, however.

Specialist speakers

There are many good reasons for using guest or specialist speakers:

1   Simple 'change of face and change of pace', breaking the routine.

2   The delegates have heard it all before from 'in house' speakers.

3   An outsider can actually say exactly the same as we would say, yet produce a

greater effect.
4 We may really want people with specialist knowledge or expertise that we do not have in the company.
5 It improves our credibility to bring in 'an expert'. The delegates feel that we care about them and it makes them feel important and worth the investment.

However, there are one or two points that we need to take care of and the following questions must be answered honestly and fully.

(a) *Exactly* what topic do we want covered?
(b) *Exactly* what aspect or emphasis of that topic do we require?
(c) At *exactly* what theoretical level do we want it pitched?
(d) Do we want it put over in a formal lecturing style or in a more participative discussion style?
(e) Do we want a humorous 'after dinner' approach or more formal style?
(f) *Exactly* how long can we allow the person to speak?
(g) Since many professional lecturers will charge by the half-day or day, can we afford to give him/her more of our precious agenda time to make it cost-effective?
(h) Since the fee will probably be a few hundred pounds, will it be worth it?
(i) How can we really capitalise on this speaker and get some positive, stimulating action plans out of his talk?
(j) Will he/she be giving handouts or shall we need to prepare some? We really can't afford the luxury of a guest speaker without something on record to which we can refer.
(k) Can we have his/her permission to record (audio or video) in full without additional charges.

We should make no move until we have answered all these questions fully. If all we want is a good laugh with a Blaster Bates or Fred Dibnah 'after dinner' approach, then no problem, go ahead, we can't really go wrong except to check on the jokes and the language. Remember not everyone likes dirty jokes, particularly in mixed company.
When we have answered the questions fully, we can decide on the speaker. If we do not know of suitable speakers, then check with the following for recommendations:

1 Colleagues or acquaintances who have organised guest speakers.
2 Appropriate departments in colleges and universities.
3 Main city libraries or college and university libraries, which maintain lists of guest speakers or local secretaries of various professional, technical or business societies or institutions. Choose the particular profession, contact the nearest local secretary and they can recommend from experience. Remember, personal recommendation is still the best guide.

The next step is to contact the person, preferably by 'phone. Ignore the fact that he/she is an acknowledged expert. Be businesslike, use the seven golden rules we established previously for telephone techniques, smile and check:

(a) Venue and date availability/logistics/convenience. We don't want to have to fly someone in and out by helicopter for a two-hour session just because of other clashing engagements.
(b) State topic.
(c) State duration of presentation and how much time for 'discussion'.
(d) Enquire fee.
(e) Negotiate!
(f) When agreement has been reached, state the width and depth requirements of topic. Get his/her acceptance of your exact requirements and request a synopsis of the talk from him/her.
(g) Write confirming all that has been agreed and *request a synopsis* of the 'talk' in writing as agreed on the telephone.
(h) Try to meet the person so that the ice is broken, and you can brief him on the type of audience, personalities, etc., and can agree the final talk content.

Many guest speakers give the same talk at every meeting, charge exorbitant fees and leave in a puff of goodwill. There is nothing wrong with that, providing we get exactly what we want.

All too often they title the talk according to our requirements, stay on line for two or three paragraphs and are then away on their favourite topic or contentious hobbyhorse. Because they are good public speakers, the switch is carefully disguised, we sit there nodding in agreement with an occasional 'Hear, hear' and two days later realise we didn't get *our* talk at all.

Pin them down. Request a synopsis and check with them about handouts and any photocopying that may be required. If they are not prepared to put a synopsis in writing, then beware. The chances are that we were not going to get the talk we wanted anyway. We should have the guts to cancel the engagement. They cannot argue, for the synopsis was an undertaking we got from them during the initial telephone call and subsequently put in writing to them.

Having agreed everything, then by all means give them some VIP treatment. Give them a decent hotel room with *en suite* facilities and a place on the top table for dinner if they have to stay overnight. The generosity need not include an open drinks account.

It is essential to check at least one week before the due date to ensure that the arrangements are firm. Then in the event of a problem a last-minute replacement can probably be found.

We must get maximum return from this item on the agenda. We can try to achieve this by applying five simple checks where appropriate:

1 We already have the synopsis agreed for the talk. If we still do not have it in written form, then we should check the synopsis by 'phone and put it in writing to the speaker.
2 Ensure that the event is announced in two or three bulletins before the due date so that people can at least be thinking about the topic and even reading around the subject. 'Talk it up' in the bulletin, giving it a positive, dynamic, motivational press, ie *sell it*.
3 For the event use a good motivational introduction. We should structure our

introduction around the following guidelines:

(a) Why we are using this person.
(b) Why we have selected this topic.
(c) Why at this place and time.

Make the audience really want to listen.

4 During previous contact with the speaker ascertain whether there is any particular aspect that is being omitted or not given in-depth coverage in his/ her opinion. This can then form a good question to be posed by you or some nominated person, and the speaker is forewarned. Circulate the synopsis beforehand to a few reliable colleagues, who can give some thought to the subject and have one or two questions ready. 'Seeding questions' is not cheating – we reap according to the seeds we sow, and it is imperative to reap a maximum harvest from this event.

5 Have a working brief or action plan assignment for some follow-through thought, study or action to be reported and discussed at the next meeting. If it is difficult to relate to your immediate business, then have some or all of your sales people prepared to give a talk in their own words on this topic.

Working within a limited budget

Whether we plan an area meeting or an annual convention, we will be expected to work within a budget. Normally the budget will impose severe limitations. It is a strange fact that the limitations are similar and just as severe whether we are planning a weekend meeting at the local *Rose and Crown* or a one-week convention in the Hawaiian Hilton, using their most expensive rooms for accommodation and a large meeting room, hiring a full range of audio-visual equipment to film the entire proceedings and a resident jazz band on call throughout the day for introductory music, breaktime music, fanfares and conclusion, a dinner dance every evening with exotic and expensive prizes, cabaret, the most expensive menu throughout the week and probably two or three days of inter-island sightseeing flights. It is only the time that we need to put into the organisation that is so very different.

Either way, both need to be a rip-roaring success. We face, however, one serious problem: whatever we did last year, this year must be better.

It is far better to plan something smaller but of top quality than try to outdo every other convention ever held – on a shoestring budget. We don't have to go to Hawaii or the Bahamas. We can stay in the UK. Some special deals on airlines and hotels, however, can make Spain and other continental venues very attractive from a cost point of view. We will survive on a sound, sensible diet and we don't need the most expensive suites.

A band for the meeting is not necessary, providing we have the appropriate music on tape and our 'technician' is properly instructed in the hotel's system and very well rehearsed. People can enjoy conventions in which they participate and make their own fun. Inter-team or inter-regional competitions, quizzes, one-act plays, charades strategically placed on the agenda to break up the formal business routine, can be very successful.

We don't have to have sightseeing tours, except perhaps one day for the wives (or husbands) if they are invited. We don't need a dinner dance and cabaret every night. People are frequently quite happy to make their own arrangements for the evening and often want to 'get away' from the company for a while.

All this is fine, providing we didn't do it better last year. It is difficult, there is no easy solution. Even if we spend a fortune organising the most lavish events, we still won't please everyone. Someone's soup will be cold or their room won't have as pleasant an outlook as someone else's.

If in doubt, cut it out. We can spend the money more wisely on other forms of sales promotion.

There is only one way to sleep easily at night, and that is to establish a series of weekly, monthly, quarterly and six-monthly objectives for every person and every team manager. The objectives must show sufficient percentage increases to pay that person's costs (for two, preferably because wives should be included). These objectives should ideally be set for each individual according to his past performance, but blanket company objectives can work.

This system puts an added strain on us for monitoring and adjudicating borderline results, and taking decisions that will be regarded as unfair by most of the sales force, and on the clerical staff for recording and working out increases. There must also be a weekly statement showing the state of the race for all competitors.

We still need to be careful. If we spend all the increased revenue on the convention, we have probably lost on the deal, because we still have to go through the whole process again for the next convention – and do it better!

41. *Dealer Meetings*

These need even more careful planning and preparation than our own sales meetings. Another management structure largely outside our control is involved and that adds to communication problems.

It is still a question of effective communication. The parameters of authority, power, rights of decision-making and policy-making are frequently indistinct and tact and diplomacy are needed.

The situation is governed to a large extent by one simple criterion: if we are the 'manufacturing' company then are we an 'innovating' or an 'imitating' company? If we are really creative, innovative manufacturers whose new products are almost always absolute winners, and if we carry out all the initial advertising to generate market awareness, spend large amounts on gaining high initial penetration, and give high percentage dealer discounts, then we are in the driver's seat and can determine the dealers' marketing strategy without question.

This is rarely the situation. Imitating competitors are usually working overtime to get around patents and undercut prices to give dealers a bigger turnover from their products. Most dealers are, therefore, fickle and greedy. When they are making good profits, they are also apathetic and lazy. Before we shout too loud, however, that sums up the majority of the human race when the money is rolling in. In their defence we must acknowledge their vulnerability in the marketing chain, their inherent fears and the fact that they have competitors, too, who are trying to cut their throats.

Dealer meetings may cover the following:

(a) Territory reorganisation.
(b) Changing methods of distribution, packaging, etc.
(c) Setting up other distributorships.
(d) Reducing distribution costs.
(e) Changing pricing structures and profit.
(f) Nursing the dealer through problem situations.
(g) Education with respect to new or improved products.
(h) Reselling the dealers on the products and the company.
(i) Helping with promotions, special items, campaigns on particular products.
(j) Additional or more aggressive sales training.
(k) Advice on inventories.
(l) Advice on cost-cutting procedures.
(m) Social 'pie and pint' evenings.
(n) Lavish dinners and entertainments.
(o) Unequivocal bribery.

Over the years companies have tried all methods to increase their outlets through distributor/dealer networks, and the simple law of supply and demand dictates the policy and procedure on both sides eventually. When we have a good product at the right price and margin, we don't need to worry too much about dealer loyalty and pushing the product.

Most companies have found that a firm policy, backed with good efficient service from the field sales force and quality in the product, is the right way to control dealers in the long term. This means Service and Quality with a deliberate capital S and capital Q. Advice and help is always there when they need it and a list of prospective dealers waiting to take over that area provide the recipe for success.

With this in mind, the dealer meetings should be business- and training-orientated, as are the meetings with our own sales force. We communicate 'with' not 'at' nor 'down at', and always try to 'make them feel important', while maintaining the control of the business, the sales campaigns and the training. Field sales staff should always be made available to help out, give advice and really push sales campaigns.

Dealers have to feel part of a successful team – that is the way of fighting the competition. If the competition sells at a lower price and gives a greater profit margin to the dealer, then we must talk even more persuasively and with conviction that selling our product is best for all in the long term because it is right for the customer and the market. That is difficult to do, but it is vital or we may find ourselves in a price war in which we may lose disastrously.

Remember, we have to 'sell' our meetings to the dealers. What are the real benefits to them, what is really in it for them? If it is just another meeting, forget it. They have to feel glad that they attended the meeting. The way to ensure that is:

(a) To make sure that they learn something that is useful to them either from the sales, product knowledge, business or theory point of view.
(b) To ensure that they participate well and let them conduct a part of the agenda.

If these objectives cannot be met, then we should not have formal meetings but step up the field activity with the sales force. People like to think that we are genuinely interested in helping them with their problems and genuinely trying to increase their sales. Under these circumstances they will give us their business on the simple basis that we have earned it – through good effective, persuasive, positive communication.

PART EIGHT

What of the Future?

This was certainly the most difficult part of our book to write. Why? Because so much of what we predict has to be pure guesswork.

We, the co-authors, have between us the best part of sixty years' experience in selling. Of those sixty years, some fifty years have been spent in management, and together we have some twenty-five years' experience in sales and management training.

There is ample evidence that a large number of clients think sufficiently well of us to pay us to train their sales forces. That would seem to indicate that our experience and our advice must be of some value.

But the key word here is *experience*, which by definition means 'personal knowledge gained in the past', ie it is retrospective and historical. Now we must try to look into the future. In the following chapters, we will attempt to predict, as accurately as possible, how the future of selling and sales management will develop. A word of warning though. Some of what we will say may be painful, particularly to the old-time sales manager.

Part of our time is spent conducting tutorials, seminars and courses at the College of the Institute of Marketing. It is interesting to note that the majority of the other tutors (both academic and practical men, old and young) seem to be of like mind about the future. We have pooled those thoughts and trust that the outcome will be a guide to the way the modern sales manager (you) should direct his energies.

42. *Your Personal Role in the Community*

The job of selling has until fairly recently been the butt of music-hall and saloon-bar comedians. The very mention of the word 'salesman' has engendered a sly wink or nudge, or both, and a comment such as 'Oh yes, company car, lunch allowance, stopping away at good hotels, all right for some!' But slowly this is changing. Somewhere, someone has realised the meaning of the old adage, 'We don't want to change the spots, we need to change the whole damned leopard!' The changing image of selling is in part due to those in it adopting a more responsible, more professional attitude to their jobs and to their role in the community.

We are going to carry out the next activity in reverse. We'll give the answers, then *ask* the questions.

1 *Answers.* 'You must be joking, I'm never home!' 'I don't have time.' 'That's all right for the office managers, but no good for me.' 'I'm never around when those things are happening.'
2 *Questions.* 'What do you do outside of work?' 'Why don't you take part in some community activity?'

Many of the sales managers we have met seem to be under the impression that to be efficient one has to:

(a) Get to work before anyone else (loyal).
(b) Rush around at work, making decisions, putting fires out (diligent).
(c) Maintain a 'busy busy busy' image (hardworking).
(d) Constantly do battle with a desk and filing trays overflowing with paperwork (important).
(e) Be the person who puts all the lights out, even after the cleaning ladies have gone home (dedicated).
(f) Go home to a bulging briefcase every night (ambitious).

No wonder such a person goes into a fit of mild hysterics when it is suggested that he join his local PTA, drama society, jogging club or whatever. But what a dull person one can become, living work twenty-four hours a day, seven days a week!

Funny how his European or American opposite numbers can lead a more civilised life and have a clear desk at the end of each day! Must be something to do with being better organised!

One thing is quite certain – being better organised will give the necessary time to enjoy out of work activities. That will lead to less stress and to a more balanced personality, which in turn mean that such a person will be a more effective sales manager.

Don't tell us your job is different. We've been sales managers and know all the pitfalls. We've done it both ways, organised and disorganised. We know which we prefer, and so do our families (that's another benefit).

It took us a long time to realise that there really wasn't all that difference between a sales manager and, say, a works manager, a technical manager or a financial manager. It was just that they were better organised and consequently had more time for the community in which they lived.

43. Staying Abreast of Change

How would you feel if you were about to be operated on by a surgeon whose techniques were known to be at least twenty years out of date? Not too good?

Equally, how do you judge other professional people (lawyers, architects, accountants, doctors, etc.). If you are currently using the services of a professional person, have a good look and see what it is about them that is attractive; why are they more successful than all the others in the same business? Almost invariably any one professional person is more successful than another because he/she bothers to keep up to date with modern practices, modern techniques.

How true is that of you? We run a regular sales management course. It is said (even by our competitors!) to be a very good course, perhaps one of the best around. To ensure that each delegate receives personal attention we close off the course once we have ten firm reservations. Fine, so what's the problem?

Approximately three weeks before the course is due to start, we sit back and wait for the phone to ring, conveying all manner of horrific reasons why the delegate cannot attend. Here are some examples of the reasons/excuses we are given:

(a) 'Terribly sorry but sales are down and I can't make the course! (the super salesman).
(b) 'My managing director has asked me to visit our principal in the States/ Australia/France/Outer Mongolia' (or I've decided to take a week off!).
(c) 'Didn't realise it clashed with the Motor Show/Caravan Show/Inter Plas, etc.' (doesn't keep a diary?).

Of course we also have the usual crop of relatives dying and babies being born unexpectedly. By the time these poor souls have finished, we are usually down to three or four delegates and we have to cancel that course and ask them to transfer to the next one.

Why are we telling you all this, you may ask. Because we suspect the real reason why people 'chicken out' (for that is what it is) of courses is due to fear on their part – Fear that they will be shown up, fear that they won't be able to cope with the work, fear that they will meet brighter people on the course.

We are not condemning these people for being afraid. We are afraid of many things. But fear is irrational and is based on ignorance. People are generally afraid of things they don't understand or have insufficient knowledge of. If one replaces ignorance with knowledge, there is a good chance that this will remove the cause of the fear.

What does all this add up to? Simply this. To maintain and improve your position in life it is essential that you stay abreast of change. To do this you should seek constantly to advance your knowledge of all those things concerning your job.

As mentioned previously, the sort of things you can do to help would be:

1 Reading (trade and professional magazines).
2 Attend seminars (the good, one-day seminars designed to fill the gaps, not the one-day stage shows designed just to get you out of the office for the day!).
3 Take courses (register for at least one residential course per year, and go for management or finance, marketing or computers).

Finally, don't forget the institute or other professional body, where you can rub shoulders with other like-minded people.

We would be the first to admit that we don't always do all the things we are advising you to do. But then who better to know what we *should* have done. When we were first practising sales managers, times were very different. We could get away with being good salesmen, having good personalities and being industrious. You are going to have to be much more dedicated to being a modern manager, which in turn means being aware of the many techniques you require to survive and prosper in a highly technical and competitive age. To do this you must not just be abreast of change, you must try to be ahead of the game.

As just one example of 'using change' rather than accepting it, let us consider the impact of the micro chip. Do we, as sales managers, really use the computer or any of its spin-offs?

Impact of the micro chip

The first generation of management to use computing effectively has just taken its 'O' levels.

The sales manager's duties take him out of the office more than any other executive; perhaps this is why new technology has made such a small impact on his job. His frequent absence tends to produce three reasons for the paucity of effective technology in the sales function:

(i)   He is not present at computer steering and development committee(s).
(ii) His job is not a tightly defined 'desk job' with the regular data needs of the accountant or production functions.
(iii) He cannot easily justify an investment which will sit idle while he is out of the office.

This section will attempt to update you on the technology that could make a significant contribution to the sales manager's job now. An attempt will also be made to assess the impact of the technology about to be unleashed!

Word-processing – a powerful sales tool

The popular image of word-processing used in a sales role is the production of 50,000 personally addressed but identical mailshots. This junk mail application has obscured the real benefit of WP, which is *flexibility*. The flexibility of WP provides a host of facilities which could make a positive contribution to the job of the sales manager. A few of the facilities are shown in Table 43.1.

TABLE 43.1   *Word-processing and sales management*

Facility	Explanation	Sample application
Simple amendments	Only the text which needs to be changed is affected.	The longest report or specification can be changed without introducing new errors!
'Personalisation'	A list of names and addresses is 'merged' with a standard letter.	A personal letter to all customers inviting them to an open day.
Search and replace	The automatic replacement of one word or passage of text with another wherever it appears in a document.	A lengthy proposal for one client can be easily changed and personalised for another.
Automatic formating	Where text is 'wrapped round' at the end of a line, an indented section is set up or the layout can be easily changed.	These benefits make even a two finger typist capable of producing professional work.
Secure filing	Letters and reports held on disc should be easier to find and take up no space.	You can quickly find documents filed some time ago and easily reproduce them.
Merge documents	Where you bring together selected text from one or more documents to produce a composite document.	A complex specification or report can be 'bolted' together from appropriate originals.
Selected mailing	Where a personalised letter is sent to only selected contacts on a name and address list.	A promotional letter can be sent to those customers with a particular product.

The real benefits to the sales manager of these powerful facilities are:

(a)   The professional quality of the documents. Format and layout techniques previously only available through typesetting are incorporated in all your letters and reports.
(b)   You control the text. You have the ability to control the content of all the information sent to customers.
(c)   No promotional opportunity is ever wasted. Promotional messages can easily be included in even the most mundane documents, such as monthly statements, specification changes or price changes.

'Off the peg' systems

The relative low cost and volume sale of small computers have led to the development of some excellent readymade systems for a wide range of applications. Even the most obscure specialist business may find that a 'package' that will cope with 90 per cent of its needs has already been developed. The Repstats system described earlier allows the sales manager to measure the effectiveness of the sales team and to analyse performance in a totally constructive way.

The purchase decision for a computer or the software should be approached in the same way as that for all other major purchases – carefully. Don't be the first. Try to be second. Avoid being last.

Why go to the office?

The ability to work from home and transmit documents and even pictures over a telephone line is now a reality. The potential savings and improvements in the quality of life that this entails provide the pressure that will make the sales manager 'homebound' in the very near future.

'Beam me up, Scotty'

The speed of innovation and development is now approaching Warp Factor 9, and the longer you stay out, the harder will be the inevitable need to catch up.

In 1963 the most popular computer cost £140,000 ($200,000). This figure excluded the necessary resident engineer and 1,000 square feet of air-conditioned specialist accommodation. The price did include a few valves and an oil-cooled central processor!

The most popular computer today sits on a desk and costs less than £800 ($1100) at 1983 prices. There are over 2,000 systems available off the shelf to make it go, and it is at least eight times as powerful as its 1963 predecessor.

The major purchase decision you will have to make in 1990 will be what colour watch strap you want your machine mounted on!

The IBM Polyanna Principle is 'Machines should work – people should think'.

44. *Your Personal Development*

It is taken for granted that, as you are reading this book, you are ambitious. The next assumption is that you have probably come up 'through the ranks' of the selling profession, which means you have been a salesperson, area manager/area supervisor, perhaps field sales manager, then the big one – sales manager.

The second assumption is based on research that was done in 1956, when it was found that of the top executives in 192 major companies, 34 per cent were from a sales background, and similar research in 1982 that discovered 57 per cent of the senior executives in large and very large companies were from selling. But in 1983 it was found that the top jobs in large companies were being filled not by ex-sales people but by accountants, engineers and marketing men. Why should that be? The research provided the answer, which was that industry is increasingly in need of senior executives who have a good grasp of the technical aspects of the product, plus an appreciation of how to *market* it (not just how to *sell* it), and, most of all, a sound knowledge of finance. Let us look at your development in two aspects: first, as a manager of sales, then as a potential chief executive.

The nature of management

There are hundreds of different definitions of management. The definition we favour most is *'The guidance, leadership and control of people and other resources towards a common goal'* or put more succinctly, *'Getting things done through others'*.

Whether the sales manager is an excellent sales person is nowhere near as important as being a good manager since he/she has to rely on others to produce the results.

The fundamental functions of management are, therefore:

1   Planning – in order to create an environment where the people they manage have the maximum chance of success.
2   Assessing – constantly measuring people and results in order to make the decisions that will ensure success.
3   Training – excellent performance by the managers' staff will only occur when they know how to do the job properly and completely. Equally, excellent performance as against average performance will only occur when motivation is maintained at a high level.

   As we have discovered training people results in motivation knowledge.
4   Directing and control – having ensured that the staff know how to perform, the managers function is to direct them into the areas of most success and control to ensure that they stay in those areas.

Success for the sales manager is therefore dependent upon:

1 Developing personal qualities that will make that manager a positive leader.
2 The constant acquisition of adequate information.
3 Decisiveness.

We have already discussed personal qualities in the leadership section of this book (see Chapter 5) but two qualities that will help enormously in all three of these areas are to be analytical in your approach – dig under the surface, perhaps the most useful question in the managers armoury is 'why' – and to develop sound common sense judgement.

Let us dwell a little longer on decisiveness.

Decision-making

It has been said that if a manager is making lots of decisions and 51 per cent of them are right, he or she is doing a good job for their company.

The malaise that effects so much of sales management is that they are not prepared to make decisions. The one line joke 'I used to be indecisive but now I can't make up my mind' is too horribly true in so many cases.

So the final Strafford/Grant technique we offer you is that of making good decisions.

1 *Recognise the symptoms* – recognise when something is occurring which requires a decision.
2 *Examine the facts* – analyse the symptoms and the circumstances in order to establish the underlying cause of the situation. Communicate with others to ensure you have got to the roots.
3 *Gather the alternatives* – rarely is there just one alternative course of action. If there was just one, decision-making would be relatively easy. So gather the alternatives, look at all the different ways you could solve this need, this situation or this problem.
4 *Project forward the effect of each alternative* – this is where most managers go wrong. They fail to look forward to see what will be the result in the future if they decide on alternative (a) or (b). As a result they solve one problem and create another.
5 *Make the decision based on step 4* – decide the course of action based on the projected effects and if you really want to improve the quality of your decision-making *write down what assumptions you made in making that decision.* Otherwise, if it goes wrong, how can you decide why?
6 *Act on your decision confidently* – you have done the best that you can to ensure that your decision is right so now communicate it positively and enthusiastically to those concerned.
7 *Monitor the results* – do not abdicate at this late stage. Monitor the results of your decision to ensure that it was the right one. If it proves correct, congratulate yourself, you have taken a giant step towards being a good manager. If it proves incorrect don't mope – act. Re-examine and find out why, then have the courage to put it right so the final step is:
8 *Be prepared to act if necessary.*

By following the advice in the previous 282 pages we can virtually assure you that you will be a successful sales manager but what of the future. If you want to go further then read on to these final few words.

Maintaining your own motivation

A good sales manager is in an excellent position to move into the job of chief executive (managing director), and with sufficient qualifications, dedication and track record as a manager, you should be in the running for such a job. With a pooling of all our experience and with advice from highly qualified people in the Institute of Marketing, the Institute of Directors and the British Institute of Management, here is a list of 'how to' points, which, if followed, will enhance your chance of success:

1   Keep your sights high enough to avoid total preoccupation with sales and selling. Start thinking *marketing*.
2   Acquire a substantial understanding of the other corporate activities, ie finance, production, engineering, personnel, promotion, distribution.
3   Balance commitment to volume with an equally intensive concern for profits.
4   Learn to analyse facts for use as the basis of decision-making.
5   Have the confidence to practise increasingly the noble art of delegation (not abdication, mark you).
6   Don't keep saying 'I haven't got time'. Well organised managers have the same twenty-four hours in each day that you have, but perhaps they make better use of them!
7   Get yourself a competent, ambitious secretary, and let her help you to get *both* of you to the top.
8   Develop and maintain an interest in subjects that will broaden your interests, eg economics, politics and industrial philosophy.
9   Keep abreast of developments in the technical world (particularly computers), and try to practise scientific management. Take courses.
10 While developing a harmonious working environment, be careful about 'close' friendships with subordinates and less ambitious/competent equals. Remember, a man is known by the company he keeps.

Reaching the top of any profession requires outstanding qualities, above-average performance, total dedication to one's job, a high standard of mental and physical health, and, above all, the motivation to succeed. Only you knows if all that applies to you.

Good luck and every success to you in the future from both of us.

Further Reading

The authors would recommend the following books to readers:

1 *Body Language: The art of seeing what others are thinking*, Dr J. Braysich, (Braysich, distributed in the UK by InTech Sales Dynamics Ltd).
2 *Further up the organisation*, Robert Townsend (Michael Joseph).
3 *Managing a Sales Force*, M. T. Wilson (Gower).
4 *Sales Management for Profit*, Peter J. Yondale (Business Books Ltd).
5 *The One Minute Manager*, K. Blanchard and S. Johnson (Fontana/Collins).
6 *The Motivation to Work*, Dr. F. Herzberg (Wiley).
7 *The Time Trap*, R. Alec Mackenzie (Amacom, a division of the American Management Association, distributed in the UK by McGraw Hill Paperbacks).
8 *The Training and Development of Salesmen*, Jan Strachan (Roger Page).

Index

Achievement, measuring, 204–14
Advancement, 221–3
Advertising for staff, 79–81
AIDA, 170–1
Application forms, 84–8
Appointment, letters of, 103
Assessment forms, 134, 135, 136, 137

Benefits, 171–2
Bulletins, 215, 259
Buying, intangible reasons, 163, 165

Change, staying abreast of, 277–80
Closing, 183–4
Committees, selling to, 178
Communication, 233–72
Communication, rules of, 248–9
Community, manager's role in, 275–6
Computers, 278–80
Consultants: recruitment/selection,
    81–2; training, 121–3
Contracts of employment, 104–5
Controlling sales operation, 14, 143–
    50
Correspondence, 259
Counselling, 222–3

Decision making, 33, 282–3
Delegation, 33–5, 218–19
Demonstrations, 179
Development personal, 281–2

Educational agencies, 82
Educational establishments, 82
Employment, contracts of, 104

FAB approach, 171–2
Field sales manager, 54–63
Field training, 124–37

Formal training, 111–20; assessment
    of, 116–17; duration, 114;
    induction, 119–20; location, 115;
    methods, 113; objectives, 111;
    syllabus, 112; teachers, 112
Forms: appointment, 103;
    assessment, 117, 131, 134–7;
    reporting, 146–50
Future, the, 273

Goal setting, 151–4
Group selection, 102
Growth, 221–3

Headhunters, 82
Herzberg, 195–8
Hygiene factors, 199–203

Incentive schemes, 208
Induction training, 119–120
Intangible reasons, 163
Internal applicants, 78
Interviewing: aims, 94; bookings, 93;
    deadly sins, 97; reports, 98;
    structure, 95–7

Job: analysis, 67; centres, 83;
    definition, 71; description, 67, 68,
    212; rotation, 219; satisfaction, 25,
    216; the selling job, 9

Key functions, 12
KISS, 237

Leadership: general, 16; qualities,
    16–18; skills, 18–20
Letters of appointment, 103
Letters, sales, 259–60
Levels in motivation, 226–9

Managers, training of, 139–41
Managing: by objectives, 152–4;
    upwards, 28
Manning and staffing, 65
Marketing, 42–4, 45–8, 50
Markets, defining, 45–6
Maslow, 193–5
Meetings: dealers, 271–2; general
    sales, 250–7; topics, 255–7
Merchandising, 156–60
McGregor, 198
Microchip, 278–80
Monitoring, 15
Motivation, 14, 22–3, 190–232
Motivators, 204–24
Motivation of motivators, 230–2, 283

Newsletters, 215, 259

Objectives, 179, 180
Objectives, managing by, 152–4
Organising, 12
Organisation, principles of, 39–40;
    structures, 49–53

Performance appraisal, 209–12;
    standards, 212
Person profile, 74–7
Personal action plan, 25
Personal development, 281–2
Phone ins, 84
Planning, 12, 41, 162
Planning sales, 161
Praise, 214–15
Pre-interview activity, 84–92
Price factor, 181
Principles of organisation, 39–40
Professional bodies, 82, 278
Proposals, 174–8
Prospecting, 164
Psychological testing, 97

Qualities: of a leader, 16–18; of a
    manager, 3, 5, 141, 282; of a
    salesperson, 184–5

Recognition of achievement, 211–16

Recruitment, 13, 65, 78–84
References, 101
Relationships, 27–9
Remunerations, 62, 200–3
Reporting systems, 146–50
Reports, interview, 98–9
Repstats System, 150
Responsibility, 219–21
Reward theory, 190–2
Rules of communication, 248–9

Sales: approach calls, 172–4;
    bulletins, 215, 258–9; conferences,
    264–70; meetings, 250–7;
    presentations, 168–70;
    professional, 161–5; sequence, 170;
    surveys, 174; to committees, 178;
    through third parties, 178
Salesforce: controlling, 14;
    motivating, 14; organising, 13;
    recruiting, 12, 65, 78, 84; setting
    up, 46–9; staffing, 13, 65; training,
    13, 107–37; types of, 46
Sales manager: basic functions, 12;
    basic role, 9; characteristics, 9;
    checklist, 8; job, 9; selection, 5
Sales person: job definition, 71–3; job
    specification, 68
Secretaries, 36, 283
Selection, 5, 94–105
Selection consultants, 81
Self motivation, 230–2
Selling process, 10, 155–61
Service calls, 182–3
Sources of staff, 78–83
Specialist speakers, 266–9
Staffing the organisation, 13
Standards: control, 144;
    performance, 212
Structure of sales force, 45–53
Supervisors, 54–63

Targetting, 204–7
Telephones, 261–3
Territory design, 51
Theory X and Y, 198
Time, 30–6, 283

Topics of mettings, 255–7
Training consultants, 121–3
Training, 13, 107–41; assessments
  forms, 117, 134–7; consultants,
  121–3; field, 124–37; formal, 111;
  induction, 119; sales force, 107;
  supervisors, 57–8; trainers, 139–41
Troughs in motivation, 225–6

Visual aids, 166–8, 252, 265

Word processing, 278
Work as a motivator, 216–19
Working with women, 28–9
Working relations, 27–9
Writing to candidates, 90;
  communication, 241–9, 258–60